**HARCOURT
BRACE**

Teaching Phonics
STAFF DEVELOPMENT BOOK

Harcourt Brace & Company
Orlando   Atlanta   Austin   Boston   San Francisco
Chicago   Dallas   New York
Toronto   London

For permission to reprint copyrighted material, grateful acknowledgment is made to the
following sources:

Folkways Music Publishers, Inc., New York: From "Put Your Finger in the Air" by Woody
Guthrie. TRO - lyrics © copyright 1954 (Renewed), 1963 (Renewed) by Folkways Music
Publishers, Inc.

HarperCollins Publishers: Cover illustration by Henry Cole from *Four Famished Foxes and
Fosdyke* by Pamela Duncan Edwards. Illustration copyright © 1995 by Henry Cole.

*Lodestar Books, an affiliate of Dutton Children's Books, a division of Penguin Books USA
Inc.*: Cover illustration from *The A to Z Beastly Jamboree* by Robert Bender. Copyright ©
1996 by Robert Bender.

MONDO Publishing: Cover illustration by Betina Ogden from *When the King Rides By* by
Margaret Mahy. Illustration copyright © 1986 by Betina Ogden. Cover illustration by John
Burge and Laurie Sharp from *Little Mouse's Trail Tale* by JoAnn Vandine. Illustration copy-
right © 1989 by Horowitz Grahame Pty Ltd.

North-South Books, Inc., New York: Cover illustration from *Five Little Ducks* by Pamela
Paparone. Illustration copyright © 1995 by Pamela Paparone.

The Center for Applied Research in Education: From *The ESL Teacher's Book of Lists* by
Jacqueline E. Kress, Ed.D. Text © 1993 by The Center for Applied Research in Education.

Puffin Books, a division of Penguin Books USA Inc.: Cover illustration from *Cat Is Back at
Bat* by John Stadler. Copyright © 1991 by John Stadler.

Random House, Inc.: "Alphabet Stew" from *The Random House Book of Poetry for
Children,* selected by Jack Prelutsky. Text copyright © 1983 by Jack Prelutsky.

*Simon & Schuster Books for Young Readers, an imprint of Simon & Schuster Children's
Publishing Division:* Cover illustration by Patricia Mullins from *Hattie and the Fox* by Mem
Fox. Illustration copyright © 1986 by Patricia Mullins.

Viking Penguin, a division of Penguin Books USA Inc.: Cover illustration by Peter Fiore
from *I See the Moon and the Moon Sees Me* by Jonathan London. Illustration copyright © 1996
by Peter Fiore.

Printed in the United States of America
ISBN 0-15-309029-4

5 6 7 8 9 10 073 2000 99 98

Contents

ALPHABET STEW

by Jack Prelutsky

Words can be stuffy, as sticky as glue,
but words can be tutored to tickle you too,
to rumble and tumble and tingle and sing,
to buzz like a bumblebee, coil like a spring.

Juggle their letters and jumble their sounds,
swirl them in circles and stack them in mounds,
twist them and tease them and turn them about,
teach them to dance upside down, inside out.

Make mighty words whisper and tiny words roar
in ways no one ever had thought of before;
cook an improbable alphabet stew,
and words will reveal little secrets to you.

Teacher's Idea Bank

Here are some ideas you may want to try out. Add to the list!

	I Do This.	I'd Like to Try This.	Doesn't Apply

1 Read to children every day. Some of the benefits are building children's
- phonemic awareness.
- vocabulary.
- sense of story.

2 Have children read and write independently every day.

3 Use word play, manipulatives, and other materials to actively engage children in phonemic awareness and phonics activities.

4 Teach the phonic elements that relate to the literature children are reading.

5 Give children many opportunities to read words, sentences, and stories containing the phonic elements they are learning.

6 Provide wait time, perhaps 10 seconds, to give children the chance to self-correct their errors.

7 Look at children's writing to find out which phonics skills they apply.

8 In addition to fiction and nonfiction books, provide a variety of reading materials, such as Big Books, poetry, chapter books, children's magazines, packages and other environmental print, electronic books, lists, and posters.

9 Use a variety of teaching methods to help children who have different learning styles.

10 For children with a home language other than English, find out about letter sounds and language patterns that are different in their first language and could cause difficulties as children learn to read and write.

11 Communicate your phonics approach to family members through a newsletter, a family night at school, or some other way. Enlist their support.

12 My idea:

Harcourt Brace School Publishers

OFTEN
Today
Suddenly
loudly
inside
Outdoors
Happily
yesterday
Soon
LATER
RARELY
Wildly

Children As Learners

"**T**he purpose of phonics instruction is **not** that children learn to sound out words. The purpose is that they learn to recognize words, quickly and automatically, so that they can turn their attention to comprehension of the text."

— Steven A. Stahl

7

What You

What You
KNOW
About Language Can Help You
TEACH

by Dr. Nancy Roser
Professor, Language and Literacy Studies, University of Texas at Austin

"One day Jenny got a letter from her best friend who had moved far away." *

To read this simple English sentence requires that you know quite a bit about your language and how it works. Even though teachers aren't linguists, they understand that language has structure—or syntax—and that the rules for describing this structure constitute the grammar of the language. For example, the structure of the sentence above tells you that it is Jenny's friend who has moved away rather than Jenny, and that a letter sent by the friend has already been received. (You know this in part because of the placement of modifiers and the tenses of verbs.) You are also aware of the meanings—the semantics—of language. Because you know that language is intended to make sense, the meaning of the word *letter* is clear to you in this sentence. You know that Jenny got a note or a card, but not a letter of the alphabet in her mailbox.

Further, you can easily pronounce the name Jenny, even if you've never had a friend or a relative with that name. You know how the graphophonic system of your language works. Whether intuitively or explicitly, you know that double consonants that separate two vowels typically signal a short vowel sound in the first syllable. You know about discourse structures, too. For example, you can readily tell this sentence is from a story (rather than an informative text or a poem), and that the story is being told by an omniscient

*from *Jenny's Journey* by Sheila White Samton (Puffin, 1993).

Harcourt Brace School Publishers

narrator. You may know, too, about the origins or stories of words—that the word l*etter*, for example, comes from the Latin word *littera*. You also know how children acquire language and that at an early age Jenny herself might have expressed the meaning of this sentence by saying, "Me. . . letter." You know about text language and natural language; you know about dialects and usage; you know about printed language conventions and how to use language appropriately across settings. You know all this and more about language.

Knowing about language helps you understand children as language learners.

It is what you know about language—the structure, meanings, patterns, usages, origins, acquisition, and so on—that lets you plan for and interpret the language growth of the learners in your classroom. For example:

- **You observe and interpret children's developing command of the written code.**

When five-year-old Roxanne drew six stick figures, she carefully wrote below them "I M U I Fe" and then read what she had written by pointing to each letter, "I am with my family." Her teacher interpreted her grasp of phoneme-grapheme match, her knowledge of word boundaries, her understanding of how print travels across the page, and her dawning awareness that longer words, such as *family* (Fe), have multiple sounds. Her teacher sees that letter names (especially vowel names) are influences on Roxanne's spellings. To Roxanne she says, "Wow! What a nice family. I'd like to hear this story read again!" At another time, she may help Roxanne with the pattern of *am* and its usage in words.

- **You interpret children's miscues, using your knowledge of language.**

When Vandee reads "I'm not surrey" instead of "I'm not sure," you use knowledge of syntax, meaning, and code to recognize what is going on. Vandee has cued on his knowledge of graphophonic relationships to a greater extent than on the sentence's meaning.

- **You encourage children to work together to make meanings through oral language.**

When these first graders were discussing their read-aloud chapter book, *The Castle in the Attic* by Elizabeth Winthrop (Holiday, 1985), the negotiated meaning was greater than any one contribution:

S: *Probably only at nighttime he can come alive.*
S: *But she touched him, too.*
S: *How come he didn't come to life when she touched him?*
S: *Because it wasn't night.*
S: *She didn't really touch him!*
S: *She only touched the box!*
S: *I know because she said "Open it alone" to him.*

There is a cautionary note to add to your language knowledge base and its use, and that is this: children don't necessarily need to know as much about language as you do. You can know more labels for grammatical terms, more sound/symbol associations, more rules for construction, and more correct spellings than you can or should teach. For example, Ms. Powers knows six spellings for the long *e* sound, but not all her first-grade children need to learn them simultaneously. And Mr. Garcia is a master at diagramming sentences, but his fourth graders may not need all of this knowledge.

If you think of your knowledge of language not as a "commodity" to transfer, but as a set of lenses that help you interpret and support children's efforts, you will be putting your language knowledge to best use. Teach children what they need, what is useful and important, and what they are already trying to learn *through* and *about* language.

Phonemic Awareness

by Dr. Hallie Kay Yopp
Professor, Department of Elementary and Bilingual Education
California State University, Fullerton

"Phonemic awareness is the most potent predictor of success in learning to read."

WHAT IS PHONEMIC AWARENESS?

Research in the past decade has revealed that phonemic awareness plays a critical role in children's reading acquisition. In fact, it is considered a necessary insight for independence in reading. But what is phonemic awareness?

It is important to note that phonemic awareness is not phonics. Phonics instruction involves teaching children that printed letters and letter combinations represent speech sounds. Children are also taught how to use this knowledge to sound out words. **Phonemic awareness** refers to an awareness of sounds in *spoken,* not written, language. It is recognizing that speech is made up of a series of individual sounds that can be manipulated. The ability to use phonics as a means to decode printed words is probably dependent upon a child's understanding that speech is made up of individual sounds, that is, his or her phonemic awareness. It makes little sense to teach the sounds represented by letters to a child who lacks phonemic awareness.

Phonemic awareness can be difficult for young children because it demands a shift in attention from the *content* of speech to the *form* of speech. It requires individuals to attend to the sounds of speech separate from their meanings.

Primary-grade teachers will find that a handful of children enter school with well-developed phonemic awareness. Others have only a rudimentary sense of the sound structure of speech. Through lots of playing with sounds in a language-rich environment, phonemic awareness emerges over time for most children.

Individuals who are phonemically aware are able to do the following:

- rhyme
- blend isolated sounds together to form a word
- tell how many sounds can be heard in a word
- segment spoken words into their constituent sounds
- substitute sounds in spoken words
- add sounds to spoken words
- delete a sound from a spoken word

Harcourt Brace School Publishers

Did you ever hear a /b/ word,
A /b/ word like *book?*

In other words, individuals who are phonemically aware are able to answer correctly the following questions:

Rhyme: Do these words rhyme?

fish   *dish* (yes)
hill   *mail* (no)
run   *ran* (no)

Phoneme Blending: What word do we have when we put these sounds together?

a-t (at)
b-i-g (big)
ch-i-n (chin)

Phoneme Counting: How many sounds do you hear in these words?

is (2)
book (3)
sit (3)

Phoneme Isolation:

What is the beginning sound in *rose?* (/r/)
What is the final sound in *pencil?* (/l/)
What is the sound in the middle of *cat?* (/a/)

Phoneme Segmentation: What sounds do you hear in these words?

dog (/d/-/ô/-/g/)
race (/r/-/ā/-/s/)
up (/u/-/p/)

Phoneme Substitution:

What word would we have if we changed the /t/ in Tommy to an /m/? *(mommy)*

What word would we have if we changed the /t/ in *hot* to a /p/? *(hop)*

What word would we have if we changed the /i/ in *sit* to an /a/? *(sat)*

Phoneme Addition:

What word would we have if we added a /g/ to the beginning of *row? (grow)*

What word would we have if we added an /l/ to the middle of *boo? (blue)*

What word would we have if we added a /t/ to the end of *ow? (out)*

Phoneme Deletion:

What word would we have if we left the /t/ out of the middle of *stand? (sand)*

What word would we have if we left the /s/ off the beginning of *spin? (pin)*

What word would we have if we left the /l/ off the end of *seal? (sea)*

PHONEMIC AWARENESS AND READING AND SPELLING ACHIEVEMENT

Research conducted during the last few decades has revealed that phonemic awareness is significantly related to success in learning to read and spell. The relationship is one of reciprocal causation or mutual facilitation. That is, phonemic awareness supports reading and spelling acquisition, and instruction in reading and spelling, in turn, supports further understanding of the phonemic basis of our speech. The relationship is so powerful that researchers have concluded the following:

● Phonemic awareness is the most potent predictor of success in learning to read. It is more highly related to reading than tests of general intelligence, reading readiness, and listening comprehension (Stanovich, 1986, 1994).

- The lack of phonemic awareness is the most powerful determinant of the likelihood of failure to learn to read (Adams, 1990).
- Phonemic awareness is the most important core and causal factor separating normal and disabled readers (Adams, 1990).
- Phonemic awareness is central in learning to read and spell (Ehri, 1984).

Why is phonemic awareness so important in learning to read and spell? Because English and other alphabetic languages map speech to print at the level of phonemes. In other words, our written language is a representation of the *sounds* of our spoken language. Therefore, it is critical to understand that our speech is made up of sounds. Without this insight, written language makes little sense.

Fortunately, research suggests that phonemic awareness can be developed in individuals by providing them experiences with language that encourage active exploration and manipulation of sounds, and training studies reveal gains in phonemic awareness and in subsequent reading and spelling performance (Ball & Blachman, 1988; Bradley & Bryant, 1983; Cunningham, 1990; Lundberg, Frost & Peterson, 1988). Many researchers encourage preschool, kindergarten, and primary grade teachers to provide linguistically-rich classroom environments where children are encouraged to play with the sounds of language (Adams, 1990; Griffith & Olson, 1992; Mattingly, 1984; Yopp, 1992). Appropriate activities for young children have a sense of playfulness about them, are conducted in social settings that encourage interaction among children, pique children's curiosity about language and invite their experimentation with it, and allow for differences among children (Yopp, 1992).

 Note: Dr. Hallie Kay Yopp has developed the Yopp-Singer Test of Phoneme Segmentation, which can be used to assess a child's phonemic awareness. This test and a Phonemic Awareness Interview can be found in the Teacher Resources section at the back of this book.

ACTIVITIES THAT STIMULATE PHONEMIC AWARENESS

Activities for stimulating phonemic awareness can be easily incorporated into any reading program. Activities such as the following should be part of the literacy experiences offered to young children:

- songs that play with spoken language, such as those found in *Oo-pples and Boo-noo-noos: Songs and Activities for Phonemic Awareness*
- riddles that draw attention to sounds in spoken language
- games that require manipulation of spoken language, such as tongue twisters, jump-rope rhymes, and hink pinks
- shared readings of stories that make use of rhyme, alliteration, or segmentation and that emphasize the sounds of the spoken language

Harcourt Brace School Publishers

Phonics Instruction for the Nineties
...AND BEYOND!

by Patricia Smith

Elementary Reading/Language Arts Coordinator,
Cypress-Fairbanks School District, Houston, Texas,
and Adjunct Professor of Education at the University of Houston-Clear Lake

It's only 8:30 in Mrs. Hodges's first-grade classroom, and already the children are productively involved in their language arts activities. Gathered around Mrs. Hodges are ten students who are engaged in a shared reading of the Big Book, *Flower Garden* by Eve Bunting. She uses a pointer to help them track the print. The discussion is rich with predictions that flow from the repetitive language, rhyming pattern, and illustrations.

During one of the repeated readings, Mrs. Hodges encourages volunteers to read the lines the way they would sound if they were spoken. As the reading becomes more fluent, she focuses their attention with a sliding mask. This teacher-made device creates an adjustable window that exposes first the word *garden* and then the letter *g* that represents a sound children are reviewing, (/g/). They decide to add *garden* to their ongoing class chart of "Words Beginning with G or g" when they rejoin the others for a full-group activity.

What are the other children doing during this teacher-directed activity? In one corner of the room, six children are listening to a tape-recorded dictation and using the sounds they hear to form words with magnetic letters on individual cookie sheets. They self-check each word formation by listening to the tape.

At another center, four children are sorting picture cards by initial consonant sounds. At still another center, a small group is busily writing sentences on personalized bookmarks to place inside books they have reread that day. There is a quiet buzz at this table because several are whispering words repeatedly, listening to the sounds before putting them into print. At times they confer with one another about spelling accuracy.

Is this a classroom where children are joyfully learning to read and write? Definitely! Is this a classroom where children are learning phonics? Again, the answer is definitely! Is it possible for both phenomena to be occurring simultaneously? You bet! Not only is it possible, but it is occurring throughout this country as we complete the nineties and enter the twenty-first century!

Should phonics be taught?

Marilyn Jager Adams, a cognitive psychologist, reviewed and interpreted the research on early reading instruction in *Beginning To Read: Thinking and Learning About Print* (1990). In her work, Adams gave phonics instruction a resounding recommendation:

> "Approaches in which systematic code instruction is included along with the reading of meaningful connected text result in superior reading achievement overall, for both low-readiness and better-prepared students."

Reading is the process of constructing meaning from written texts. This construction of meaning occurs when readers use their background knowledge and the words from the text to create new meaning. Without the recognition of words, there would be an incomplete foundation for constructing meaning. Phonics, along with the use of context, word parts, syntax, and automaticity, enables a reader to recognize words.

How should phonics be taught?

Instruction should be direct within the context of real reading and writing.　Let's look again at Mrs. Hodges's first-grade classroom and observe phonetic instruction within a literate environment.

Mrs. Hodges: We've been reading about many different kinds of homes. Today, you've enjoyed following the print, looking at the illustrations, and talking about the poem, "A House Is a House for Me," by Mary Ann Hoberman. Let's read the first part again. Where does the ant live?

A hill is a house for an ant, an ant.
A hive is a house for a bee.
A hole is a house for a mole or a mouse.
And a house is a house for me!

Class: Hill. (Mrs. Hodges writes *hill* on a large sheet of chart paper. She repeats the same procedure for *hive, hole*, and *house*.)

Mrs. Hodges: Let's read these four words on the chart. What do you notice about the words?

Class: They all begin with the letter *h*. (Mrs. Hodges underlines the *h* in each word.)

Mrs. Hodges: Does anyone's name begin with the same sound we hear in *house* and *hill*?

Class: *Heather* and *Hardy*. (Mrs. Hodges writes both names on the chart. Volunteers suggest more words.)

Mrs. Hodges: Let's read all the words on this chart. Now open your picture dictionary notebook to the *h* page. Choose words from our chart to write on your page. You may sketch a reminder picture for each word. Knowing how words often sound when they begin with *h* can help us when we read and write. As we read words that begin with this letter, let's add them to our chart.

Phonics instruction should be demonstrated as one of multiple cueing systems that are used in conjunction with one another.   Children will use phonics along with the context and syntax of the text, the illustrations, and the words they recognize automatically. As Mrs. Hodges reads with her students, she frequently discusses and demonstrates the use of these many sources for cues. She asks children to cross-check their pronunciations. *Does it look right? What would you expect to see in the word if it were pronounced that way? Does it make sense?*

The use of multiple cueing systems allows children to achieve successful approximations. Since our language is not completely phonetic, there are times when the first attempts at spelling or pronunciation are approximate. When children are shown how to adjust and are praised for adjusting their initial attempts at spelling and reading, they are able to use their graphophonic knowledge flexibly.

Marie Clay reminds us that our goal is to produce independent readers whose reading and writing improve each time they encounter print. We need to help children learn how to
- monitor their reading.
- search for cues.
- cross-check one source of cues against another.
- self-correct to gain meaning and accuracy.
- become increasingly fluent as they read more-challenging materials.

Instruction should be aimed at developing automaticity.   Samuels (1988) suggests that achieving accuracy is not enough if the process is time-consuming and laborious. Fluent readers need to identify words quickly so they can devote their energy and attention to comprehension. He recommends developing automaticity in word recognition by giving children sufficient instruction and practice with print conventions.

Should phonetic rules be taught?
Clymer (1963) found that only 45% of the phonics rules worked as often as 75% of the time. Children should not see rules as absolutes but rather as a way to note patterns within words. For example, the silent final *e* is not always consistent, but knowing about it does help the reader note the pattern. Rules should not be taught for recitation.

What might be the advantage of learning common word families?
Even though phonetic rules are not highly reliable, Adams (1990) noted that sounds are stable in the part of the word from the vowel forward. She referred to the part with the vowel as the "rime." She called the part before the rime the "onset." Adams found that 95% of the 286 phonograms that appear in primary-grade-level texts are consistent. She identified the 37 most common rimes from which children could form 500 words through the substitution of onsets.

-ack	-all	-ain	-ake	-ale	-ame	-an
-ank	-ap	-ash	-at	-ate	-aw	-ay
-eat	-ell	-est	-ice	-ick	-ide	-ight
-ill	-in	-ine	-ing	-ink	-ip	-ir
-ock	-oke	-op	-ore	-or	-uck	-ug
-ump	-unk					

What is the role of invented spelling?
Adams found that classroom encouragement of invented spellings is a promising approach toward the development of phonemic awareness and understanding spelling patterns. Further, it clearly indicates which of the phonetic principles have been internalized by the learner.

Harcourt Brace School Publishers

What is the role of phonemic awareness in teaching phonics?

Phonemic awareness is awareness of the sounds in *spoken* words. Phonics is awareness of the relationship between letters and sounds in *written* words. Marie Clay (1993) includes practice in phonemic awareness in the 30-minute Reading Recovery lesson. Children are taught to move markers to signal the sounds they hear in a spoken word, for example, moving three markers to show the sounds in *leaf*, /l/, /ē/, /f/. When teachers lead children in the enjoyment of rhymes, poems, chants, and songs, they are helping children develop phonemic awareness.

Should time be devoted to teaching children the names of letters?

Children often come to school having "overlearned" the names of letters through experiences such as the alphabet song, according to Adams. This over-learning of the names gives them pegs on which to hang the knowledge of letter sounds. It keeps them from being confused by having to learn letter names and sounds simultaneously.

What do letter reversals by young children indicate?

Adams found that letter reversals are usually not a sign of neurological dysfunction or immaturity but of insufficient knowledge of how print works. When children were shown the contrasts between similar letters and given repeated experiences with reading and writing print, the reversals disappeared.

When is instruction in phonics the most productive?

Instruction in phonics is most successful when children have a context in which to learn the code system. Children who have experienced hours of exposure to print during their preschool years come to school with a solid foundation for learning to read. For children lacking this foundation, schools provide kindergarten activities such as listening to stories, shared reading of Big Books, matching print in nursery rhymes on charts, and other language experience activities. This whole-language base gives children a context of what reading and writing are and the uses that sound-letter knowledge might have. It makes the learning of the graphophonic code meaningful.

There is no sequence of phonics instruction that is clearly superior. To plan their instruction, conscientious teachers note the needs of children, the appearance of patterns in the texts to be read, and the organization of generalizations from more reliable to less reliable. One such sequence with rationale follows.

Phonetic Principle	Rationale
Consonants—initial then final	Most reliable and useful sounds
Short vowels—introduced one at a time after every four or five consonants	Allows for formation of words
Consonant digraphs (Examples: *ch, sh, th*)	Unique sounds that appear often
Consonant blends	Promotes concept of blending
Long vowels formed with silent final e	Teaches the concept of a silent final vowel, causing the first vowel to be long
Long vowel patterns formed with two vowels together (Examples: *ai, ay, ee, oa*)	Most reliable of the two-vowels-together generalization
Variant vowel patterns (Examples: *r*-controlled, *oi, oy, ou, ow, oo, au, aw*)	Useful for children reading at late second-grade level and above

WHAT TYPES OF PRACTICES SEEM THE MOST PROMISING IN LEARNING TO USE PHONICS?

- Big Books
- Language experience activities
- Many books for reading and rereading
- Sentences to cut up and re-form
- Songs to promote phonetic sounds
- Sorting activities
- Books that contain many words with previously taught phonic elements
- Individual chalkboards for practicing words from dictation
- Ongoing class-composed phonic charts
- Individual word books of child-composed pages, arranged alphabetically

- Invented spelling activities
- Magnetic letters
- Posters showing mnemonic sound/letter associations such as the s in the form of a snake
- Hand-held mirrors to note the way the mouth looks when making a particular sound
- Individual reading inventories by teachers to note children's use of decoding strategies
- And, most important, an environment that encourages risk-taking and growing independence!

Using Cueing Systems to Unlock New Words

by Patricia Smith

"Jeff, what do you do when you come to a word you don't know?" asked first-grade teacher, Mrs. Ames.

"Well, I sit up very straight and listen to my brain whisper it to me."

Intrigued, Mrs. Ames asked, "Does that work—are you then able to read the unknown word?"

"Sometimes, but not always. My brain doesn't always whisper loud enough, no matter how straight I sit or how hard I listen. What should I do then?"

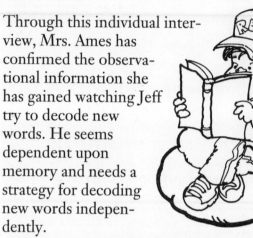

Through this individual interview, Mrs. Ames has confirmed the observational information she has gained watching Jeff try to decode new words. He seems dependent upon memory and needs a strategy for decoding new words independently.

What strategies should he and other readers use when encountering new words? To answer this question, we can look at the strategies accomplished readers use.

A MULTI-PRONGED APPROACH FOR INDEPENDENTLY DECODING NEW WORDS

When strong readers encounter a new word, they actively problem-solve the translation of the unknown word by using all the available information about the unknown word. The available information comes from various cues, as shown in the graphic.

By teaching children to combine information from these sources, we enable them to read new words independently, regardless of the phonetic regularity of the unknown word or the amount of context available for decoding.

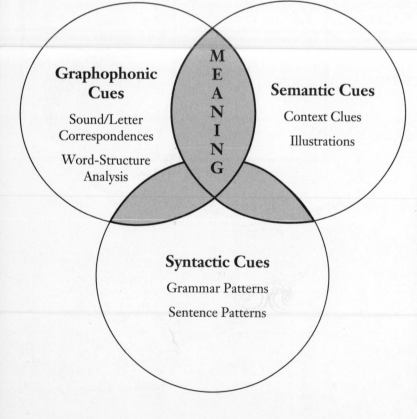

Graphophonic Cues

Sound/Letter Correspondences

Word-Structure Analysis

MEANING

Semantic Cues

Context Clues

Illustrations

Syntactic Cues

Grammar Patterns

Sentence Patterns

Harcourt Brace School Publishers

PROMOTING SUCCESSFUL DECODING

Teachers can provide direct instruction, modeling, discovery activities, and numerous opportunities for children to practice using the cueing systems.

What Does the Teacher Do?	What Do Children Learn About Decoding?
• Models decoding by reading aloud to children.	• Print conveys meaning. • Reading progresses left to right, top to bottom. • Each printed word can be matched one-to-one with a spoken word.
• Directs children's attention to difficult words and guides the decoding by using information from a variety of sources.	• Words can be read by using the sounds letters represent, the meaning (context), the picture clues, and the language patterns.
• Teaches children to associate sounds with letters and to blend the sounds to form words.	• Phonetic sounds, common word patterns, and sound blending can help in decoding.
• Provides numerous opportunities for children to independently read and decode new words.	• Some words become known automatically through repeated reading.
• Promotes making approximations and adjustments, if needed, to read the author's words accurately.	• Reading new words involves searching for cues, taking risks, monitoring trials, and confirming/self-correcting.

PROMPTING THE USE OF ALL CUEING SYSTEMS FOR DECODING AND SELF-CORRECTING

When strategic readers encounter a new word, they often use all the cueing systems—graphophonic, semantic, and syntactic—to decode it. When children are stymied by a new word, it usually indicates they are stopping too soon in their use of cues. Additionally, when readers make a decoding error and seem unable to adjust their attempt, they are probably relying on too few of the cueing systems.

We can prompt children to use all the cueing systems. Eventually, the prompts can become less specific and more apt to promote independent decoding. The chart on the next page provides some examples of prompts.

Goal of the Prompt	Prompt for Decoding	Prompt for Confirming or Self-Correcting
One-to-one matching	• Point to the words and make them match your spoken words. • Read it again with your finger and make it match.	• Did your words match? • What did you notice? What wasn't quite right? Try again.
Use of graphophonic cues	• Get your mouth ready. • Read it with your finger. • Read all the way through the word.	• Does that look right? • What sound would you hear at the beginning of __?__ • That makes sense, but look at _____.
Use of context (semantic) cues	• Where could you look? • Think about what would make sense. • Think about what is happening.	• Does that make sense? • You said, _____. Does that make sense?
Use of syntax cues	• What would sound right in that sentence? • Reread the sentence and make it sound like "talk." • Try that again.	• Does that sound right? • Do we talk like that?
Use of word parts	• You know _____. Change the beginning [ending] to read this word. • Read it in parts.	• Do you know another word that is almost like this one? • What do you know that will help?

Praise children for their independent use of decoding strategies.

- I like the way you worked to read that word all by yourself.

- That was a very tricky part, and you kept trying until you made it sound right.

- You did what good readers do. You used the sounds, the pictures, the meaning, and made it sound like talking.

- What a good job you did of rereading when you came to the hard part!

By promoting this strategic use of the cueing systems, readers will be able to successfully decode most of the words they have in their listening/speaking vocabularies. They will not have to rely upon their "brain whispering to them," as young Jeff did in the opening example. They will know what good readers do when they encounter new words.

Harcourt Brace School Publishers

Achieving Fluency

by Dr. Nancy Roser

Six-year-old Kris had just finished her first week in first grade. Excitedly, she described to me on the phone "the great books" she was reading. With the soft sound of South Carolina in her voice, she enthused, "The best is *Did You Find the Dog?* It goes like this: 'Did *you* find the dog?' '*I* din't find the dog.' 'Did *you* find the dog?' '*I* din't find the dog.' And on and on until . . . guess what? They FIND the dog, and [in a squeal] it had *puppies*!!" Her joy for the story's ending seemed boundless.

Then, a pause. "But," she continued, "it doesn't sound that way when *we* read it."

"Oh?" I asked. "And how does it sound when you read it?"

"Well," Kris explained patiently, "we have to use our pointers (she pronounced it "poy uhn tuhs"), and it sounds like, 'Did . . . you . . . find . . . the . . . dog?' 'I . . . din't . . . find . . . the . . . dog.'"

It's a funny, typical first-grade anecdote. At first blush, it seems that Ms. Patton, Kris's teacher, is encouraging her children to become *less* fluent first-grade readers, by having them slow their reading rate so that their words no longer "sound" like normal speech. Actually, Ms. Patton is reinforcing growth toward more *mature* reading. As Jeanne Chall describes it, Ms. Patton is working to make certain her children become "glued to the print."

> To advance . . . beginners have to let go of pseudo-reading. They have to engage, at least temporarily, in what appears to be less mature reading behavior— becoming glued to the print—in order to achieve real maturity later. They have to know enough about the print in order to leave the print. (Chall, 1987)

By slowing to point, the children are no doubt learning word boundaries and voice/ print matching, and are coming to understand that printed stories, unlike oral ones, stay the same, no matter how many times they're reread. Eventually, Kris must regain the fluency that her memory of the story allowed her to demonstrate on the phone.

Children gain reading fluency when they can read at a steady rate, recognizing words accurately and achieving correctness in phrasing/intonation *(prosody)*. Teachers know that fluent readers comprehend better than less-fluent ones. They also know that readers must become "automatic" in word recognition so that struggles with words don't claim attention from making meaning. But, teachers know that fluency takes practice, and practice is one of the best ways that readers, especially beginners, come to understand how written language works. That is, with her voice matching the print in repeated visits to her "great book," Kris is more likely to attend to the patterns of written language, and to observe how the code works.

How else can teachers help to ensure that beginners become fluent readers? Here are some ideas:

Model fluent reading. There is probably no better way to learn to be a fluent reader than by listening to fluent models. Be conscious of your expression, your inflections, and your phrasing when you read aloud. Pay attention to the books you select and be sure to read them well.

Provide stories on audiocassettes for the classroom Listening Center. One good way to provide models of fluent oral reading for children is through your Listening Center. Offer children taped read-alouds of their current favorites, especially the books and stories they are reading for themselves. Encourage listeners to follow the print with their eyes or with a marker.

Provide manageable texts. Fitting the appropriate "level" of text to the child's ability is critical to supporting reading fluency. If the story is too hard, the child must slow down to struggle with the words and ideas. If the story is too easy, the child may become too quickly "unglued" from the print.

Monitor reading rate. When the text "fits" well, first-grade children typically read at 60 words per minute, and increase by 10 words per minute each year (Guszak, 1992). A quick rate check can indicate whether the texts you provide children are manageable for them.

Harcourt Brace School Publishers

Include children in shared reading.

Children who read together in Big Books are provided the opportunity to become fluent in a risk-free activity. That is, chiming voices mask individual errors until the struggling reader gains familiarity, confidence, and fluency.

Put songs, rhymes, and chants on charts.

Every jump-rope jingle and playground chant provides opportunities to promote fluency. When familiar songs, poems, and rhymes become the material of instruction around the classroom, children can revisit them, matching their voices with the print and attending to the way in which written language records sounds.

Teddy Bear, Teddy Bear, turn around.

Teddy Bear, Teddy Bear, touch the ground.

Teddy Bear, Teddy Bear, turn out the light.

Teddy Bear, Teddy Bear, say "Good night."

Make poetry/rhyme notebooks.

Children enjoy putting copies of their favorite poems into personal poetry books. They can both illustrate the poems and share them with others in "Poetry Performances." Best of all, personal choices encourage more reading and rereading, creating greater likelihood of fluent reading.

Encourage readers to rehearse.

Because readers demonstrate increased fluency when they are allowed to practice, let your children read silently before they read aloud. Very young or struggling readers may need to read aloud with you or with a friend before they read aloud to others. In all cases, fluent performances depend upon rehearsal.

Promote rereadings.

Reading and rereading the same text greatly benefits fluency. Evidence attests to positive gains in reading rate and accurate word recognition between children's first and last reading of the same passage. However, experts caution that rereadings can also diminish children's interest in the text. The following suggestions are ways to keep interest alive while promoting rereadings:

▶ **Provide for buddy reading.** Children can take turns reading with a buddy every other page or paragraph. Reading to a "cross-age" buddy can also motivate practice (and thereby increase fluency).

▶ **Offer scripts for Readers Theatre.** Even the simplest text can be turned into a Readers Theatre script in which children take roles and exchange them. By taking roles, young readers are challenged to make reading "sound" like normal speech. Because the roles are fun to interpret, the scripts are read and reread. For example, some beginners reread *The Perfect Pet* (Harcourt Brace, 1997) dozens of times because of the big sneezes of allergic pet seekers and because of the manageable language patterns:

First child:	Achoo! We *can't* get a dog.
Second child:	Achoo! We *can't* get a cat.
Both children:	Achoo! Achoo! We *can't* get a mouse.

Even though this book is only seven pages long, it invites rereadings because it is humorous, because of its dialogue, and because it can be enacted easily.

▶ **Provide books to take home.** Because readers must practice in texts that are manageable, there should be opportunities to take home books that "fit." Published trade books and child-made books that are carried home allow children to demonstrate their developing skills in another setting. In addition, readers who read both in school and at home are more likely to become fluent.

PHONICS AND THE DIVERSE LEARNER

by Dr. Marguerite Cogorno Radencich
University of South Florida, Tampa, Florida

LEARNERS WITH VARIED LEARNING STYLES

We all learn differently. We once thought of such differences as modalities—visual, auditory, and kinesthetic. We now think more in terms of learning styles, from the work of educators such as Rita Dunn and Marie Carbo, and multiple intelligences, from the work of Howard Gardner. These concepts are all related. Your students will use various learning styles, and *your* learning style will not match those of all your students. It is essential that you regularly include activities that match different learning styles and intelligences.

The following suggestions are based on a framework of multiple intelligences, initially comprising seven intelligences—verbal/linguistic, logical/mathematical, visual/spatial, bodily/kinesthetic, musical/rhythmic, interpersonal, and intrapersonal—and now expanding to include additional intelligences. Those most commonly used by schools are verbal/linguistic and logical/mathematical intelligences. Alternate intelligences are the focus here, particularly kinesthetic, musical, and artistic intelligences.

1. Allow children options in activities and in the formation of groups, when possible. One pair might work well together reading-around-the-room or writing-around-the-room, using a clipboard. Another student might enjoy making letters on the chalkboard with a wet paintbrush. Yet another might find success working with a phonics computer program.

2. Young children can become actively involved in activities that require them to manipulate sounds and letters. Word play is an excellent way to promote phonemic awareness and to increase phonics knowledge.

   ❧ Students can manipulate sounds through rhymes, raps, and music. For example, *Fe, fi, fiddly-i-o* can be sung, ending with "Now change it to the /z/ sound," leading to a chorus of *Ze, zi, ziddly-i-o* (Yopp, 1992). Because the effectiveness of phonics rests on students matching what they see with what they hear, you may want to record or have children record the target letters as you sing along. You can use *Oo-pples and Boo-noo-noos: Songs and Activities for Phonemic Awareness* to help children develop phonemic awareness.

   ❧ Write on the board the pattern word *care*. Children can manipulate individual letters (Cunningham, 1995) or write words as you dictate modifications:

   Change one letter and make *dare*.

   Rearrange the letters to make *dear*.

   Take away one letter and leave *ear*.

   Rearrange those letters and make *are*.

3. Capitalize on interpersonal intelligence through the use of a buddy system. Sometimes children will learn from others what they do not learn from you.

Harcourt Brace School Publishers

4. Use concrete learning. Children who seem not to learn a sound from a passive worksheet may learn the sound quite well if there is a picture associated with the letter, such as a fish drawn at the top of an *f,* or by using manipulatives such as gluing beans onto a large letter *b.*

5. Find creative ways to engage parents and guardians in supporting children's learning styles. Most homes have food labels and junk mail that children can use to cut out words and letters. Then they can sort them and combine them as they explore and learn different sounds. Encourage the use of letter manipulatives, phonics songs, and chants of word spellings.

LEARNERS WITH DIVERSE LANGUAGES AND DIALECTS

The more you know about children's languages and dialects, the better you can deliver phonics instruction. If children do not hear certain sounds in their dialect or language, teaching the sounds may be ineffective. Another consideration is interference between any two of the following: (a) your pronunciation, (b) standard American English sounds, and (c) sounds spoken in a child's native language or dialect. Thus, Cambodian children may have difficulty with the letter *c,* which is pronounced /ch/ in Cambodian, or a teacher from Boston working with children in the South will find that they have different vowel pronunciations.

Following are some examples of patterns to watch out for. (See also the chart on page 24.) It would be helpful to use information like this to figure out the sounds in English that children with other native languages might find confusing. Keep in mind that dialects of each language result in variants just as dialects of English do.

Spanish Vowels each have one sound: *a* as in *father, e* that sounds similar to *eh* as in the name *José, i* like the *e* as in *me, o* as in *no,* and *u* as in *zoo.* The sounds /j/, /z/, /sh/, and /th/ do not occur in Spanish. Also, in Spanish, the letter *j* sounds like the English /h/, the letters *c* and *g* have only the hard sounds, the letter *h* is silent, and the *ll* sounds like the English /y/. Finally, *b* and *v* are sometimes pronounced almost identically.

Chinese English sounds not used in Chinese are /b/, /d/, /j/, /g/, /s/, /v/, /z/, /ch/, /sh/, /th/, and /o/. In one system of Chinese, the Wade system, certain rules differ from English. For example, *k* and *h* at the beginning of a syllable never combine with /i/ or /ü/. Also, syllables which end with /i/, /u/, or /ü/ must be written with *y, w,* or *yü* if they are not preceded by a consonant.

As with all areas of language, issues of phonics and pronunciation must be handled with great tact. There is little that is so personal to us as our language!

When working with children who are learning English, use the following tips, as applicable to age and English proficiency:

- Use Total Physical Response (TPR). Developed by James Asher, the idea is simple. Give a command that involves an overt physical response. At first, you also perform the action in the command. For example, "Make a *c,*" and students move their bodies to form a *c,* or "Be a cat," and students crawl and meow. Ask students then to think of words that use the target sound.

- Second-language learners need exposure to topics and concepts that they can understand. Use concrete objects whenever possible, such as keeping a shoe box with manipulative objects for each letter that children can relate to the letters they represent.

Encourage children to experiment with sounds from their home language as well as sounds from English. Celebrate children's languages. After all, English words derive from as many as 100 other languages!

Focus on clearing up confusion rather than on correcting pronunciation. If a child says *ban* for *van*, just repeat the correct pronunciation, "Yes, that's a *van*."

Avoid phonics activities with no oral component.

Use masks and puppets to help increase risk-taking as students pronounce new sounds.

Consider your work in meeting diverse needs as an opportunity to stretch yourself and make yourself an ever-better teacher. Embrace the challenge!

The following chart shows similarities across languages which can result in confusion with reading and spelling.

Problem Contrast	Chinese	French	Greek	Italian	Japanese	Korean	Spanish	Urdu	Vietnamese
/ā/-/a/			X	X	X	X		X	
/ā/-/e/			X	X	X	X	X	X	X
/a/-/e/	X		X	X	X	X	X	X	X
/a/-/o/	X	X	X	X	X	X	X	X	X
/a/-/u/	X		X	X	X		X	X	
/ē/-/i/	X	X	X	X	X	X	X	X	X
/e/-/u/	X		X	X			X	X	
/ō/-/o/	X		X	X	X		X	X	X
/o/-/ô/	X		X		X		X	X	X
/o/-/u/	X		X	X	X		X		X
/u/-/o͞o/	X	X	X	X			X	X	X
/u/-/o͝o/	X		X		X		X		X
/u/-/ô/	X		X	X	X	X	X	X	
/o͞o/-/o͝o/	X	X		X		X	X	X	
/b/-/p/	X					X	X		X
/b/-/v/			X		X	X	X		
/ch/-/j/				X		X	X		X
/ch/-/sh/	X	X	X		X	X	X		X
/d/-/th/	X				X	X	X	X	X
/f/-/th/				X		X	X	X	X
/l/-/r/	X				X	X	X		X
/n/-/ng/	X	X	X	X	X		X	X	
/s/-/sh/			X	X	X	X	X		X
/s/-/th/	X	X	X	X	X	X	X	X	X
/s/-/z/	X		X	X		X	X		X
/sh/-/th/			X		X	X	X	X	X
/t/-/th/	X		X	X	X	X	X	X	X
/th/-/th/	X	X	X		X	X	X	X	X
/th/-/z/	X	X	X	X	X	X	X	X	X

From *The ESL Teacher's Book of Lists,* © 1993 by The Center for Applied Research in Education

Harcourt Brace School Publishers

ACHIEVING BALANCE IN OUR LITERACY PROGRAMS

by Dr. Dorothy S. Strickland
State of New Jersey Professor of Reading, Rutgers University

New insights into learning and teaching have brought about numerous changes in literacy instruction in recent years, particularly in the early grades.

Greater emphasis on writing and its relationship to reading, greater use of trade books, and increased attention to the integration of the language arts are among the most noticeable changes. Most would agree that there is much to celebrate. But, as with anything new, the changes have also brought about some confusion and frustration. A variety of factors may account for this.

★ At times, new ideas were embraced and implemented before they were clearly understood.
★ At other times, change was only nominally accepted, and more-familiar methods were imposed on the new curricular frameworks and materials.
★ In still other cases, too many changes were imposed at once.

As a result, many educators were made to feel as though they were struggling in a morass of change.

Today, in districts throughout the country, educators are once again reexamining the direction they have taken. They are wondering, "Have we gone too far in one direction or another? Have we abandoned some of the tried-and-true good practices of the past?" They want to know how they can take advantage of the best research and methods available today in a way that makes sense and is more effective for children, teachers, and parents. They are searching for balance.

When educators search for balance in their literacy programs, certain issues inevitably surface. Following is a list of some of these issues and suggestions for how they might be addressed.

BALANCING A *SKILLS* EMPHASIS WITH A *MEANING* EMPHASIS

Neither skills nor meaning need ever be abandoned. Indeed, skills are learned best when taught through meaningful use. For example, after sharing a story that includes many examples of the same sound/letter relationship, such as /b/*b* or the inflectional ending *-ing*, point out the relationship and discuss it with children. Help them make a chart of other examples they find in their reading, and encourage them to use what they have learned in their own writing.

Harcourt Brace School Publishers

BALANCING DIRECT AND INDIRECT INSTRUCTION

Direct instruction usually refers to the explicit transmission of knowledge. Indirect instruction involves providing opportunities for children to discover new ideas and strategies, to apply skills they have learned, and to assist one another as teachers and learners. Effective teaching will make use of both. For example, minilessons are key elements of contemporary literacy instruction. These are systematically planned, brief instructional episodes that focus on a single strategy for learning and that employ direct instructional methods. Minilessons make heavy use of the modeling and demonstration of skills. Teachers not only *tell*; they *show*. Showing how something is done is one of the most effective methods of direct instruction available. Still, that is not enough. For children to "own" a skill or strategy, they need opportunities to try it out on their own and to "discover" opportunities for its use. The most adept teachers are those who know how to provide a variety of opportunities for children to learn and to apply their learning in a meaningful way.

BALANCING CONTENT AND PROCESS

Although the desire for information frequently inspires us to learn, learning involves much more than accumulating information. If we overemphasize content, children are left not knowing how to get information or to learn on their own. When teachers plan for instruction in science or social studies, for example, they need to keep both content and process goals in mind.

Content goals refer to the knowledge we hope children will gain from the topic under study, such as how plants grow or the kinds of helpers in the neighborhood. **Process goals** refer to what we hope children will be able to do at the end of the study—specifically, how to observe and chart the growth of a seedling over a period of time or how to interview a neighborhood helper and write a brief paragraph to share with the class. Process goals take children beyond the specific subject matter, helping them become skillful learners no matter what content is under study.

BALANCING TRADE BOOKS AND TEXTBOOKS

In many school districts, textbooks continue to be the core materials in various curricular areas, providing a sense of continuity across grade levels. An effective literacy program embraces a wide variety of materials, including separately bound trade books. It may be helpful to think in terms of several layers of texts in the classroom. One layer might involve the literature selected by the teacher for read-aloud purposes. Another might be the core literacy program in which all children are involved, providing many opportunities for extension to trade books and technology. Yet another layer might involve a variety of self-selected materials that children read independently. While these layers relate specifically to the literacy program, children should be involved with both core and trade book materials in every subject area. Each layer has an important role in a balanced program.

Harcourt Brace School Publishers

BALANCING INFORMAL CLASSROOM ASSESSMENT AND NORM-REFERENCED STANDARDIZED TESTS

Shifting the balance away from standardized tests in favor of authentic classroom assessment methods is a goal that most educators applaud. Standardized tests are useful in rank-ordering pupils and, frequently, teachers and schools as well. However, they do little to help teachers focus on instructional needs. Schools are seeking to make greater use of performance-based assessment procedures, which are closely linked to the curriculum and also serve to inform the public about how well students are doing. For example, portfolios that include samples of a child's writing over time help both teacher and child get a sense of specific strengths and weaknesses. Probably most important, this type of ongoing assessment tends to make the criteria more clear to both child and teacher.

Achieving balance in our literacy programs should not imply that there is such a thing as The Balanced Approach. Nor should it imply a sampling method in which a teacher selects a little of this and a little of that. Finally, it should not imply two very distinct, parallel approaches coexisting in a single classroom—for example, literature on Mondays and Wednesdays and skills the remainder of the week.

Ultimately, a teacher must make instructional decisions based on how children learn and how he or she can best teach them. More than likely, this will never mean throwing out all of the methods used by any single teacher or school district. Needless to say, it will also not mean maintaining the status quo. Finding the balance takes knowledge, time, and thoughtfulness.

Harcourt Brace School Publishers

A balanced literacy program makes use of the various ways and conditions under which children learn to read and write. This chart offers sound ideas for achieving balance.

FACTORS TO BE CONSIDERED	ELEMENTS THAT MUST BE BLENDED or COMBINED
INSTRUCTIONAL EMPHASIS	Skills and meaning are blended so that they reinforce and support children's learning.
INSTRUCTIONAL FORMATS	Flexible grouping provides for regular use of whole-group, small-group, and personalized instruction; homogeneous and heterogeneous groups; and grouping for various purposes, such as needs, interests, and for research.
INSTRUCTIONAL MODES	Teacher-led, direct instruction is accompanied by teacher-planned, indirect instruction, which allows children many opportunities to practice and reinforce skills in ways that are meaningful and purposeful.
INSTRUCTIONAL STRATEGIES	Instruction is delivered through several basic strategies, which are modified according to purpose: reading and writing aloud (teacher demonstrates); shared/interactive reading and writing; guided reading and writing; independent reading and writing.
MATERIALS	The total literacy program includes a core literacy program; individually bound trade books; technology; and content-area materials, charts, journals, manipulatives, and other supplementary materials.
ASSESSMENT	A planned assortment of assessment means are used for various purposes: ongoing classroom assessment tools (both formal and informal), summative end-of-unit measures, portfolio assessment, and district-wide summative assessment.
CURRICULUM INTEGRATION	Every attempt is made to connect literacy learning in all content areas, such as social studies, science, math, health, and the arts.
THEMATIC FOCUS	Themes are organized around big ideas, such as universal themes (making new friends, exploration), content-area topics, topics of interest, authors, or textural forms (literary and expository).
READING OPPORTUNITIES	Children read widely among literary and expository forms: stories, plays, poems, essays, letters, and others. Through reading, they are exposed to authors with many different writing styles.
WRITING OPPORTUNITIES	Children write stories, plays, poetry, letters, short and long reports and essays, and a variety of other types of texts.
MULTICULTURAL FOCUS	Children are exposed to diversity among authors, locales, and groups of people from varied backgrounds.
SCHOOL-HOME CONNECTIONS	Children are given many opportunities to connect learning at home and school; they build upon home experiences in school and extend school learning to the home.

NOTE: For more information about achieving balance in literacy programs, see Dorothy Strickland's article in *Reading Today* (October 1996).

Helping Children

Learn

"**Y**ou can engage the children's minds and hearts in reading good literature and finding their own voices as authors and, at the same time, teach them how our alphabetic language works!"

Patricia M. Cunningham

Managing Phonics in the School Year and the School Day

by Dr. Marguerite Cogorno Radencich

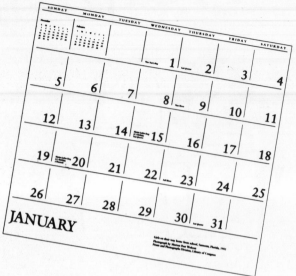

JANUARY

Girls on their way home from school, Sarasota, Florida, 1941
Photograph by Marion Post Wolcott
Prints and Photographs Division, Library of Congress

"...your management plan for phonics instruction can be both systematic and flexible, direct and incidental, whole group and individualized."

Start your school year with a blueprint that includes careful attention to your students' phonics needs. Then think about specific ways of fitting phonics into your busy school days. Select and adapt ideas from the following to make the organization of your phonics program work for you.

FITTING PHONICS INTO THE SCHOOL YEAR

As you plan to systematically introduce children to needed phonics, consider the following:

☆ Provide ample opportunity for children to develop phonemic awareness, the understanding that spoken language is composed of a series of separate sounds and the ability to segment language into phonemes. Keep a file of resources you can turn to for each sound. Include tongue twisters, children's books that repeat a given sound, alphabet books, and songs. Don't forget old favorites like the *e-i-e-i-o* in "Old MacDonald" or the *K-K-K-K* in "K-K-K-Katie."

☆ If your children are just beginning with phonics, rather than designating a sound a week, try a two-pronged strategy that allows for both direct and incidental learning:

1 Directly focus on two or three sounds at a time—working those sounds into words.

2 Simultaneously bombard children with exposures to sounds in a print-rich environment. Fill the room with print and spend a few minutes with daily reading-around-the-room. You will then find children using these words in temporary or conventional spellings. Celebrate this risk taking, and you will have children who practice a lot and then progress through the stages of developmental spelling—a prime way of learning phonics.

Harcourt Brace School Publishers

If you recognize that each child is likely to know the initial sound in his or her name, you will use children's names as an important part of the literate environment. Thus, in your News of the Day, Toby will be able to help with the initial letter of *today* whereas Wendy will be able to help with *we*. Enhance this incidental learning also by posting several charts of children's names for their reference (e.g., an "I can tie my shoelaces" shoe-shaped chart and an "I ride the bus" chart) and including activities such as laying out children's names printed on large cards and helping children find their own and, later, those of others.

☆ If your children are at a level to learn phonograms, keep handy—perhaps as a laminated bookmark in your planbook—the following list of the most common rimes (phonograms) (Wylie & Durrell, 1970). Plan both to work with rhyming words and to regularly incorporate these patterns into children's reading and writing. For example, Rose Robart's *The Cake That Mack Ate* is a predictable language book that provides practice with *-ake, -at, -ack*, and *-ate*. Shared reading with this book followed by class-made innovations on the story would provide contextualized practice for several of the most-frequent phonograms.

High-Frequency Phonograms

-ack	-ale	-ain	-ake	-all	-ame	-an
-ank	-ap	-ash	-at	-ate	-aw	-ay
-eat	-ell	-est	-ice	-ick	-ide	-ight
-ill	-in	-ine	-ing	-ink	-ip	-it

FITTING PHONICS INTO THE SCHOOL DAY

To be sure that you include any needed phonics in busy school days, organize phonics activities into your basic flexible grouping patterns. Many options are possible. The chart that follows provides some possibilities:

GROUPING OPTIONS

	Whole Class	Teacher-Facilitated Small Group	Cooperative Group or Pair	Individual
News of the Day with emphasis on certain phonic elements	X			
Phonics through attempts at temporary spelling		X	X	X
Phonics songs, rhymes, and tongue twisters	X	X		
Phonics manipulatives	X	X	X	X
Trade books that repeat phonic elements		X	X	X

These and other activities can fit into regular routines:

Individual Allow children to engage in phonics play as they enter the classroom in the morning. You might have magnetic letters on cookie sheets, sides of file cabinets, or an overhead projector; felt letters on a felt board; and clay ready to be formed into words.

Cooperative Group or Pair Provide boxes of books from which children can choose during a buddy-reading time. Include a rich supply of titles that focus on phonic elements, such as Dr. Seuss's *Hop on Pop* and Diana Epstein's *Buttons.*

Harcourt Brace School Publishers

Teacher-Facilitated Small Group Set aside time for teacher-facilitated small groups. To help Lupe, Bill, and Kenesha in developmental spelling, you might use Elkonin boxes (Clay, 1985) with a focus on the sounds in

chat | ch | a | t | and *brick* | b | r | i | ck |.

Children use each box to represent a sound, first placing a marker in each box as they say the sound and then recording the sounds in the boxes.

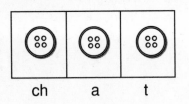

ch   a   t

Later, you might bring Bill back and form a new ad hoc group with Barbara and Amy, with all three students needing to develop some other phonics skill. Bill might need this double duty.

Close observation and good record keeping, essential in all teaching, will be particularly important for you as you attempt to form ad hoc groupings supportive to all your students.

Whole Class Use your News of the Day to work on sounds. For example, when you record that "Mario had a visitor," you can, depending on children's levels, have those students stand whose names begin like Mario's, have Mario tell you the first letter in *visitor*, or have students find in the finished product all the words that have the same beginning sound as *had*.

As you see, your management plan for phonics instruction can be both systematic and flexible, direct and incidental, whole group and individualized. Enjoy your children's discoveries and be ever ready to prompt each a little further. There is little in a teacher's life so satisfying as teaching a child to read.

A Note for Teachers of Multi-Age Classes

Multi-age classes have many definitions and names, but generally they entail children from a range of two or three grades who are taught according to their developmental needs rather than as grade groupings within a class. The variety of levels in a multi-age class can thus be quite large.

If you teach a multi-age class, you know that you need to be organized to meet the needs of all your students. Many teachers find it helpful to use the following strategies:

☛ Regroup children for some degree of homogeneity during language arts and math instruction. In a K-2 combination, this might result in K-1 and 1-2 groups.

☛ Have children who are more comfortable with phonemic awareness and phonics help their less-proficient peers. A pair might work together on a good computer program or co-write a story. Or, the more-proficient student might read aloud a trade book that repeats a phonic element, with the less-proficient student chiming in for a second reading. Then the two together could make up their own story innovation.

☛ From time to time, allow children to reflect on their learning in a group of their same-age peers. It will help them express their ideas freely, especially children who may be intimidated by older classmates.

On the Grouping Options chart provided in this article, you may find that fewer whole-class activities are practical, and you may prefer to use more of the other grouping patterns.

Harcourt Brace School Publishers

Word Building

Discovering How the Alphabetic System Works!

by Judy Giglio
Educational Consultant and Writer

What is word building?

Word building is an active, hands-on, manipulative activity in which children are given sets of letters that they can arrange to make words. This activity is designed to require a response from every child, since they are working independently to build words and look for patterns. Children learn how replacing one letter or changing the location of a letter changes the whole word. And they have *fun* in the process!

Very few materials are needed. You can use a pocket chart to display words as you model word building. Children can use *Word Builder Cards*, which is a set of individual letter cards and selected phonogram and digraph cards.

- Letter cards can be used to build words.

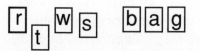

- Letter cards can be combined with phonogram cards and digraph cards.

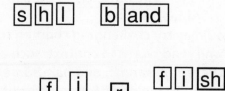

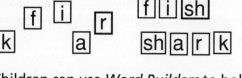

- Children can use *Word Builders* to hold the cards as they manipulate them to build words.

If you wish, you can help children make Word Builders by folding a heavy-grade paper to form a one-inch pocket. Staple or tape the sides. Draw an arrow on the pocket to show left-to-right progression.

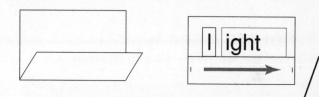

- Two more options are magnetic letters on a metal surface and transparent letter and phonogram cards on the overhead projector.

How does word building help children decode words and increase fluency?

When young children attempt to decode an unknown word, they often use one of two strategies:

1. Children may look at the initial letter in the word and say the letter sound followed by the rest of the word—for example, /p/ - /ot/, *pot*. This strategy suggests that children naturally tend to divide words into *onset* (initial consonant or consonant cluster) and *rime* (vowel plus the rest of the word).

2. Children may look for a familiar or pronounceable word part to begin reconstructing the entire word. For example, *grand* might be read as

> *an-ran-gran,* **grand**
> *gran-d,* **grand,** or
> *ran-gran,* **grand.**

Word building capitalizes on the same two strategies of using onset and rime or using pronounceable word parts to make words that follow a pattern. Through word building, children are shown how to use phonic elements to figure out unknown words.

Word building should be used along with daily writing activities that include opportunities for children to try out their phonics knowledge. The more support systems and word-recognition strategies children can rely on, the more efficiently they will be able to decode unknown words. As children are better able to decode words in context while reading or figure out how to spell words when writing, the more fluent readers and writers they will become.

What are some typical word building techniques?

The following sample lessons demonstrate effective word-building techniques. They can be adapted to focus on the phonic elements you wish to teach.

Lesson 1: Word Building by Adding the Onset

Provide children with: Word Builders, letter cards *r, t, m, n, p, s*, and phonogram card *-ail*.

- Place the phonogram card *-ail* in a pocket chart, and ask children to do the same in their Word Builders.

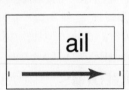

- Ask children to add a letter to *-ail* to make the word *mail*. Then have them tell you what to add in the pocket chart. Read the word *mail* together.

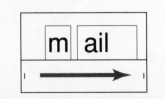

- Write *mail* on a large sheet of paper to begin a word list or on an index card to add to a classroom word file or Word Wall.
- Continue by having children make the words *pail, tail, rail, trail, sail, nail,* and *snail,* followed by reading and writing the word each time.
- Read together the list of *-ail* words. Ask what is the same about all the words. Ask volunteers to add more *-ail* words.
- Later, you may try challenging children to decode words such as *detail, trailer,* or *railway* in context. Ask them, "Is there any part of this word that you know?" After they attempt to read the word, cross-check its use in context to determine if it makes sense.

Lesson 2: Word Building by Adding the Rime

Provide children with: Word Builders, letter cards *c, h, l, r, s,* and phonogram cards *-ap, -at, -and.*

- Place letter card *c* in the pocket chart. Children do the same with their Word Builders.
- Invite children to add a phonogram card to make the word *cat*. Then have them tell you what to add in the pocket chart. Say the word in parts, /k/-/at/, and together, *cat*. Write *cat* on an index card to add to a Word Wall or a classroom word file.
- Follow a similar procedure to build the words *rat, hat, sat; lap, sap, cap, rap; land, sand, hand*.
- Encourage children to add other words that follow the same patterns to the Word Wall or word file.
- Later, you may try challenging children to decode and read words in context, such as *chat, rattle, scrap, sandal,* and *handsome*. Remind them to look first for any part of the word they know.

Harcourt Brace School Publishers

Lesson 3: Word Building and Sorting

Provide children with: Word Builders and letter cards *a, c, c, h, r, s, t.*

In this more complex lesson, help children discover patterns for two vowel sounds as well as words that rhyme. Write the words on cards as they are made, and place these word cards in a pocket chart. As children make words, emphasize word meaning as well as structure.

- Invite children to use three letters to make *art* in their Word Builders.
- Have them move the same letters around to make *tar*. Ask if they have seen workers using *tar* to pave roads.
- Tell them to change a letter to make *car*.
- Invite them to make a four-letter word by adding a letter to *car* to make *cart*. Say *cat* and *cart* together. Ask how the middle sounds are different.
- Tell them to change one letter so *cart* becomes *cars*. Ask what a *cart* and *cars* have in common. *(They both have wheels and carry people or things.)*
- Have them move the same letters around to make *scar*. Explain that a cut on your skin might leave a *scar*.
- Continue having children add or rearrange letters to form these words: *star, scat, cash, rash, trash, crash,* and *chart.*
- Challenge children to arrange all the letters to make a word that names an action you do when you have a mosquito bite! *(scratch)*

Your pocket chart will look like this:

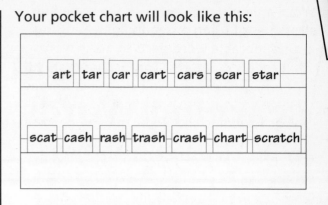

| art | tar | car | cart | cars | scar | star |

| scat | cash | rash | trash | crash | chart | scratch |

Ask volunteers to read and sort the words in the pocket chart to show words with short *a*, with *ar*, and words that rhyme. These groups of words can then be added to a Word Wall or classroom word file.

How can I plan my own word building lessons?

When planning a word building lesson, decide which words children will make and in what order so that they will be guided to discover common spelling patterns and variations in clusters of words. Depending on ability, children can gradually increase the number and length of words they build. Focus on groups of words that contain a vowel-consonant pattern that can be presented as a unit. The following chart lists high-frequency phonograms. This list can be supplemented with any rimes or syllable patterns your children need to know. Refer to the lists of phonograms beginning on page 173 for example words for these and more phonograms.

HIGH-FREQUENCY PHONOGRAMS

-ack	-an	-at	-eep	-id	-ing	-op	-ug
-ad	-and	-ate	-eer	-ide	-ink	-ope	-um
-ag	-ang	-aw	-en	-ig	-ip	-ore	-ump
-ail	-ank	-ay	-ent	-ight	-it	-orn	-un
-ain	-ap	-ead	-est	-ike	-ock	-ot	-unk
-air	-ar	-ear	-et	-ill	-og	-ound	-up
-ake	-are	-ed	-ew	-im	-oke	-ow	-urry
-all	-ark	-eed	-ice	-in	-old	-oy	-ust
-ame	-ash	-eel	-ick	-ind	-ook	-ub	-ut

Often-Asked Questions About Learning Words

by Dr. W. Dorsey Hammond

Dr. W. Dorsey Hammond, Professor of Education at Oakland University in Rochester, Michigan, is a recognized authority on comprehension and emergent literacy in children.

Below are questions that educators often ask about how words are learned and the best strategies for teaching words to young children. Although there are different views about how words are learned, there are some very common-sense approaches to word learning.

How do children learn words?

Children learn words in many ways: by seeing words in their environment, by developing phonics generalizations about how letters and letter combinations represent sounds, and most importantly by doing lots of reading. Just as it is true that we learn words in order to read, it is also true that we read in order to learn words. The more students read, the more words they learn. Thus, strategies such as using predictable books, experience stories, choral reading, shared reading, and repeated reading all contribute to the learning of words.

What is the most important idea about learning words?

The most important idea is a caution not to equate word learning with learning to read. Learning to read is much more than the learning of words. The focus must always be on teaching children to read, with the learning of words as a *part* of that process.

Where does phonics fit in?

Phonics is important. Phonics allows children to develop generalizations about words and letter combinations. It allows children to decode unknown words. It allows them to go from a known word to an unknown word. For example, if as a young reader I know the words *game, same,* and *ten*, I can use the beginning sound and letter in *ten* to recognize the word *tame*. Or I can use the *un* from *fun*, change *her* to *der*, use the *st* in *stop*, and add *and* to recognize the word *un der st and*.

So should I teach phonics first before I do anything else?

A more balanced approach is to teach phonics while involving students in other reading activities, such as shared reading, reading experience stories, reading a variety of literature, reciting poems, reading predictable books, and also writing on a daily basis. In this way, phonics is learned more easily, in the context of language and other reading activities. Many words will be learned and reinforced through exposure to meaningful print.

Harcourt Brace School Publishers

Why are high-frequency words difficult for children to learn?

First, we have to recognize that this is indeed the case. Words such as *the, said, what, was, saw, to,* and *has* are often difficult for beginning readers. This should not surprise us. Simply because these words occur frequently and are usually "little" words does not mean they are easier to learn.

There are a number of reasons why high-frequency words are difficult. They tend to be abstract rather than concrete—it's difficult to picture a "said" or a "the" or a "was" in your head. It's much easier to picture a "mother" or a "sister" or a "pizza." Secondly, these high-frequency words are little. They have fewer features than do longer words, such as *Tyrannosaurus, roller coaster,* and *spaghetti.* Big words of high meaning interest children more than little words of low meaning. In addition, the high-frequency words tend to be phonetically irregular, as in *was, the, of, what, to,* and *said.* Because of these combinations of factors, we should not be surprised that high-frequency words often present problems for young children.

Should high-frequency words be the first words children learn?

That is the viewpoint in some circles. But there is a better approach. We should not begin by teaching children what is most difficult for them to learn. The priority should be on learning to read. It makes little difference what words children are learning as long as they are learning. Careful observations of children learning to read indicate that interesting and high-meaning words are often learned first, followed shortly by some of the high-frequency words.

What are some ways for children to learn words?

In addition to strategies such as choral reading and reading predictable books, there are a variety of ways to enhance word learning.

First, encourage children to look for words in their environment: advertisements and labels on buildings, and signs, boxes, containers, and packaging. Encourage children to search in magazines and newspapers for words they know, and to cut them out and make a word collage or poster with the words. More-advanced students can find words they know that relate to a particular theme or subject area.

Second, have students in the early reading stages keep a word file or word bank of words from their reading experiences. Students at a more-advanced stage of reading could keep a record of a select number of interesting words they are learning. Words children learn from the literature they are reading can be written on small cards and kept in a recipe box, or have them keep their known words in a small notebook. As children learn new words, they can add these words to their existing file.

Third, have a Word Wall in your classroom. As children learn new words, they can be added to the Word Wall. *Words on Word Walls should be chosen by the children and should be words they have initially learned.* The words are exhibited on a wall to help with retention and to remind children of interesting new words they are learning.

Fourth, encourage students to organize and categorize words they know either by some meaning relationship or a common phonic element, such as beginning sounds, words that rhyme, or words beginning with a certain consonant cluster.

It is not necessary to do all of these activities, though. Different teachers and students prefer different activities. Of course, the more children read and write, the more words they will learn.

What if students don't know enough words to read the text?

The options here are relatively straightforward. One option is to move to an easier text, particularly a text that is more predictable in terms of ideas and sentence patterns—the kind of text typically found in Big Books.

In addition, you could read the text to the student or students first and then have them read along with you. Here is a good rule from the *child's* perspective: the teacher reads *to* me, then *with* me, and then I read by myself.

Children could also read chorally with other class members. Or, they could practice repeated readings during which the same segment of text may be read or rehearsed several times until fluency is reached.

Isn't it important for students to write words?

Writing is very important—indeed, essential. As children write stories and construct words as best they can, they are not only constructing meaning but using their phonics ability to decide which letters represent particular sounds.

Note that the emphasis here is not on copying words but on writing words as best they can to communicate ideas. We know that writing and reading are best learned together.

How do children learning English as a second language learn words?

Actually, they learn words in very much the same way as described above. Using predictable books, repeated readings, experience charts, phonics activities, and environmental print activities are the easiest and most natural ways to learn words and to develop language.

Why do students often appear to be careless when they read and miscall "easy" words?

We need to remember that what appears to be an easy word to us as adults may not be easy to the child. High-frequency words or little words are really not easy for the young reader. When children are reading in the early stages, they have several things to pay attention to. They are trying to recognize words. They are trying to sound good and perform for themselves or for their teacher and classmates. And, they are trying to make sense. That is a lot to do all at the same time.

In summary, what are some basic guidelines to remember in helping children learn words?

Here are seven basic guidelines for word learning.

1. Introduce words in context rather than in isolation. Context provides the support that young readers need to be successful. Trying to learn words in isolation is difficult and frustrating for many children.
2. Provide every opportunity for students to participate in activities such as reading predictable books, creating experience stories, and rereading familiar stories. Children learn words best by reading.
3. Encourage students to use meaning clues when reading sentences and stories. Words in context are easier to recognize and understand than words in isolation.
4. Encourage young children to write and to construct their own spelling approximations.
5. Celebrate words! Talk about words. Encourage students to find words they know. Keep a word bank or Word Wall of *known* words.
6. Be positive. Focus on what children know, not on what they don't know. Talk about the "new and interesting words we have learned."
7. Be patient. Some children will learn to read relatively quickly. Others will take more time. Persistence and positive attitudes are the keys.

Harcourt Brace School Publishers

How Can I Help Students Identify Unknown Words?

"We hope that our students will choose to read because they love to read."

As teachers, we know that the goal of reading instruction is to produce successful, life-long readers. We hope that our students will *choose* to read because they *love* to read.

Successful readers can identify the majority of unknown words they encounter in their reading. They have developed a system of strategies that they can apply to make sense of a new word. For some difficult words, they know to try more than one strategy.

The chart that follows lists many of these strategies. You may want to post one in your classroom. Encourage students to share with each other the strategies they use, and add any new ones to the chart, such as *Ask a friend*.

What Good Readers Do

1. Try out a word to see if it makes sense in the sentence. Use the letters of the word to check it. Reread the sentence to be sure the word makes sense.

2. Look at the letters. Use what you know about the sounds of letters to figure out the word.

3. Look for small words or word parts that you know to help you read the word.

4. Look in the sentence or paragraph for clues that tell what the word means.

5. Skip the word. If the sentence makes sense without it, keep reading.

6. Look up the word in a dictionary.

1. Try out a word to see if it makes sense in the sentence. Use the letters of the word to check it. Reread the sentence to be sure the word makes sense.

Unrecognized words can fall in two categories: words that are already a part of a student's oral vocabulary but that have not previously been encountered in written form and words that are completely unknown. The same strategies can be applied to decoding both kinds of words, but success will be more rapid with words that are already known, because the student has a context into which such a word fits, like a needed puzzle piece.

Often, the best way to decode these words is to make an "educated guess" based on context. Letter sounds may be used to confirm the guess. One teacher modeled this strategy with a sentence from "The Twelve Dancing Princesses":

The twelve princesses pretended to go to sleep.

Hmm. That's a big word. *The twelve princesses* something *to go to sleep*. What did they do? *Tried?* No, the word starts with *pr. Pretty? Pretty to go to sleep?* No, that doesn't make sense. *Pretended? The twelve princesses* pretended *to go to sleep*. That makes sense.

---

2. Look at the letters. Use what you know about the sounds of letters to figure out the word.

Sometimes, the context of the sentence may not offer enough clues. Research shows that when this happens, even very good readers process a new word letter-by-letter (Adams, 1990). Often individual letter sounds can be put together to produce an approximate pronunciation that will lead to the correct word.

3. Look for small words or word parts that you know to help you read the word.

Some long words are easy to decode because they are compound words. The English language tends to coin words by putting together two shorter words. Many times the new word is very descriptive of the word's meaning. This is particularly true of words that are specific to a subject area.

Remind students to look for whole words within a long word. Sometimes they can use the meanings of the two small words to help them figure out its meaning.

Long words that are not compounds may contain word parts, such as affixes, that students recognize. When they know a prefix or word ending, they can concentrate on the base word. Notice how a teacher modeled this strategy with a sentence from a social studies text:

Many inventions make work easier.

I see the ending *-tions* on this word. How is the ending *-tion* pronounced? (*shun*) Okay, I'll cover up the *-tions* part and look at the rest of the word. I see the small word *in* and I can sound out the middle part *v-e-n*: *in-ven-tions*.

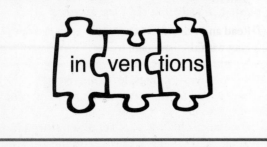

---

4. Look in the sentence or paragraph for clues that tell what the word means.

Sometimes students will meet words that, even when pronounced correctly, will not be part of the student's known vocabulary. For those words the student needs additional strategies to unlock the word's meaning. Often the text itself will give the meaning of the word, as in the following example:

Soon the new business had more than fifty competitors. Everyone wanted to sell the same product.

The teacher modeled his thinking to show how to use the context to figure out the word *competitors* as follows:

The business had more than fifty competitors. I wonder if that means it made fifty different things. That makes sense. I'll keep reading. *Everyone wanted to sell the same product*. Oh, competitors are people who want to sell the same product. Just like competitors in a race all want to win.

---

5. Skip the word. If the sentence makes sense without it, keep reading.

From time to time a long or difficult word will not be vital to the meaning of the text. One third-grade student read and enjoyed the book *Hitty, Her First Hundred Years*. When asked to tell about the story, the student began, "Hitty is a wooden doll that was carved for a girl named Foe-eb." The student had read and understood the book without knowing that the girl's name was Phoebe—and it really didn't matter!

6. Look up the word in a dictionary.

The last method is one students should learn. But, since it requires leaving the text, it interrupts the flow of reading and is therefore not the first choice of most students. However, when a word is vital to the meaning of the text, and the student is not having success with other strategies, he or she should know how to use a dictionary, including how to select the most precise meaning if more than one is given.

Harcourt Brace School Publishers

Developing Phonemic Awareness with Trade Books

by Dr. Bernice E. Cullinan
Professor of Reading, New York University

I f you ask a young child, "What sound do you hear at the beginning of this word?" you may get a puzzled look in reply. If the child seems to not have any idea what you are talking about, he or she may not be phonemically aware, or aware that speech is made up of separate sounds. Before children acquire phonemic awareness, they do not know that sounds can be segmented—that you can hear one sound at the beginning of a word. Just as most children crawl before they walk and babble before they talk, young readers need to develop phonemic awareness before they can learn about phonics.

Children learn language the way they learn to swim—by getting into it (water/language), sloshing around in it (water/language), and seeing what they can do with it (water/language). Children learn with their whole bodies; they need to touch, taste, feel, smell, and hear everything. They need to experience language to learn to use it. That is why playing with the sounds of language and writing down the sounds they hear is the best way that children can develop phonemic awareness and, for that matter, learn to read.

BOOKS TO DEVELOP PHONEMIC AWARENESS

Children develop phonemic awareness when they have many opportunities to hear different sounds in words. They come to recognize that speech is made up of a series of sounds (phonemes) that can be said separately, or segmented. Characteristics of certain texts help foster phonemic awareness in beginning readers, which is important to their success in becoming independent, fluent readers. These texts provide scaffolding, or support, for children who are new to reading. Children who do not know how to read (decode) figure out more quickly how reading works when they see words that rhyme, words that begin with the same sound, words that appear in patterned sentences, and words repeated in cumulative stories. Many books contain more than one such supportive language feature.

WHY USE THESE BOOKS?

We don't teach language rules to very young children who are learning to speak; they learn to use language in context by being surrounded with it, by hearing it, and by experimenting with it. Expose children to fun-filled books so that they can hear and play with the sounds of language that they need to distinguish.

GENERAL STRATEGIES

The following strategies to develop phonemic awareness may be used with any books that have the characteristics mentioned above:

* Drench children in language with discernible sound patterns.
* Choose books with explicit language play.
* Read and reread favorite stories, songs, and poems.
* Play with the language features used.
* Encourage predictions.
* On repeated readings, let children read more words as you read fewer. Have them take increasing responsibility for reading texts.
* Encourage children to write or tell story variations, using the language patterns from the literature.

BOOKS WITH SUPPORTIVE LANGUAGE FEATURES

The following books, which represent four kinds of supportive language features, are favorites with many teachers and children. For additional books that promote phonemic awareness, see the annotated bibliography on pages 167–172 in the Teacher Resources section in this book.

Rhyming Books

> **Rhyming books have words with the same ending sound.**
> Carlstrom, Nancy White. *Jesse Bear, What Will You Wear?* Alladin, 1996.
> Hennessy, B. G. *Jake Baked the Cake.* Viking Penguin, 1990.
> Paparene, Pamela. *Five Little Ducks: An Old Rhyme.* North-South, 1995.
> Scarffe, Bronwen. *Oh No!* Mondo Publishing, 1994.
> Vandine, JoAnn. *Little Mouse's Trail Tale.* Mondo Publishing, 1994.

How to Use Rhyming Books

❋ Read and reread the rhyming books aloud.
❋ Write rhyming words on separate word cards. Ask children to match their word cards to words in the story.
❋ Prepare word charts with basic rhyme segments, such as *-ake, -ip, -ent,* or *-ing*. Write the segment at the top of the chart, and ask a group to list words that rhyme. Encourage children to add words to the chart any time they discover ones that rhyme. Individuals can also create lists.

Books with Alliteration

> **Alliterative books have words that repeat initial consonants.**
> Anno, Mitsumasa. *Anno's Alphabet: An Adventure in Imagination.* HarperCollins, 1975.
> Bender, Robert. *The A to Z Beastly Jamboree.* Lodestar, 1996.
> Carle, Eric. *All About Arthur.* Franklin Watts, 1974.
> Charles, Donald. *Paddy Pig's Poems.* Simon & Schuster, 1992.
> Edwards, Pamela Duncan. *Four Famished Foxes and Fosdyke.* HarperCollins, 1995.
> Enderle, Judith Ross, and Stephanie Gordon Tessler. *Six Creepy Sheep* (1992); *Six Sleepy Sheep* (1991); *Six Snowy Sheep* (1994). Boyds Mills Press.

How to Use Books with Alliteration

❋ Show alphabet books, such as *Anno's Alphabet*, and have children find the objects whose names begin with each letter featured or hidden in the artwork.
❋ Play with beginning consonant sounds. Make up phrases that begin with the same sound. Give children a chance to experiment with sounds, using songs, games, riddles, tongue twisters, shared reading, and dramatization. Say tongue twisters: **Peter Piper picked a peck of pickled peppers. She sells seashells by the seashore.**
❋ Substitute consonants. Change the first letter of a child's name to create a nonsense rhyming syllable; for example, change *Maddie* to *Waddie*. Then sing the rhyme, leaving a blank for the name: **Waddie, Waddie, the elephant sat on _____.** [Children say *Maddie*.] **Wommy, Wommy, the elephant sat on Tommy.**

* Play guessing games. Say: "Riddle, riddle, ree. I see something you don't see, and it starts with /d/-/d/-/d/" (use the sound, not the letter). "I'm thinking of an animal that begins with /r/-/r/-/r/. It has long ears and hops. What is it?"

* Read *Six Sleepy Sheep* or another alliterative story. Help children make up other phrases in which all the words start with the same sound. Ask children to draw pictures containing as many objects as possible whose names begin with the same sound.

Books with Patterned Language

Patterned books have language that repeats words and sentence structures.

Galdone, Paul. *Little Red Hen*. Clarion, 1974.

London, Jonathan. *I See the Moon and the Moon Sees Me*. Viking Penguin, 1996.

Martin, Bill, Jr. *Brown Bear, Brown Bear, What Do You See?* Henry Holt, 1964, 1983, 1992.

Stadler, John. *Cat Is Back at Bat*. Puffin, 1996.

Vaughn, Marcia. *Hands, Hands, Hands*. Mondo Publishing, 1995.

How to Use Books with Patterned Language

* Use shared reading. Read aloud from print that children can see, using materials such as Big Books, transparencies, and charts. Point to the words. When you come to a word that is predictable and decodable—a word children should know—stop and allow children to say the word. Read the same text repeatedly, each time turning over more of the reading responsibility to children.

* Read and reread the story.
* Sing the story.
* Substitute new words in the patterned sentences.
* Have children repeat patterned phrases—for example, in *Little Red Hen:* "'Not I,' said the dog.' 'Not I,' said the cat.' 'Not I,' said the mouse.'"

Cumulative Stories

Cumulative stories have repeated successive additions to a story or verse.

Domanska, Janina. *If All the Seas Were One Sea*. Alladin, 1971.

Fox, Mem. *Hattie and the Fox*. Scholastic, 1987.

Hogrogian, Nonny. *One Fine Day*. Macmillan, 1971.

Mahy, Margaret. *When the King Rides By*. Mondo Publishing, 1995.

Traditional. *This Is the House That Jack Built*. Childs Play, 1977.

How to Use Cumulative Stories

* Present stories orally by performing them as a group.
* Read the story as a script in Readers Theatre style.
* Speak the story as a choral group. Volunteers may choose parts.
* Write the text on strips of paper. Give each sentence strip to a small group of children. Have them read their part.

Reading aloud books with supportive language features is one of the most practical—and enjoyable—ways to develop phonemic awareness in beginning readers. By using fun-filled activities to build on children's experiences with the sounds of language, you will start children on the road to becoming successful readers.

Harcourt Brace School Publishers

ANSWERS to Parents' Often-Asked Questions About Phonics

by Dr. Dorothy S. Strickland and Dr. Nancy Roser

"In an effective reading program, instructional emphasis must be placed not only on phonics but also on the other skills that help to make the use of phonics work for readers and writers."

Parents, educators, and the general public perceive reading ability to be the most critical skill contributing to school achievement. When learning to read is discussed, the topic of phonics is certain to emerge. Concerns about phonics have been with us for a very long time. But today, perhaps more than ever before, teachers are likely to be confronted with questions regarding phonics instruction. Below are some of the questions that parents are most likely to ask and some suggestions as to how they may be answered.

WHAT EXACTLY IS PHONICS ANYWAY?

Phonics refers to teaching the sound/letter relationships used in reading and writing. It involves an understanding of the alphabetic principle upon which the English language is based and a knowledge of which sounds are associated with a particular letter or combination of letters.

The ability to learn phonics is largely determined by the development of *phonemic awareness,* the ability to discriminate between and manipulate sounds in words and syllables of speech. It is also important to distinguish the teaching of phonics from instruction in *structural analysis,* which involves a knowledge of the structural changes that differentiate words having common roots, such as inflectional endings *(-s, -ed, -ing),* prefixes and suffixes, and compound words. Parents should know that phonemic awareness is a key part of the kindergarten and the primary grades programs and that structural analysis continues throughout the grades.

WHY IS THERE SO MUCH TALK ABOUT PHONICS?

Historically, there has always been a great deal of attention given to phonics. It is generally the first thing discussed when parents are concerned about a child's progress in reading and is often looked to as a possible causal factor when the public is concerned about reading scores. Indeed, phonics has come to mean much more than what is expressed in the definition above. For many, phonics stands for the preservation of "the basics." It is considered to be a highly concrete and visible skill, one whose presence or absence can easily be determined. Parents need to know that their concerns about phonics and reading are important and that phonics is a key part of an effective beginning reading program. They also need to know that reading involves a set of highly complex skills, all of which influence one another. In an effective reading program, instructional emphasis must be placed not only on phonics but also on the other skills that help to make the use of phonics work for readers and writers.

WHY DON'T THEY TEACH PHONICS ANYMORE?

First, parents need to know that the teaching of phonics has never been abandoned. But, in some ways at least, instruction probably looks different from the way it was taught to them. For example, more attention is given to teaching phonics as a part of a total reading program, so that children not only learn sound/letter relationships but also know when and how to use them. Today's young learners are more likely to use phonics in writing as well as in their reading. In writing, students apply their knowledge of phonics when they

Harcourt Brace School Publishers

spell words, using invented and conventional spelling. In reading, students are taught how to use phonics clues in conjunction with word meaning and sentence structure in order to figure out unknown words.

IS THERE A CERTAIN AMOUNT OF PHONICS THAT ALL CHILDREN SHOULD HAVE?

Children come to the task of learning to read with varying backgrounds and abilities. Nevertheless, they should all have access to a systematic program of phonics instruction that is organized in terms of a sound developmental sequence. There will always be some children who "catch on" to the alphabetical principle immediately and use it to figure out the patterns of our language with a minimum of instruction, and some will need extensive extra support. An effective reading program has built-in accommodations for all these differences.

HOW WILL I KNOW WHETHER MY CHILD IS GETTING ENOUGH PHONICS?

There are two very important windows into a child's knowledge and use of phonics. One is the kind of reading errors made during oral reading. The other is the application of phonics during attempts at independent writing. Beginning readers are likely to first pay attention to the sounds that the initial letters in a word represent. In their early writing, they will continue to demonstrate what they understand about sound/letter relationships. Parents have reason to be concerned if, over time, they don't see steady development, for example, increasingly more accurate use of word spacing, final letters, letter pairs, and vowels.

WHAT IS THE CONNECTION BETWEEN PHONICS AND SPELLING?

Knowledge of phonics is a major spelling strategy. Young children are released to communicate their ideas through writing, using whatever sound/letter relationships they know. It is important to remember, however,

that visual memory and structural knowledge are also extremely important. As children encounter more and more words visually and become acquainted with the common spelling generalizations in our language, they should rely less on phonics and more on a combination of these strategies.

SHOULD PHONICS INSTRUCTION CONTINUE THROUGHOUT THE GRADES?

Most experts agree that phonics instruction should be concentrated in the first few grades, with alternative strategies or special instructional programs considered for those who have not mastered it sufficiently by third grade. Instruction in structural analysis, which is often confused with phonics, continues throughout the grades.

PHONICS IS BEST LEARNED WHEN:

* Children come to it with a strong base in phonemic awareness.

* Instruction focuses on reading and writing words, rather than on rote memorization of sound/letter correspondences or the memorization of rules.

* It is taught in conjunction with other important word-recognition strategies, such as attention to word meanings (*semantics*) and structure (*syntax*).

* Children perceive it as a useful tool for reading and writing, rather than something that is learned for its own sake.

* It is taught as one important part of children's growing understanding of how our language system works.

* Children are given ample time to practice what they know through independent reading and writing.

* It is taught as part of a *total* reading/ language arts program.

Harcourt Brace School Publishers

Helping Children Learn 45

From School to Home: Phonics Is All in the Family!

by Judy Giglio

Family members can give younger children a real boost toward being successful learners by engaging them in all sorts of literacy activities at home. Here are some ideas for activities to help children read and write. Adapt these ideas to create your own handouts for families or to make suggestions during conferences with family members.

You can also duplicate the School-Home Newsletters found on pages 102-112 to send home. Each newsletter relates to one or two specific phonics concepts and is filled with phonics activities for family members to do together.

PLAY GAMES WITH WORDS, LETTERS, AND LETTER SOUNDS

Family members can create simple games that will reinforce children's knowledge of words, letters, and letter sounds.

Change-a-Word   While reading a familiar book or nursery rhyme to children, change the beginning sound in a word or change a significant word and have the child make the correction.

Jack be nimble,
Jack be quick,
Jack jump over
   the candlestick

Mack be nimble,
Mack be quick,
Mack jump over
   the candlestick

Sound Search   Children can hunt around the house for objects whose names contain a certain consonant or vowel sound. Family members can write the name of each found object to verify.

One variation of this activity might center on environmental print found in the kitchen. For example, on a short *o* sound search, *hot dogs, chopped broccoli, hot chocolate mix, hot sauce,* and *popcorn* might be just what junior sound/letter hunters are looking for.

Alphabetize the Grocery List   Ask children to help make a family grocery list. Items can be listed in alphabetical order. Saved empty food containers can be a reference for spelling. As the order is filled in the store, child helpers can find the name of each item on the list and cross it off.

Harcourt Brace School Publishers

Word Hunt   After reading a story or a poem together, children can hunt in the literature for words that begin or end the same, words that rhyme, or a favorite word or phrase.

New Life for Old Games   Give a new twist to familiar games:

- For "Simon Says," have children say words that *begin with s-s-s-s* or *rhyme with hat*, in place of doing actions.
- For a game of hopscotch, write letters or words in the spaces in place of numerals. Children can say words that begin with the letters or read the words as they hop.
- Write words on a sheet of cardboard for a new game of "Tiddlywinks." Flip up the tiddlywink and read the word it lands on.
- If "Red Rover" is a favorite, you can play it like this:

"Red Rover, Red Rover, send [child's name] on over."
[The child says a word that begins with /r/ and then runs over.]

"Ted Tover, Ted Tover, send [child's name] on over."
[The child says a word that begins with /t/ and then runs over.]

Scavenger Hunt   Each family member is given a different letter. Then the members hunt through newspapers and magazines, in books, or on food labels to find words that begin or end with their assigned letters. Set a timer. At the end of the hunt, see who has found the most words.

Play Word Games   Families can play games that require the building of words, such as Scrabble®.

Travel Bingo   Make Bingo cards with letters or words in place of numerals. Play while traveling in the car, and see who can be the first to find five letters or words in a row while looking at objects such as vehicles, buildings, plants, signs, and license plates. To make the cards reusable, use small self-stick notes to cover the spaces. The letters or words can be read aloud by players as they cover the game card.

CREATE A WRITING BOX

Promote writing at home with a box filled with colorful, appealing items that can be used for writing all sorts of things. A child's writing box can be a durable, plastic container filled with the following items. Items can be added or changed periodically.

* lined and unlined paper	* scissors
* construction paper	* see-through ruler with cut-out templates
* blank books	* small chalkboard, chalk
* index cards	* pencil sharpener
* pencils	* alphabet chart
* erasers	* stencils
* crayons	* rubber stamps, stamp pads
* scented markers	* stickers
* tape	* recycled greeting cards
* glue	* envelopes
* small stapler	* paper fasteners and clips

WRITE "LIKE CRAZY" AT HOME

Children will want to use their "very own" writing boxes to write at the kitchen table, in their bedrooms, at a desk, at a parent's desk, in the corner of the family room, on the deck, under a tree, on a family trip . . . all over the place! Children will not have any problem thinking of things to write, but just in case they do, some ideas follow.

On Their Own: stories, signs, greeting cards, letters, diaries or journals, poems, plays, maps, cartoons, jokes, riddles, puzzles, games, surveys

With Help: grocery lists, menus, recipes, thank-you notes, calendar events, invitations, birthday cards

Ask children to read what they have written. Tell them to feel free to ask for help with spelling, but encourage them to write the words the way they sound. It would be a good idea to have a child's dictionary available for use in copying and checking words.

RAISE A BOOKWORM

There are many ways family members can encourage active and sustained interest in reading at home. The following are some practical ideas to pass on to families:

Library Card Sign-Up   Encourage parents or other adult family members to take younger children to the nearest public library to sign up for a library card. September is "Library Sign-Up Month" and might be a good time to promote this idea.

Personal Book Shelves   Suggest that each family member have his or her own special space to keep books. They can be books that are bought or given as gifts and those that are borrowed from a library. Arrange the books in alphabetical order or according to topic.

Involve Older Family Members   Does the local public library have special programs? If so, encourage children to invite older family members, grandparents, and uncles or aunts to accompany them. Do the same for school programs. If a special program is being advertised in your community, send home notices to tell families beforehand.

Family Take-Out Service   When you have enjoyed a story, poem, rhyme, or song at school, provide copies that can be taken home and shared with family members. Children will feel proud that they can be the ones to teach family members a new action rhyme or song. If audiocassettes are available, lend them to families for overnight use.

Family Puppet Party   Provide families with directions or patterns for easy-to-make puppets, using household materials like paper bags, paper cups, plastic spoons, kitchen utensils, envelopes, egg cartons, paper plates, socks, mittens, drinking straws, cardboard tubes, and folded paper. A simple stage can be made with a blanket over a table or between two chairs, a table turned on its side, or a three-sided panel of cardboard. Family members can then plan their own puppet shows to perform at home.

Integrating

Instruction and

Assessment

"**T**he bottom line in selecting and using any assessment should be whether it helps students."

→ Dr. Roger Farr

STRATEGIES FOR ASSESSMENT

"The three main purposes for assessment are (1) finding out what children know; (2) determining if they can apply what they know; and (3) learning about children's ability to self-assess."

—Dr. Roger C. Farr

An assessment program should be integral to instruction. By using assessment tools and methods, you can get a good look at where children are instructionally and plan your program accordingly.

A variety of assessment options can be used to find out how well a child has acquired the understanding of phonics and other skills necessary to be a successful reader and writer.

FORMAL ASSESSMENT

Placement tests can be used with individual children or large groups to estimate their levels of proficiency in the areas of reading, comprehension, and writing skills. The scores from a placement test can then be used as a guide to determining placement levels.

Skills assessment tests are diagnostic tests that measure what children know. They can be used to assess a child's level of phonemic awareness, as well as skills in phonics and decoding, vocabulary, comprehension, literary appreciation, study skills, and grammar.

Holistic reading assessment measures whether children apply what they know. This kind of tool can consist of fiction and nonfiction reading passages with multiple-choice and open-ended questions that assess children's ability to apply their skills as they comprehend literature and respond in writing.

Integrated performance assessment can be reading-writing tasks that help you gain a comprehensive view of children's skills. Children read literature passages and then respond in writing to demonstrate their ability to apply writing skills in meaningful situations. Holistic scoring gives an overall picture of reading and writing proficiency.

Phonemic awareness tests can test children's level of phonemic awareness, an important predictor of reading success. The Yopp-Singer Test of Phoneme Segmentation and the Phonemic Awareness Interview can be found in the Teacher Resources section in this book.

Harcourt Brace School Publishers

INFORMAL ASSESSMENT

Informal assessment is your ongoing observation of children's progress. It probably is not possible for you to evaluate every child's reading and writing skills every day, but try to observe each child individually on a regular basis. Following are some strategies you can use.

Kid watching is the process of monitoring children's ongoing development as they participate in daily activities. You can

- observe a child working independently or groups in centers. For example, note what a child does when he or she comes to an unfamiliar word while reading aloud.

- interact with a child during brief encounters or "teachable moments."

- observe during shared reading or writing to assess whether a child understands concepts such as sound/letter relationships.

  Write notes on a sheet of paper, or use self-stick notes, index cards, or adhesive labels to jot down your impressions in the child's folder or portfolio. Look at your records of several observations over time, watching for patterns. This information will help confirm what you may already know intuitively.

Running records can be used to assess a child's phonics knowledge—decoding and word-recognition skills and strategies. As the child reads aloud, record on a copy of the selection any errors the child makes, or tape-record the oral reading for later listening and analysis. Consider the following questions as you analyze errors:

- How many errors did the child make?

- What types of errors did the child make? Are they letter/sound-based errors? What strategies did the child use to decode unfamiliar words?

- Does the child self-correct?

- How fluently does the child read?

Anecdotal records can be used to track a child's progress. Anecdotes are brief, dated notes about observations made as the child engages in activities, such as reading, writing, and working in cooperative groups. When you take notes,

- focus on strengths.

- be objective and specific. Record actions—what the child is doing.

- include the context of the event. Is it independent reading time? Shared reading?

- collect the anecdotal records systematically. They will be more effective if you focus on one or two skills or strategies for a week. Don't try to observe everything.

- later, go back through your notes to discern patterns of development, specific needs to help you plan instruction, and evidence that concepts are being applied.

Retellings (by children) of stories help you gain knowledge about a child's ability to understand a story, identify important information, make inferences, and organize and summarize information.

- Before conducting a retelling, tell children that when they have finished reading or listening, you are going to ask what they remember about the story.

- When conducting a retelling, ask children to tell the story in their own words.

- If a child needs prompting, try generic prompts such as "Tell me more," and "You're doing a nice job."

Harcourt Brace School Publishers

SELF-ASSESSMENT AND PEER ASSESSMENT

Student self-assessment helps a child gain insight about his or her own strengths and weaknesses and take responsibility for his or her own learning. Student self-assessment can take the form of

- checklists.
- pictures, diagrams, and other graphic organizers filled in with notes.
- discussion.
- reading and writing journals.
- attitudes and interests inventories.

Peer assessment, or peer conferences, can teach children how to ask questions of others so that they will then ask these questions of themselves. A peer conference also

- helps children think about standards and develop criteria for judging their own work and the work of others.
- gives children a chance to see a task from a different perspective.
- builds critical thinking and speaking skills.
- provides for cooperative learning.

Explain that a "critical friend," or peer assessor, is supposed to

- encourage and praise.
- share opinions, but also listen and respond to others' ideas.
- provide constructive feedback.
- raise questions.

PORTFOLIO ASSESSMENT

"Portfolio assessment is student-centered, providing an environment where learning flourishes."

Portfolios are ongoing collections of children's writing and other work. A portfolio can be an easily accessible folder, box, space on a shelf, or computer disk in or on which children's writing is collected. A working portfolio provides opportunities for assessment, instruction, and development. A child's carefully kept portfolio

- can include finished and unfinished work, first drafts, and notes, as well as lists of ideas, pictures, and other materials.
- encourages reflection about reading and writing development.
- serves as a springboard to more reading and writing activities.
- supplies continuous informal assessment opportunities and reveals whether instructional goals are being met.
- provides many opportunities for children to show what they can do and what they are proud of.

- You also might want to keep your own portfolio of each child's work to track his or her progress, selecting pieces of work that you feel represent the child's successes and continuing instructional needs.

Portfolio conferences provide you with an opportunity to learn about a child's reading and writing interests, attitudes, and habits and ability to use language strategies and conventions. Children benefit from a portfolio conference because it promotes reflection and self-assessment of their reading and writing. This helps them gain confidence in their own ideas and empowers them to take responsibility for their own progress and growth.

> **TIPS FOR PORTFOLIO CONFERENCES**
> - ALLOW CHILDREN TO DO MOST OF THE TALKING.
> - AVOID MAKING JUDGMENTS OR BEING EVALUATIVE.
> - COLLABORATE ON A LIST OF GOALS.
> - TAKE NOTES DURING THE CONFERENCE AND REVIEW THEM TOGETHER AT THE END.
> - PUT THE NOTES AND LIST OF GOALS INTO THE PORTFOLIO SO THAT THEY CAN BE REVIEWED AT THE NEXT CONFERENCE.

Sharing portfolios can be a perfect way to strengthen the connection between school and home. Encourage children to share their portfolios with family members because family involvement will often generate more child involvement. Also, encourage children to add to their portfolios stories and other pieces written at home.

Harcourt Brace School Publishers

Strategies Guide for Phonics Instruction

by Dr. W. Dorsey Hammond

Even as competent educators, we sometimes need an additional strategy to use; or perhaps we need to be reminded of a workable strategy that we may have overlooked. Below are ten situations, each accompanied by teaching strategies that are usually successful in helping students learn.

Problem/Situation	Considerations	Suggested Instructional Strategies
Has minimal knowledge of phonics.	The issue is how to begin. Phonics and phonemic awareness are learned best while children are having extensive experiences with print.	• Begin with basic sounds in the environment such as clapping, snapping fingers, or tapping, and ask "Are these sounds the *same* or are they *different?*" • Make sure students have concepts of *likeness* and *differences*, and *beginning, rhyming,* and *endings*. • Deal with sounds in context of words. • Use poetry, chants, songs, and so on, to focus on beginning sounds or rhyming sounds. • Use predictable books, Big Books, and nursery rhymes. • Model for students the tracking of print by moving your hand or finger along the print as you read aloud.
Has difficulty recognizing words in isolation.	Recognizing words in isolation is more difficult than recognizing words in context.	• Provide extensive opportunities to see and hear words. • Encourage students to recognize individual words within context of story or sentence. For example, after reading a page, ask students to find and point to a certain word. • Build a word bank or file of known words.
Seems confused by phonics instruction.	Some students find phonics overwhelming.	• Check students' understanding of concepts of *likeness, differences, beginning, ending,* and so on. • Address sounds in the context of words. • Chunk sounds as in f*ast,* l*ast,* p*ast*. • Say words *to* students or show the words boldly on the board or on a transparency. Have them say the words. • Keep activities light and enjoyable.
Tends to reverse letters and words.	Reversals do not usually indicate a learning problem. Reversals tend to be a natural part of the early learning-to-read process.	• Continue with appropriate instruction in reading and writing. • Put words in context. Students make less reversals when they have meaning to support their word recognition. • Encourage students to look carefully at the beginning letters of words. • Model for students the left-to-right process of reading words and sentences. • Display the letters of the alphabet.

Problem/Situation	Considerations	Suggested Instructional Strategies
Miscalls words when reading.	This behavior often occurs with young readers. It is possible that students need to mature in their phonics ability. It is also possible that students need to pay more attention to the meaning, that is, what would make sense.	• Remind students to make sense of what they are reading. • Refrain from correcting the reader until he or she has had time to self-correct. • Intervene by asking the student to look carefully at the whole word. You might ask "What part do you already know?" or "Which part of the word is giving you trouble?"
Seems to honor beginning sounds and then says *any* word with that particular sound, for example, *d*og for *d*one or *s*un for *s*and.	When reading, students often feel pressured to produce a word very quickly by looking at the first letter and then guessing.	• Encourage students to make sense of what they are reading. • Give students several words that have a common beginning and ask them to read the words with you, as in *friend, from, free,* and *fry.* These activities encourage young readers to look beyond the first letter. • Sort words by endings.
Has difficulty with ending sounds.	This situation occurs with some emerging readers.	• Encourage reading in context where the sentence structure will help determine the appropriate ending. • Identify a base word and show students how to change endings to produce a new word. Examples: *fast, faster, fastest* • Encourage students to listen carefully to the endings of words. Use rhyming words, phonograms, and rhyming couplets.
Has difficulty with vowel sounds.	This is a common comment from classroom teachers and from parents. Vowels are highly unpredictable unless they are in context of other letters or letter combinations. As students mature in reading, their knowledge of vowel patterns will increase.	• Increase students' amount of reading. • Encourage students to write and think about which letters represent particular sounds. • Work with vowels in clusters or phonograms, such as *fast, last, past.* • Do word sorts. Encourage students to group or organize words by sound and letter patterns.

Doesn't apply what he or she knows.	Application needs to be taught as part of the process of learning phonics.	• Model for students the thinking process of what to do when they come to a word they don't know.
		• Discuss the process, and make a chart:
		    a. Think about what would make sense.
		    b. Look at the beginning.
		    c. Find the part of the word I already know.
		    d. Think of another word that looks almost the same.
		    e. Then ask for help.

Has difficulty recognizing words quickly. Reads slowly word-by-word.	Immediate recognition of words develops with maturity. There are many ways to enhance fluency and automaticity.	• Have students read familiar or predictable texts. • Read *with* children in choral-reading situations. Read poetry and rhyme. • Practice repeated readings—reading a segment of text several times until fluency is reached. • Encourage students to combine groups of letters to produce sounds, as with phonograms, rhyming words, base words, and affixes. • Encourage students to think about their reading. Reading for meaning increases word accuracy.

Harcourt Brace School Publishers

Intervention Strategies

by Dr. Bernice E. Cullinan

Intervention strategies = *prevention* strategies. They are steps teachers take to help children who may be at risk for difficulties in reading and writing and children who are already beginning to have difficulties in these areas. Alert teachers use intervention strategies as good teaching practice to prevent trouble before trouble begins. In reading and writing, a stitch in time does save nine!

WHO MAY NEED EXTRA SUPPORT?

Watch for these children, who are likely candidates for intervention:

- Immature, inexperienced learners
- Children who speak a regional or an ethnic dialect that differs from the prevailing dialect or accent used in the classroom.
- Children who have hearing problems
- Children who do not articulate clearly
- Children with low self-esteem
- Low achievers

ASSESSING THE NEED FOR INTERVENTION

Children differ in their levels of phonemic awareness and phonics knowledge. The following assessment methods can be used to identify specific sound/letter correspondences that children have mastered and ones they are struggling with.

- *Observations During Shared Reading* Read together cumulative stories and books with patterned language—ones that repeat phrases or that have many words that contain the same phonic element, such as beginning sounds or spelling patterns. Note whether children recognize words that contain a certain phonic element and whether they figure out the story pattern and join in. (For lists of these kinds of books, see the article "Developing Phonemic Awareness with Trade Books.")

- *Running Records* Listen to a child read aloud. Tape-record the reading and listen again later. Record miscues: omissions, insertions, substitutions, mispronunciations, self-corrections, repetitions, punctuation missed or added, and hesitations. Running records show you what children know—they indicate a child's level of expertise with decoding and phonemic awareness.

- *Journals and Learning Logs* Examine children's writing. Phonetic spelling shows you which sound/letter correspondences children know. If you do not have a broad sample of a child's writing, dictate a list of words to spell, including words with phonetic elements that concern you.

- *Anecdotal Records* Jot down notes about a child's behavior. The notes eventually form a mosaic and create a picture of a child's abilities. Record the date, place, and a live-action description of the child's behavior or talk. Write phrases or brief comments on self-stick notes, on cards, or in a spiral notebook.

- *Tests of Phonemic Awareness* Administer a test such as the Yopp-Singer Test of Phoneme Segmentation or the Phonemic Awareness Interview, both found in the Teacher Resources section at the back of this book.

Harcourt Brace School Publishers

INTERVENTION STRATEGIES AND ACTIVITIES

Literature can be used for language and literacy development in various ways. Poetry, songs, chants, and prose can be used effectively for intervention, as in the following activities involving speaking, dramatization, reading, and writing.

Speaking and Dramatizing

◎ ***Call-and-Response Rhymes*** Use rhymes and chants from sources such as *Juba This and Juba That* by Virginia Tashjian (Little, Brown, 1969, 1995). The leader chants a phrase, and children repeat it exactly. They clap hands and tap feet in rhythm. Try using some of the verses from this song by Woody Guthrie.

PUT YOUR FINGER IN THE AIR

Put your finger in the air, in the air;
Put your finger in the air, in the air;
Put your finger in the air
And leave it about a year,
Put your finger in the air, in the air.

Put your finger on your head, on your head;
Put your finger on your head, on your head;
Put your finger on your head.
Tell me, is it green or red?
Put your finger on your head, on your head.

Put your finger on your cheek, on your cheek;
Put your finger on your cheek, on your cheek;
Put your finger on your cheek
And leave it about a week;
Put your finger on your cheek, on your cheek.

◎ ***Choral Reading*** Assign each child or small group a line or part to say from a verse, such as "If All the Seas Were One Sea." Have children act it out.

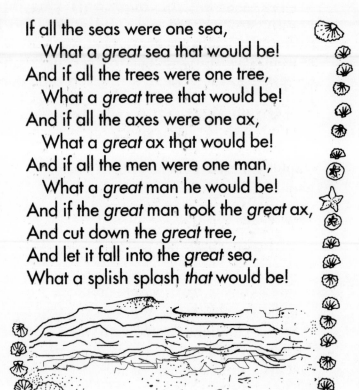

If all the seas were one sea,
 What a *great* sea that would be!
And if all the trees were one tree,
 What a *great* tree that would be!
And if all the axes were one ax,
 What a *great* ax that would be!
And if all the men were one man,
 What a *great* man he would be!
And if the *great* man took the *great* ax,
And cut down the *great* tree,
And let it fall into the *great* sea,
What a splish splash *that* would be!

◎ ***Pattern Games*** Have children repeat patterns after you, as in the game "Little Sir Echo":

Teacher: Higgledy Piggledy pop.
Student: I want to go to the top.
Student: Put my hat on a mop.
Student: My sister likes to shop.

Harcourt Brace School Publishers

Reading

◎ *Cut Up Story Sentences* On sentence strips, write key sentences from a previously read story or sentences a child dictates. Read each sentence with the child, cut up the sentence into individual word cards, and let the child arrange the word cards to form the sentence again and read it. Then, encourage the child to explore language by rearranging the word cards to form new sentences.

◎ *Word Building* Ask children to form new words by substituting sounds, such as consonant clusters. Display sets of words and read them with children.

star, stick, step, stone
tree, try, truck, train
flake, flag, flea, flat

After each set of words, say "What part of these words is the same? Use that part to make a new word." Children can use letter cards to form the words or list the words on paper. Ask children to continue the activity, choosing new patterns.

◎ *Shared Reading*
- Read aloud stories with patterned language, such as *"I Can't" Said the Ant* by Polly Cameron (Coward-McCann, 1961). Ask children to join in as soon as they figure out the pattern. Read and reread Big Book versions of the stories, tracking the print for children and discussing the words and language. Then, ask children to participate in an oral presentation of the story. Ask them to repeat dialogue, sentences, or phrases.
- Read alphabet books, simple concept books, and books with labels and environmental print. Help children find words (and pictures of words) that begin with the same sound. Point to signs and show children they know how to read them. Build confidence and skills with activities like these.

- As you read, help children predict what a word will be. Model how to use the context of the story, beginning consonants, and the rest of the letters in a word to confirm predictions.

Writing

◎ *Shared Writing* Work with children to create stories and other forms of writing. During the writing process, you can do the following:
- Repeat words, stretching out the sounds of the letters as you write them down. Ask a child to tell you what letter should begin a word or come next in a word.
- Make line spaces for each letter of a word. Ask a volunteer to fill in any letters he or she knows. Fill in the letters the child does not know. Use correct spelling and give reasons for the spelling.

◎ *Sound/Spelling Pattern Stories*
- Have children write and illustrate sentences and stories using words that share the same sound/spelling pattern, for example:

I'll <u>bake</u> a <u>cake</u> if you come to the <u>lake</u>.
My <u>cake</u> will have coconut <u>flakes</u>, but it won't have a <u>snake</u>.
A <u>cake</u> with a <u>snake</u> would be <u>fake</u>.

- Ask a child to dictate a sentence. Write the same sentence again, changing one word, for example, *The <u>monkey</u> climbed up the tree. The <u>cat</u> climbed up the tree.* Ask the child to continue using the pattern.

◎ *Create Poems* Encourage children to write or dictate poems. Discuss line breaks, rhyme, rhythm, and other interesting things they discover about how to use language.

by Dr. Marguerite Cogorno Radencich

About
MINILESSONS

How do minilessons fit in with systematic, direct instruction in phonics?

Minilessons are short lessons, taking 10 to 20 minutes or even less time, delivered to a whole class or a small group to meet specific instructional needs. Teachers use minilessons both in systematic, direct instruction as well as during teachable moments. A systematic program has a scope, but there is room for some flexibility in the sequence. For example, you could rearrange the order in which you teach consonant clusters to work with children on the *br* cluster while reading Bill Martin, Jr.'s *Brown Bear, Brown Bear, What Do You See?*

You will find the balance between systematic, direct instruction and use of teachable moments that seems most comfortable to you. While minilessons cannot be the sole tool for delivering phonics instruction, they are invaluable because they can respond directly to children's enthusiasm and their needs.

How do I fit minilessons into my schedule?

There are many ways. Mornings might begin with your recording on the chalkboard or chart paper children's dictated News of the Day while you prompt children to use their phonics knowledge to help you spell some of the words. Then during your Reading/Language Arts block of time, you might pull groups of children who need a particular skill, while other children engage in individual, paired, or cooperative activities that do not require your direct attention. You might also integrate phonemic awareness and phonics minilessons anytime you share rhymes, poems, and songs with children.

How do I know what minilessons to teach?

Teachers decide on minilessons based on the expected curriculum and ongoing observation. Go "clipboard cruising" around the room, observing the use of phonics and other skills as children read aloud, work with literacy manipulatives, write or "drite" (Patricia Cunningham's term meaning "drawing and writing") in journals, or work in learning centers. Record children's needs on a checklist or with brief notes, also known as anecdotes, to help guide your instruction.

If you use anecdotal records, you may want to choose one of the following teacher-tested methods to help you stay organized. Each option allows you to record notes only when you have an important notation to make.

- Use a loose-leaf binder with a page for each child.

- Jot down notes on index cards attached to a clipboard. Then put the note cards into a recipe box that has a section for each child.

- Have a file folder for each child. Record notes on labels or self-stick notes, and later affix these to the appropriate folder. For example, you might write on 9/27 that Julio "writes one letter for each syllable" and on 10/15 that he "has begun to add vowels to some words."

How do I take advantage of teachable moments?

Teachers can deliver minilessons during teachable moments throughout the day, in any curriculum area. Taking advantage of a teachable moment may mean shortening or changing a planned activity. But children march to their own drummers, and we ignore those drummers at our own peril! Perhaps Sam will spot an interesting beetle outside and note that *beetle* starts like *Ben*. Maybe Jamal will form his body into a *J* during playtime and lead a group of copycat letter makers. These might be times to pause and playfully extend the children's play. Older children might puzzle over the spelling of difficult words while writing content-area reports, spawning minilessons on particular sound patterns.

Be on the alert for teachable moments, and try to be flexible enough to make good use of them as they appear.

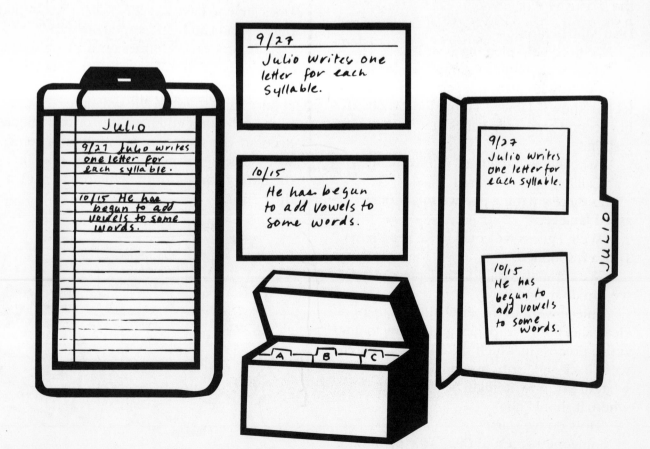

SHARED WRITING

by Dr. Dorothy S. Strickland

"Shared writing provides a risk-free opportunity for children to engage in the writing process."

Dear Mrs. Benton,

   We need help planting a garden.

   "If we want Ashley's mom to come and show us how to plant our garden, how can we let her know?" Janiece Turner looked out at her second graders as hands flew in the air to respond.

   "Ask Ashley to tell her," replied Josh.

   "Call her up," answered Angel.

   "Is there anything else we might do?" asked Janiece.

   "Well, I guess we could write her a letter," Tonya responded.

   "We certainly could," said Janiece. "And we can do it together."

   Janiece went to the easel, flipped to a clean sheet of chart paper, and began an interactive process in which she and the children went back and forth, making decisions about what to say, how it might be spelled, and where it should go.

   "How do we start?"

   Someone suggested *Dear Mrs. Benton.*

   "Does anyone besides Ashley know how Benton begins?"

   "Yes, with a B," someone offered.

   "Good, James. Will you spell the rest of your name for us, Ashley? Notice that I'm putting a comma after *Benton.* Now, it would be very nice to include the date on our letter. Does anyone have any idea where we should put it? Who can help us spell *March?*"

   The process continues until a draft of the letter is completed. The children review what they have said. Janiece asks for comments about changes. Later, she will enter the letter in the computer and have one or two children decorate the stationery before it goes home with Ashley. Janiece will hang the draft in the library corner for the children to read at their leisure.

What is shared writing?

Shared writing is an interactive group writing process in which teachers and children work together to compose or record meaningful messages and stories. The teacher often acts as a scribe as he or she thinks through with children what they want to say and the best way to say it. Individual children may also act as scribes as they fill in letters and words that they know. Everyone works together to draft, revise, and edit as appropriate. Shared writing provides a risk-free opportunity for children to engage in the writing process.

The term interactive writing is usually reserved for shared writing in which children actually hold the marker or chalk and do the writing themselves. Obviously, this will probably produce a text that is structurally less uniform than one written by an adult. Even so, interactive writing offers an excellent means to closely guide and scaffold the work of an individual or a small group of children. It is especially useful as a personalized strategy with a child who is experiencing difficulty.

Any kind of writing may be the focus of shared writing: response to reading, group stories, Big Books, poems, informational notes and books, class charts, and written retellings are just a few.

Why is shared writing important?

- Writing is shown to be a functional, meaningful way to communicate.
- Teachers model reading and writing during the creation of the text.
- The entire writing process, from brainstorming during prewriting to proofreading and editing, may be modeled to the extent that it is appropriate.
- A variety of writing strategies are developed as children get first-hand demonstrations and rehearsal from participating with others.
- Specific skills may be explained in context as children help to produce a finished piece.

What happens during shared writing?

Prewriting

Stimulus Shared writing is generally stimulated by a common experience of some kind, such as a class trip, a school assembly, or a book that the teacher has read aloud to the whole group.

Discussion Actual writing is usually preceded by a brief discussion: Who is our audience? What form of writing should we use? What should we say?

Drafting

Writing The teacher guides children as they "think through" the process together. The teacher acts as a scribe, soliciting children's ideas and their help with writing letters, words, and punctuation. A way to involve young writers is to ask questions like the ones below as the group composes.

How to Teach Phonemic Awareness, Phonics, and Language Conventions Through Shared Writing

Shared writing makes the application of skills visible to young learners. Here are some types of questions that help children both acquire skills and learn how to use them.

- How will we start?
- What else do you hear at the beginning? at the end? in the middle?
- What letter(s) would you expect to see at the beginning of _____? at the end of _____?
- Let's read what we have so far.
- What will we write next?
- The first letter of the next word is one we talked about yesterday. Who thinks they know how [the word] begins?
- The next word begins like [George]'s name. [George], do you know what letter that is?

Harcourt Brace School Publishers

Revising/Proofreading

Refining The teacher rereads the piece aloud periodically and again at the end. Throughout the writing, the teacher constantly solicits help by asking questions like the ones below and by thinking aloud about needed wording, punctuation, spelling, and so on.

- Did we say everything we needed to say?
- Did we leave anything out?
- How can we make this part better?

Upon completion of the piece, the teacher and children review it together for final polishing, and then publish it.

PERFORMANCE ASSESSMENT

Use children's independent writing to assess application of the following, which they have learned and practiced through shared writing.

Children show evidence of

✔ Interest in writing activities
✔ Awareness of left-to-right progression
✔ Need for spaces between words
✔ Awareness of the many purposes of writing
✔ Willingness to take risks in approximating sound/letter relationships
✔ Understanding that words are composed of letters
✔ Ability to use vocabulary appropriate to the topic and task
✔ Willingness to "try out" writing independently
✔ Ability to match often-repeated words and phrases
✔ Understanding of the language used in the act of writing and in discussion of writing: *title, story, word, letter, line, sentence, beginning, end,* and so on
✔ Ability to contribute relevant ideas
✔ Ability to consistently apply what has been taught about
      sound/letter relationships
      punctuation
      capitalization
      other language conventions

Opportunities for Shared Writing

- Group retellings
  - Story read aloud
  - Story maps
  - Facts remembered from a nonfiction text
- Group compositions
  - Alternative texts based on stories read aloud
  - Original stories
  - Big Books
  - Poems
  - Letters, invitations, notes, messages
  - Posters
  - Class journal entries
  - Class observations, such as during science experiments
  - Observations from shared experiences, such as field trips
  - Original recipes
  - Descriptions
  - Newsletters
  - News of the Day
  - Reports about information
  - Book reports
  - Learning log entries
- Class charts
  - Class jobs
  - Class rules
  - Directions
  - Planning charts
- Captions
  - Bulletin boards
  - Collections
  - Student-created displays
  - Objects in the classroom

Harcourt Brace School Publishers

Phonics in Action

by Patricia Smith

Beginning writers progress through predictable, recognizable stages of spelling that vary in duration for individual children. Each stage provides insight into what a child knows about phonics, learned through reading and applied in spelling, and what remains to be learned. Examples from more than one stage often appear in the same piece of writing.

1. **Pre-alphabetic** Scribbling, or pretend writing, is not necessarily random marks on the page (Figure 1). It may be a child's first attempt to approximate the print he or she encounters naturally all day long. Listen for the running monologue that may accompany a child's scribbling; this child is well aware that written symbols contain meaning!

2. **Alphabetic** Letter strings, or random letters, are a child's attempts to mimic the forms of our alphabet (Figure 2). At this pre-phonemic stage, letters do not yet represent sounds. More often than not, the child uses capital letters. You may notice that a child at this stage is already practicing left-to-right and top-to-bottom progression on the page.

3. **Early Phonetic** One-letter spelling is a common occurrence in this stage (Figure 3). Here, a child uses the initial consonant and perhaps another distinctive consonant to represent an entire word, such as *b* for *baby* or *bl* for *believe*.

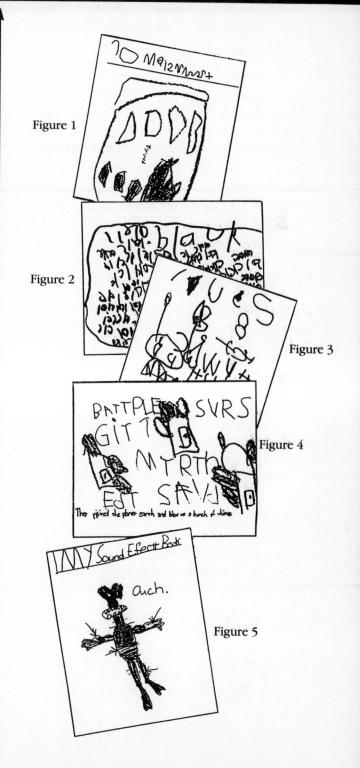

Figure 1

Figure 2

Figure 3

Figure 4

Figure 5

4. **Phonetic** Invented spelling, or *temporary spelling*, is a window on a child's understanding of sound-symbol correspondences (Figure 4). Children, encouraged to "spell a word the best they can," experiment with using their phonemic awareness to write the sounds they hear in the order they hear them. Accuracy of the phonetically reliable consonant and short vowel portions of the words, such as *candee* for *candy*, makes the words readable and shows phonemic awareness.

5. **Transitional** The use of more sophisticated phonetic generalizations and adjustment of phonetic approximations to match spellings seen in reading facilitate the transition to conventional spellings (Figure 5). At this stage, there still are many approximations of irregular words, such as *speshel* for *special*, but the errors indicate knowledge of more sophisticated phonetic generalizations. At this stage, children also begin to make adjustments to match visual memory of high-frequency words.

6. **Conventional** The accurate spelling of words, regardless of their phonetic regularity, characterizes this stage. The speller uses phonemic awareness, phonetic generalizations, and a strong visual memory to produce accurate spellings of frequently seen words. When spelling attempts do not satisfy the conventional speller's visual memory, a mental red flag is raised, and the child enacts a plan to achieve conventional spelling. These fix-up strategies might include use of a word bank, a dictionary, a spelling buddy, an alternate attempt, or a computer spell-check option.

EVALUATION OF SPELLING MISCUES

When *evaluation* of spelling is viewed as an opportunity to find *value* in what children know about phonics and conventional spellings, teachers are provided with instructional anchors and targets. This type of miscue analysis of spelling is similar to the miscue analysis of reading. The following form can be used to illuminate the strengths and targets for instruction.

SPELLING ANALYSIS

STUDENT: _____ DATE: _____
EVALUATOR: _____
OF TOTAL WORDS: _____
% OF CONVENTIONAL SPELLING: _____
% OF MISCUES: _____

EXAMPLES OF CONVENTIONAL SPELLING:
EXAMPLES OF SPELLING MISCUES:
PHONETIC STRENGTHS:
INSTRUCTIONAL TARGETS:

Stages in Spelling Development

Stage	Characteristics	Examples of Miscues	Knowledge Indicated	Instructional Targets
Pre-alphabetic	Scribbling or pretend writing	*Mqi2Vhrst* (handwritten)	Written symbols contain meaning	Alphabet
Alphabetic	Letter strings or random letters	*L xxx OM*	Importance of letters; possibly directionality	Sound/letter correspondences
Early Phonetic	Initial consonants	*b* for *baby*	Letters represent sounds	Phonemic awareness of initial, medial, and ending sounds
Phonetic	Invented (temporary) spelling	*candee* for *candy*	Consonant and short vowel sounds; letter sequence	Expanded knowledge of phonetic generalizations
Transitional	Words spelled using visual memory and phonetic generalizations	*speshel* for *special*	Expanded use of phonetic knowledge and visual memory	Use of visual memory and fix-up strategies
Conventional	Difficult, but frequently used words spelled correctly	*sinthesis* for *synthesis* (example of a difficult word seen infrequently)	Importance of visual memory and correction of spelling approximations	Increased visual memory of words

Harcourt Brace School Publishers

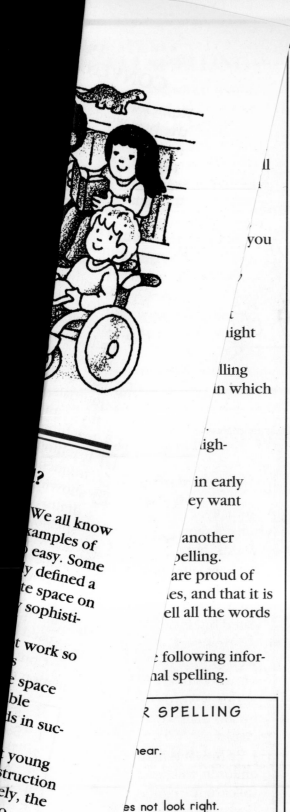

Partial text visible on left torn page fragments:

you

light

lling
in which

igh-

in early
ey want

We all know
xamples of
easy. Some
defined a
te space on
sophisti-

t work so

space
ble
ds in suc-

young
struction
ely, the
to

another
pelling.
are proud of
es, and that it is
ell all the words

following infor-
nal spelling.

R SPELLING

near.

es not look right.
n. If it appears right, go

is already printed.
help you spell it.
rrectly on your paper and in
al.

🍎 TEACHING TIP

Word Sorts Provide children with the tactile/kinesthetic activity of sorting words into categories formed with a common phonetic pattern.

Spelling /ûr/

perch	bird	burn	earth	worm
herd	whirl	turn	learn	world
fern	third	hurl	search	worth

The word-sort activity can be extended to the formation of class word charts and word walls. Prompt children to add words they notice in their reading to the appropriate column. Class charts can lead to individual word charts in a child's writing folder or spelling journal.

Word Sorts ◊ Class Charts ◊ Individual Charts

All three of these activities help a child develop the practice of noting how words work.

IN CONCLUSION . . .

Celebrate children's increasing use of conventional spelling patterns, as well as their ability to note and find ways to correct initial misspellings. Their familiarity with print, developed through numerous opportunities to read and write, will allow them to monitor their own spelling. This independence, coupled with an attitude of pride when conventional spelling is achieved, will enable them to successfully continue a lifelong pursuit of good writing and communication.

How Children Learn About Words

by Dr. W. Dorsey Hammond

In a first-grade classroom early in the school year, Ms. Stimson is sharing a Big Book with the children. The students are looking at the pictures and reading along with her as she tracks her finger across the line of print: *"I will build my house of sticks," said the first little pig.*

"Deidre, can you point to the word *house?*" asks Ms. Stimson. Deidre tracks her finger across the entire sentence. And when Marcus tries, he points to a specific letter.

In both cases, these children have not yet developed the concept of word, as distinguished from the concept of a sentence or a letter. It is not so much the case that Deidre and Marcus are unable to identify the word *house*; rather, it appears that they may not be sure what a word is.

Even though children enter school knowing a great deal about how to use language, their experiences with language are primarily oral. Many of our concepts about words come from our experiences with print.

What is a word

Actually, a word is hard to define. [   ] what a word is, and we can give e[   ] words, but to define *word* is not s[   ] language authorities have laughing[   ] word as a group of letters with whi[   ] each side. This definition is not very[   ] cated but is helpful nonetheless.

However, this definition does no[   ] well for oral language. As we expres[   ] ourselves orally, we often place mor[   ] within a word (for example, at a sylla[   ] break) than we do between two wor[   ] cession.

Thus, it is natural to anticipate tha[   ] children will need experiences and in[   ] to learn the concept of word. Fortunat[   ] concept of word, or wordness, is easy [   ] teach. In addition, young children enjo[   ] learning about words.

How do children learn about words?

As children learn how to read, they need to be able to track print, that is, visually focus on the word they are saying, as they read phrases, sentences, and stories. Note the following example:

Text: **The first little pig said. . .**
Child reads: **"The first lit tle pig. . ."**

Notice that the young reader elected to move <u>to</u> <u>the</u> <u>next</u> <u>word</u> <u>of</u> <u>print</u> at the syllable break in the word *little*. This is a common practice for early emergent readers and should not be viewed with alarm. With appropriate modeling and instruction, children soon learn to track print effectively.

Developing the concept of word and tracking print are two related behaviors. Below are activities that can help children learn about words and how to track print.

Shared Reading   Read a Big Book or chart story with children, deliberately moving your hand or finger along each word as it is read in a natural context. This experience should be repeated with children many times with a variety of stories. As you continue to model, children can be encouraged to track the print themselves.

Finding Words in Context   Using a Big Book or chart story, encourage children to find individual words by asking them questions like these:

- Who can find the word *turkey?*
- Who can find the word that means "yummy?"

Ask a volunteer to bracket the word with his or her hands or to draw a line under the word. Encourage the volunteer to explain how he or she knew the word.

Finding Words in the Environment
Encourage children to find words they know in their environment, such as logos, labels, and advertisements. Have children build word collages of words they know, using old magazines and newspapers.

Building a Word Bank or Word File
Encourage children to identify individual words they know and write the more interesting words on small cards. Then children can put the words into a word box, add selected words to a word wall, or write them on a word chart.

Using Word Sorts   Have children group word cards by some common element, such as words that rhyme or words that begin with a particular letter. For example, *pizza* and *popcorn* go together because they begin with the same letter; *farmer* and *doctor* go together because they end with the same sound.

Building Phrases and Sentences   Have children combine words they know to express an idea or to create a phrase or sentence. For example:

I	like	popcorn	.

I	go	to	the	movies	.

Building Words   Show children how they can make new words by changing letters. For example, change *g* in *game* to an *s* and make *same*, or change to an *f* and make *fame*. Children soon learn that they can use words they already know to create "new words."

Instruction in Phonics

As children mature in phonics ability, their knowledge will help them track print better. They will use context and the beginning sounds to match what they are seeing with what they are pronouncing as they read. There is considerable evidence that basic knowledge of beginning sounds facilitates tracking and thus reinforces the concept of word.

Encourage children to write. As children write and attempt to represent with letters the sounds they hear, they learn to focus on when a new word is beginning and ending and when the next word begins. Children use their phonics knowledge as they spell words, using invented spelling that gradually becomes more conventional as they gain more experience with print in reading and writing situations. The power of early writing is that it helps produce not only better writers but also better readers and better spellers.

Henderson (1981) and Bear (1990) have proposed that there are parallel stages in reading and spelling.

- **Emergent readers** have little concept of word. When they write, they use scribbles and random letters to "spell" words.
- **Beginning readers** are developing a concept of word. They read with support and finger-point as they read. When they write, they use logical beginning and ending consonants and some vowels, such as *BD* for *bed,* *FLT* for *float,* and *DRIV* or *JRIV* for *drive.*
- **Transitional readers** are approaching fluency and can read easy chapter books. In their writing, they spell many short-vowel words correctly and are experimenting with long-vowel patterns. They will probably spell *bed* correctly. They may write *FLOTE* for *float* and *DRIEV* for *drive* or spell the words correctly.

In learning to read, the learning of words is important. But also of great importance is for children to learn *about* words, to develop the concept of word. Learning *about* words is a major stepping stone to learning to read with fluency and comprehension.

"The power of early writing is that it helps produce not only better writers but also better readers and better spellers."

Harcourt Brace School Publishers

101 Ways to Make Your Students Better Decoders and Readers

"*Appropriate activities for young children have a sense of playfulness about them, are conducted in social settings that encourage interaction among children, pique children's curiosity about language and invite their experimentation with it, and allow for differences among children.*"

Dr. Hallie Kay Yopp

INTRODUCTION

What is your main reason for teaching phonics? One of your goals may be to provide children with strategies they can use to help them learn to read and write. A strategy is not something children know, such as a rule; rather, it is something children do! Young children are limited in what they can read, so they need to develop the ability to figure out words. This introduction offers some strategies you can model and teach children to use so that they can become better decoders and readers.

Keep these tips in mind when teaching phonemic awareness and phonics:

- Plan activities that will keep children actively engaged. Avoid activities that have the child sit passively.
- Plan activities that include variety so that children's different learning styles are considered. Activities might involve children with singing, rhythm, movement, drama, games, writing, drawing, and manipulating visual props.
- Keep the use of phonics jargon and rules at a minimum. Instead, model strategies that children can use when they read and write.
- Offer activities that have something for everyone. Begin an activity with a warm-up to review or reinforce, and end with a challenge. Offer one-on-one or small-group instruction for those who need extra support and more challenging interactive games and activities for those who can work on their own.
- Engage children in daily reading and writing activities so that they use what they learn.

How can we help children hear sounds in words?

Develop Phonemic Awareness   The phonemically aware child knows that the spoken word pig has three sounds that can be segmented into /p/-/i/-/g/. This child can identify that the word begins with /p/ and ends with /g/. This child can also name other words that have the same beginning, middle, or ending sound as *pig.* Making children phonemically aware will help them recognize that speech is made up of a series of individual sounds. This awareness will lay the foundation for children to eventually be able to use phonics as a means to decode printed words. Activities that build phonemic awareness include rhymes, songs, riddles, and games that require the child to match sounds in words; blend sounds to form words; count phonemes in words; isolate or segment sounds in words; and delete, add, or substitute sounds to form new words.

How can we help children see patterns in words?

Word Building Strategy   Give children letter cards to make words. Start with a vowel such as *a* or a phonogram such as *-at.* Use letter cards to form words such as *bat, rat, sat, mat, fat, cat, hat, chat,* and *flat.* A child who can use letters to form *at* and *cat* can be guided to read and spell other *-at* words.

Word Sorting Strategies   Word sorts help children discover spelling patterns. First, you can model the word sort, using familiar words. Group the words into categories, and then help children think of other words that fit the categories. These categories might include words that rhyme, begin with the same sound, end with the same sound, or share the same spelling for a given vowel sound. After guided practice, children can sort their own sets of word cards independently or with partners. These sorts might later be written

Harcourt Brace School Publishers

on a Word Wall or in columns in a notebook, or filed together in a word file. Following are some different kinds of word sorts:

Closed Sort Teacher selects the categories and models the procedure.

Open Sort Children sort words according to their own categories. They explain their choice of categories.

Blind Sort In this variation of the closed sort, the teacher determines the categories. Then one child or the teacher can call out a word while another child points to the key word it would follow. Children are not using written words, so more attention is paid to sounds than visual patterns.

Writing Sort In this variation of the closed and blind sort, the teacher calls out a word while the child writes it in the proper category.

Speed Sort Once children are proficient at sorting, they can time themselves during each sorting activity and chart their progress.

Word Wall Strategies   The building of a Word Wall develops children's ability to see words in terms of letters and patterns that will help them become effective decoders. Word Walls provide opportunities for children to generate words and become an accessible resource for troublesome words and checking words in writing. Play guessing games with words on a wall, or have children make Wordo (a form of Bingo) games. Or, choose words from the wall to form different kinds of sentences for children to write each day. Some examples of different kinds of Word Walls follow:

Key Words on a Wall As children are introduced to high-frequency words, add them to a Word Wall in alphabetical order. Draw a shape box around each word to emphasize its configuration, one strategy children use to recognize words.

Tricky Words on a Wall Make a wall of words that are most often misspelled. List them alphabetically. Do at least one daily activity in which children find, write, and chant the spelling of some of these words. Use the words in context to check meaning.

Rhyming Words on a Wall Words are listed in groups by spelling patterns, for example, words with the phonograms -*eet* and -*eat*. Play riddle games and write rhymes, using the list as a resource.

Portable Word Walls Children can copy the words from the Word Wall onto file folders that can be carried to a desk, the library, or another classroom. As words are added to the Word Wall, do the same to the portable version.

 Use these resources, along with the activities that follow, to help all of your learners!

- *Oo-pples and Boo-noo-noos: Songs and Activities for Phonemic Awareness* and Audiocassette
- *Big Book of Rhymes*
- *Phonics Practice Book*
- *Phonics Game Board Pattern Book*
- *Word Builder*
- *Word Builder Cards*
- *Magnetic Letters*
- *Alphabet Cards*
- *High-Frequency Word Cards*

Harcourt Brace School Publishers

Rhyming Activities

Rhyme-a-Day

TEACHER DIRECTED Start each day by teaching children a short rhyme. Periodically throughout the day, repeat the rhyme with them. Say the rhyme together, have them say it alone, pause and leave out words for them to insert, or ask volunteers to say each line. Children will develop a repertoire of favorite rhymes that can serve as a storehouse for creating their own rhymes.

Rhyme in a Line

TEACHER DIRECTED Have children form a line. Give the first child in line a picture card. Ask the child to say the picture name and a word that rhymes. The card is passed to the next child, who does the same. If some children need encouragement, provide a beginning sound for them. Once several words have been given, continue with a new picture card.

Scavenger Hunt

INDEPENDENT Place around the classroom several picture cards of things that rhyme. Send a **small group** of children on a scavenger hunt to retrieve the pictures and then sort them into groups according to names that rhyme. You may also want to try an "open sort" by having children create categories of their own to sort the picture cards.

Puppet Parade

TEACHER DIRECTED Use the Finger Puppets patterns on page 123 to assess children's ability to recognize words that rhyme. Invite a **small group** to make puppets by drawing certain objects or animals whose names rhyme with words you will say. For example, children in a group of four can decide who will make a finger puppet of a cat, a dog, a pig, and a cow. Then say words such as *frog, wig, sat, now, jig, bat, bow, hog, hat, how, log,* and *big*. The child who is holding the puppet whose name rhymes should wiggle it.

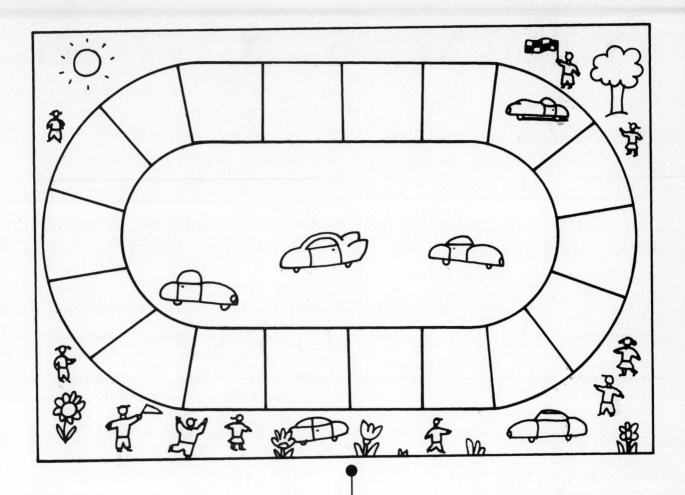

Rhyme Pairs

TEACHER DIRECTED To assess children's ability to recognize pairs of words that rhyme, say a list of twenty or more pairs of words. Half of the word pairs should rhyme. Children tell which word pairs rhyme and which do not. If working with a **small group,** have children indicate *yes* with a smiling face card or other symbol. If working with **one child** (or a small group), help children make a Racetrack Game Board using the pattern from page 113. For each correct response, the player can move a marker ahead one space. Provide word pairs until the player has finished the race.

What Word Rhymes?

TEACHER DIRECTED Use theme-related words from across the curriculum to focus on words that rhyme. For example, if you are studying animals, ask: *What rhymes with snake? bear? fox? deer? ant? frog? goat? hen? fish? whale?* If a special holiday is approaching, ask: *What rhymes with trick, treat? mask? scare? night?* Use these word groups for sound matching, sound blending, or sound segmenting activities.

Sound Matching Activities

Sound Seats

TEACHER DIRECTED Arrange chairs in a circle with the backs facing inward. Include a chair for each child. Explain that you want children to listen for words that begin with the same sound as in *march*. Direct children to march around the chairs as you slowly say a list of words, some of which begin with the sound of *m*. Each time children hear a word that begins like *march*, they are to sit in the nearest chair. Say words such as *march, sing, moon, ball, cat, monkey, man, top, nest, mouse, seal, mop, fish, zebra, fan, milk,* and *map*. Continue the game, focusing on a different action and a new initial sound, such as flapping their arms if a word begins like *fly*.

Picture Slide Show

INDEPENDENT Have children work in **pairs** or **independently** to draw pictures or search through magazines for pictures whose names begin with a given sound. The pictures can be cut out and glued on the slide from any Word Slide pattern on pages 124–128. Tape additional strips together to make a longer slide. Once the slides have been put together, suggest that children exchange slides with one another, naming each picture as the slide is pulled. Then children can work together to make up alliterative sentences and stories about the pictures.

Odd Word Out

TEACHER DIRECTED Form a **group** of four children. Say a different word for each group member to repeat. The child with the word that does not begin (or end) like the other words must step out of the group. For example, say *ball, bat, cow, box*. The child whose word is *cow* steps from the group. The odd-word-out player then chooses three children to form a new group and the procedure continues.

Head or Toes, Finger or Nose?

TEACHER DIRECTED Teach children the following rhyme. Be sure to say the sound, not the letter, at the beginning of each line. Recite the rhyme together several times while touching the body parts.

> */h/ is for head.*
> */t/ is for toes.*
> */f/ is for finger.*
> */n/ is for nose.*

Explain that you will say a list of words. Children are to touch the head when you say a word that begins with /h/, the toes for words that begin with /t/, a finger for words that begin with /f/, and the nose for words that begin with /n/. Say words such as *fan, ten, horn, hat, feet, nut, ham, nest, toy, fish, note, tub, nail, time, fox,* and *house*.

Harcourt Brace School Publishers

Say and Sort

INDEPENDENT Have children work in **small groups.** Give each group a set of picture cards whose names begin with two or three different beginning consonant sounds. Group members are to say the picture names and sort the cards according to beginning sounds. The same activity can be used for sorting picture cards into groups whose names have the same medial or ending sound. As an alternative, allow children to create their own categories to sort a group of picture cards. A group of objects, such as toys, can be used in place of picture cards.

Souvenir Sound-Off

TEACHER DIRECTED Have children imagine that a friend has traveled to a special place and has brought them a gift. Recite the following verse, and ask a volunteer to complete it. The names of the traveler, the place, and the gift begin with the same letter and sound.

My friend [person] who went to [place] brought me back a [gift].	My friend Hannah who went to Hawaii brought me back a hula skirt.

After repeating this activity a few times, ask **partners** to recite the verse to each other, filling in the missing words. With older children, you can focus on words with initial blends and digraphs. Children can focus on social studies and phonics skills by using a world map or globe to find names of places.

Match My Word

TEACHER DIRECTED Have children match beginning or ending sounds in words. Seat children on the floor in a circle, with **pairs** sitting back-to-back. One child in each pair will say a word. His or her partner will repeat the word and say another word that begins with the same sound. To invite each child to give a word, the group sings the following song to the tune of "The Farmer in the Dell."

> (Child's name) will say a word.
> Then you say the word.
> Think of another word to say
> That starts (ends) in the same way.

Begin with one child and move around the circle clockwise until each pair of children has had a turn to give a word and match a sound. Then repeat the activity, reversing the roles of partners and focusing on ending sounds.

Coin Toss

INDEPENDENT Have children make a game board using the pattern for the 16-square grid on page 122. They should use rubber stamps or stickers to fill each space with a picture. **Partners** toss a coin or button on the grid, name the picture landed on, and say another word that begins (or ends) with the same sound.

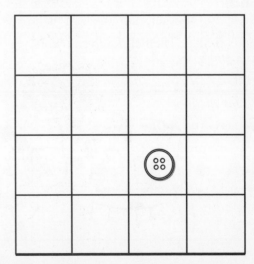

Sound Isolation Activities

What's Your N-N-N-Name?

TEACHER DIRECTED Invite children to say their names by repeating the initial phoneme in the name, such as *M-M-M-Michael* or by drawing out and exaggerating the initial sound such as *Sssssssss-erena*.

R-r-r-repeat the S-s-s-sounds

TEACHER DIRECTED Sing a song that makes use of alliteration in the beginning sounds of words. "Hippity Hop to Bed" is an example that repeats the /h/ sound throughout. As you recite or sing the song, emphasize the /h/ sound by repeating it each time it occurs in the initial position.

H-h-h-hippity h-h-h-hop to bed,
I'd rather stay up instead.
But! When Daddy says "must,"
there's nothing else, just
H-h-h-hippity, h-h-h-hoppity;
H-h-h-hippity, h-h-h-hoppity,
H-h-h-hippity, h-h-h-hoppity;
H-h-h-hippity, h-h-h-hoppity, h-h-h-hop!
To bed!

You can also use songs from *Oo-pples and Boo-noo-noos: Songs and Activities for Phonemic Awareness* and the accompanying audiocassette.

Sound-Off

TEACHER DIRECTED Model how phonemes can be isolated in a word: *jam* starts with /j/; *goat* ends with /t/; and *cat* has the /a/ sound in the middle. Form **groups of three** children. Have them form a line, and designate which child will listen for the beginning, the middle, and the ending sound in words you say. Say a word and point to a child, who will then isolate and say the sound he or she is responsible for.

Singling Out the Sounds

INDEPENDENT Form **groups of three** children. Children can decide who will name the beginning, the middle, and the ending sounds in one-syllable picture names. Given a set of *Picture Cards*, the group identifies a picture name, and then each group member isolates and says the sound he or she is responsible for. Group members can check one another.

Chain Reaction

TEACHER DIRECTED Have children form a circle. The child who begins will say a word such as *bus*. The next child must isolate the ending sound in the word, /s/, and say a word that begins with that sound, such as *sun*. If the word is correct, the two children link arms, and the procedure continues with the next child isolating the final sound in *sun* and giving a word that begins with /n/. You will want all children to be able to link arms and complete the chain, so provide help when needed.

Sound Addition, Deletion, or Substitution Activities

Add-a-Sound

TEACHER DIRECTED Explain that the beginning sound is missing in each of the words you will say. Children must add the missing sound and say the new word. Some examples follow.

Add:

/b/ to *at (bat)*	/f/ to *ox (fox)*	/k/ to *art (cart)*
/f/ to *ace (face)*	/p/ to *age (page)*	/h/ to *air (hair)*
/w/ to *all (wall)*	/j/ to *am (jam)*	/r/ to *an (ran)*
/b/ to *and (band)*	/d/ to *ark (dark)*	/f/ to *arm (farm)*
/d/ to *ash (dash)*	/s/ to *it (sit)*	/s/ to *oak (soak)*
/h/ to *eel (heel)*	/b/ to *end (bend)*	/m/ to *ice (mice)*
/n/ to *ear (near)*	/f/ to *east (feast)*	/b/ to *each (beach)*
/fl/ to *at (flat)*	/sk/ to *ate (skate)*	/tr/ to *eat (treat)*
/gr/ to *ill (grill)*	/sh/ to *out (shout)*	/pl/ to *ant (plant)*

Remove-a-Sound

TEACHER DIRECTED Reinforce rhyme while focusing on the deletion of initial sounds in words to form new words. Ask children to say: *hat* without the /h/ *(at)*; *fin* without the /f/ *(in)*; *tall* without the /t/ *(all)*; *box* without the /b/ *(ox)*; *will* without the /w/ *(ill)*; *peach* without the /p/ *(each)*; *nice* without the /n/ *(ice)*; *meat* without the /m/ *(eat)*; *band* without the /b/ *(and)*. Continue with other words in the same manner.

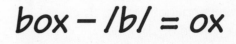

box – /b/ = ox

Rhyming Riddles

TEACHER DIRECTED Play a word riddle game to focus attention on initial sounds in words and to reinforce rhyme and sound substitution. Ask children rhymes such as these:

- What color name rhymes with **bed** and begins with /r/? *(red)*
- What animal name rhymes with **hat** and begins with /k/? *(cat)*
- What food name rhymes with **Sam** and begins with /h/? *(ham)*
- What body part rhymes with **go** and begins with /t/? *(toe)*
- What furniture name rhymes with **fed** and begins with /b/? *(bed)*
- What number word rhymes with **hive** and begins with /f/? *(five)*

Continue the game with riddles of your own. Encourage children to create riddles too.

Sounds in Songs

TEACHER DIRECTED Substitute sounds in words that occur in songs familiar to children. Choose songs that have adaptable refrains or make use of nonsense words.

"Old MacDonald Had a Farm"
    Ee-i, ee-i, oh
    Tee-ti, tee-ti, toh!
    Me-my, me-my, moh!

"Looby Loo"
    Here we go looby loo;
    here we go looby light...
    Here we go dooby doo;
    here we go dooby dight...
    Here we go gooby goo;
    here we go gooby gight...

Just for fun, when a child's birthday occurs, sing the words to the birthday song, substituting each beginning phoneme with that in the child's name:

    Mappy Mirthday mo mou!
    Mappy Mirthday mo mou!
    Mappy Mirthday mear Margie.
    Mappy Mirthday mo mou!

Mixed-Up Tongue Twisters

TEACHER DIRECTED Think of a simple tongue twister such as *ten tired toads*. Say the tongue twister for children, but replace the initial letter in each word with another letter, such as *p*, to create nonsense words: *pen pired poads*. Explain to children that you need their help to make sense of the tongue twister by having them replace /p/ with /t/ and say the new tongue twister. Use the same procedure for other tongue twisters. Then ask **partners** to do this activity together.

The Name Game

INDEPENDENT Occassionally when a new sound is introduced, children might enjoy substituting the first sound in their names with the featured sound for the day. Children will have to stop and think when they call one another by name, including the teacher. For example, if it is /p/ day, *Ms. Vega becomes Ms. Pega, Carmen becomes Parmen, Jason becomes Pason*, and *Kiyo becomes Piyo*. Just make certain beforehand that all the names will be agreeable.

To make certain that children remember the sound of the day, have each child make a finger puppet with a picture whose name begins with the sound. Use the Finger Puppets patterns from page 123. For example, on /p/ day, everyone can make a pig finger puppet. The puppet can then go home with children to share with family members.

Harcourt Brace School Publishers

Sound Blending Activities

Do You Know Your Name?

TEACHER DIRECTED Occasionally when it's time for children to line up for lunch, for dismissal, or to travel to another room, call their individual names aloud by segmenting the sounds. The child then blends the sounds to say his or her name and gets into line.

**/j/ - /e/ - /n/ -/i/ - /f/ - /ər/
Jennifer!**

As an alternative, you could provide an initial sound, and invite children whose names begin with that sound to line up.

Listen to the Sounds

TEACHER DIRECTED Sing the following song to the tune "Frère Jacques" to focus on blending sounds to form a word.

**Make these three sounds;
Make these three sounds:
/k/-/a/-/t/.** (Children repeat:
/k/-/a/-/t/.)
**Can you say the word?
Can you say the word for
/k/-/a/-/t/?** (Children repeat:
/k/-/a/-/t/.)

After a volunteer responds, repeat the song, inserting new sounds for words.

Show Me the Picture

TEACHER DIRECTED **INDEPENDENT** Display a set of *Picture Cards* or big *Alphabet Cards*. Make certain children know the name of each picture. Model how to say the name of one picture by segmenting the sounds, and ask children to identify it: *Show me the picture of the /f/-/r/-/o/-/g/*. As the picture is identified, have the **group** say its name by blending the sounds (*frog*). Continue until all the pictures have been identified. Provide new *Picture Cards* for children to continue this activity in **small groups.**

I Bought Me a Cat

TEACHER DIRECTED Display picture cards of animals, including one of a cat. Recite or chant the following Mother Goose rhyme:

**I bought me a cat and the
   cat pleased me.
I fed my cat by yonder tree;
Cat goes fiddle-i-fee.**

Ask a volunteer to find and hold the picture of the cat. Then explain that you will say a new verse, but that you will say the next animal name in a special way. Ask children to figure out the name by blending the sounds together:

I bought me a /d/-/u/-/k/...

Pause for children to blend the sounds to say *duck*. Then a volunteer can find the picture of the duck to hold. Recite the verse together, asking the child with the picture to suggest the sound the duck makes. Repeat the verse, inserting a new animal name each time.

Harcourt Brace School Publishers

Sound Segmenting Activities

How Many Sounds?

TEACHER DIRECTED Provide children with concrete representations of sounds in words by having them use buttons or plastic counters. Each counter they show will represent one sound in a given word. For example, say the word *cat* and have the child repeat it. The child would represent the sounds in the word with three counters, and the word *flat* by four. The counters will gradually give way to letter cards.

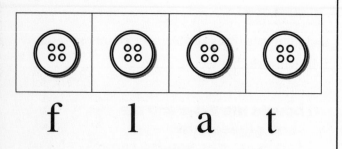

f l a t

Sound Counters

INDEPENDENT Provide **partners** with big *Alphabet Cards* and a set of counters. Children say each picture name together, decide how many sounds they hear in the name, and indicate the number of sounds by placing the same number of counters on the picture card.

Pull the Word Apart

TEACHER DIRECTED Provide **each child** with plastic tokens or buttons. Children will use these tokens to represent individual sounds in words. Recite this rhyme:

> Listen to my word.
> Tell me all the sounds you heard.
> [Say a word such as *stop*.]

Children will then separate and say each spoken sound in the word, /s/-/t/-/o/-/p/, and indicate the number by showing four tokens.

Sound Game

INDEPENDENT Have **partners** play a word-guessing game, using a variety of *Picture Cards* or big *Alphabet Cards* that represent different beginning sounds. One child says the name of the card, separating the beginning sound, as in **d-og**. The partner blends the sounds and guesses the word. After children are proficient with beginning sounds, you could have them segment all the sounds in a word when they give their clues, as in **d-o-g.**

Harcourt Brace School Publishers

Activities for Consonants

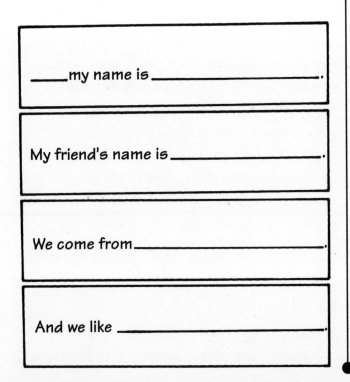

You can duplicate and send home School-Home Newsletter 1, page 102, to provide families with fun, easy-to-do activities for reinforcing consonants.

Jump-Rope Jingles

TEACHER DIRECTED Children can start with their own names to review initial consonants in words. Write each line of the following jump rope jingle on separate strips of tagboard, and place them in a pocket chart.

```
_____my name is_____.

My friend's name is_____.

We come from_____.

And we like _____.
```

Model how children are to complete the rhyme, using the initial letter in your name.

> *K my name is Kathy.*
> *My friend's name is Kevin.*
> *We come from Kansas,*
> *And we like kangaroos.*

Provide blank cards for children to write the initial letter in their names and words that begin the same to complete the rhyme. Take turns inserting the cards into the pocket chart and chanting one another's rhymes. Use with a jumprope to chant during recess.

Children may also enjoy making a pop-up book of their rhyme with the final word written and drawn inside the book on the part that can be popped up. Use the Pop-Up Book pattern from page 131.

Kangaroos

Alphabet Puppet

TEACHER DIRECTED Provide copies of the Finger Puppets patterns on page 123. Have each member of a **small group** make two letter puppets. Tell them the consonants they should write. As you say words, the child holding the puppet with the letter that stands for the beginning sound should wiggle it. Follow a similar procedure to reinforce ending consonant sounds in words, as well as consonant clusters and digraphs.

Consonant Tic-Tac-Toe

INDEPENDENT Make copies of the 9-Square Grid on page 121. Make sure children know how to play the game Tic-Tac-Toe. Invite **pairs** of children to play, but in place of using X's and O's, assign a consonant to each player. Players can write the conso-

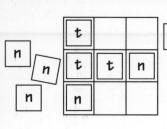

nant on each of the game playing cards (five each). To make a move, the player must say a word that begins with the letter sound and then place the letter card on the board. For each new game, children can change partners and trade letter cards. Older children can use the game to reinforce words with consonant clusters, digraphs, and *r*-controlled vowels.

Happy Birthday to Me!

INDEPENDENT Provide patterns for the Step-Page Book from page 132. Once the books are assembled, invite children to wish themselves a *Happy Birthday* by giving themselves presents whose names begin with the sounds of four letters given by you. As you name each of the four letters, chil-

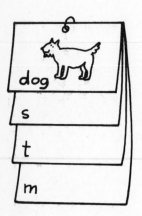

dren can write one on the bottom of each of the four pages. Then they can draw pictures or cut pictures from magazines of four gifts they would like. Later, have them finish writing the name of each present.

Beginning or Ending Sound?

TEACHER DIRECTED Provide **each child** with a plastic marker or button and a grid with three boxes. Say words that contain three phonemes and begin or end with the sound of a consonant you wish to reinforce. For example: *Where do you hear the /d/ sound in* red?

The child can indicate where the sound occurs in the word by placing the token on the corresponding box. To verify, have a volunteer form the word using *Letter Cards*.

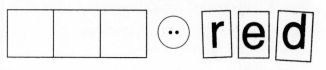

Beginning and Ending Match

INDEPENDENT Use a picture sort to match initial and final consonant sounds in word pairs; for example, the beginning sound in *red* matches the end sound in *bear*. Provide the picture cards. Make certain that children can recognize the pictures and identify the beginning and ending sounds in each picture name. Model saying words that make a match. Then have **partners or a small group** work independently to sort sets of pictures. Provide an answer sheet with word pairs for checking. Here are two sample sets to get you started:

Set One:

bug / tub	*rain / door*	*goat / rug*	*king / rock*
lock / hill	*nest / pin*	*pig / mop*	*tape / tent*

Set Two:

pan / cup	*rose / pear*	*seal / lips*	*tent / hat*
girl / dog	*lake / doll*	*nail / sun*	*duck / road*

Test Your Memory

TEACHER DIRECTED Display a group of objects. Choose objects with simple names. Have children identify the objects whose names begin with the same sound and remove the others. Then choose one of the following activities to do:

- Have children close their eyes as you remove one object. After they open their eyes, they can write the name of the missing object on paper. Reveal the object, and ask a volunteer to write the name on the board and underline the letter(s) that stand for the beginning sound(s).

- Cover the objects, and challenge children to write the names of as many objects as they can remember. As volunteers write each name on the board, show the object again. Have the volunteer underline the letter(s) that stand for the beginning sound(s).

Use more difficult words with older children to reinforce initial consonant clusters, digraphs, or names with like vowel sounds, including vowel variants.

Begin-and-End-the-Same Game

INDEPENDENT Make copies of the Racetrack Game Board on page 113, and assemble the track. In each section, write an easy word that begins and ends with a consonant. **Two or three players** can use game markers and a numbered spinner, found on page 120, to move along the game board. Players must read the word landed on and then say a word that begins with the same letter and sound. Next they say a word that ends with the same letter and sound. Play until everyone has circled the track.

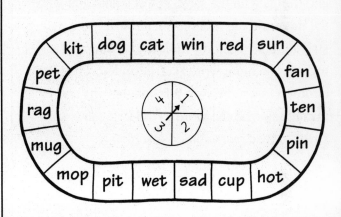

Activities for Short Vowels

You can duplicate and send home School-Home Newsletter 2, page 103, to provide families with fun, easy-to-do activities for reinforcing short vowels.

Animal Word Slides

INDEPENDENT Patterns are provided on pages 124–128 to make animal Word Slides featuring words containing each of the short vowel sounds. Children can cut out the animal and the strip. Working **independently or with a partner,** they can name the animal and other people, places, and things with the same vowel sound and write the names in the sections on the strip. Make the strip longer by taping additional sections of paper together so more words can be added. Then have children insert the strip through the slits and pull through to read the words. Children can trade strips to read one another's words.

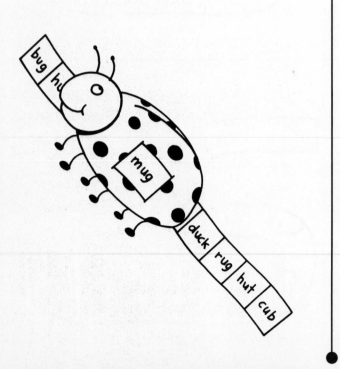

Scavenger Hunt

INDEPENDENT Scatter around the room picture cards whose names contain short vowel sounds. Have children form **small teams,** and provide each team with a list of picture names. Team members must read the words on the list and hunt for the corresponding picture cards. When the hunt has ended, ask each group to match their words with the pictures they found to verify. This same activity can be used for words with long vowel sounds or initial consonant clusters. If you wish to make this a rhyming word activity, scatter word cards around the room, and provide a list of words that rhyme to match.

Word Puzzlers

INDEPENDENT On the board, make several word puzzle boxes, with three boxes across and three down. Fill the first two boxes in the row going across with a consonant and vowel. **Pairs** of children can add letters to the puzzle to form two words. Repeat the activity, providing only the vowel in the middle box. Then have children start their own puzzle boxes for one another. Older children can create puzzles with more boxes for longer words and ask each other to write the words.

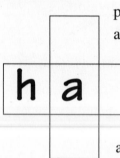

Wordscopes

INDEPENDENT Have children use the Wordscope pattern on page 130. A phonogram can be written in the box on the scope, and letters that stand for beginning sounds are written on the strip, which is then pulled through the scope and read.

Harcourt Brace School Publishers

Rhyming Tic-Tac-Toe

INDEPENDENT Provide **partners** with copies of the 9-Square Grid found on page 121. Each player must choose a short vowel phonogram to use in place of X's and O's. Children can refer to the *Phonogram Cards* in the set of *Word Builder Cards* as a resource. Players can write their chosen phonogram on each of the game playing cards (five each). To make a move, a player must say a word that ends with the chosen phonogram, spell the word aloud, and then place the *Phonogram Card* on the board. For each new game,

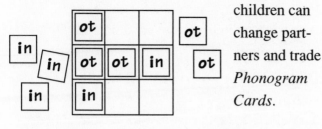

children can change partners and trade *Phonogram Cards*.

Flip-the-Flap Books

INDEPENDENT Use the Flip Book pattern found on page 133 to have **individuals** make flip books that features a short vowel phonogram, such as *ot*. Model by writing the letters *ot* on the larger strip. Write consonants, clusters, and digraphs on the smaller strips (*n, c, g, h, d, l, p, r, bl, sl, tr, sh*). Show children how to assemble the book by stapling the stack of smaller strips onto the left side of the longer strip.

Plan which phonogram each child will do or have children decide. Then they can create a collection of different books for everyone's use. Suggest that children share their book pages with several partners before stapling them. **Partners** might suggest additional letters that can be added

to form words. Children can use the *Word Builder Cards* as a resource.

Trail Blazers

INDEPENDENT Make copies of the S-Shape Game Board on pages 115–116. In each section on the game board trail, write the beginning and ending letters to form a short vowel word. Insert a blank to indicate the missing vowel. Provide a numbered spinner, found on page 120, and game markers for each **group** of players. The object is to have players make as many words as possible.

1. First player spins and moves the number of spaces indicated.
2. All players look at the unfinished word and write a word on paper by inserting a vowel. Each player reads the word on his or her list. Players should brainstorm to determine if any other words can be made and written. The game continues with the next player spinning.
3. Play until everyone has reached the end of the trail.

These word frames could be used in the spaces on the board:

h _ t	f _ n	p _ g	b _ g	c _ t	p _ n
d _ g	s _ d	l _ ck	r _ g	r _ ck	h _ m
b _ d	c _ p	l _ d	m _ t	n _ t	p _ t
r _ d	s _ n	t _ p	t _ ck		

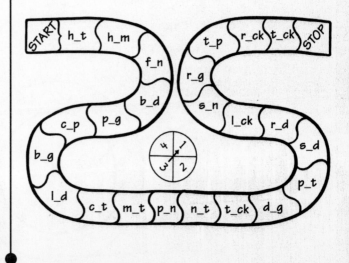

Activities for Long Vowels

You can duplicate and send home School-Home Newsletter 3, page 104, to provide families with fun, easy-to-do activities for reinforcing long vowels.

Making Words with Long Vowels

TEACHER DIRECTED Follow the directions from previous activities to make flip books and wordscopes. Focus on long vowel spelling patterns.

Long-Vowel Word Wheels

INDEPENDENT Duplicate the Word Wheel pattern on page 129. Have children cut out and assemble the wheel with a paper fastener. Have **each child** write letters that spell a long vowel pattern on the left side of the top wheel. Suggestions: *ade, ail, ain, ake, ame, ate, ave, ay, eak, eam, eed, eel, eep, ice, ide, ight, ike, ind, ine, ite, oke, old, ole, one, ope.* Children finish the wheel by writing consonants, consonant clusters, and consonant digraphs on the bottom wheel to form words. Have a wheel exchange so that children can read words on several wheels.

Picture These Rhyming Pairs

TEACHER DIRECTED **INDEPENDENT** Write the following thirty words on index cards, or use the Word Cards pattern from page 135. To help children focus on the long vowel spelling pattern/rhyme relationship in words, have them match words to form rhyming pairs. Include these pairs:

beast feast	*pink drink*	*brain strain*	*fly pie*
bright light	*clay tray*	*cold gold*	*dry fly*
fake snake	*fine pine*	*free bee*	*nice price*
pale whale	*rock clock*	*snail jail*	*weak beak*

Invite **each child** to choose a word pair to illustrate in a funny manner. Children can also create rhyming word pairs of their own and illustrate them. Note that the long vowel spelling does not always have to be the same—for example, *sweet treat* and *cheap sheep*. This same activity can be used with short vowel words. These illustrations can be published using the Pop-Up Book pattern on page 131. Children can write the rhyming word pair on the front and have their picture pop up from inside.

Harcourt Brace School Publishers

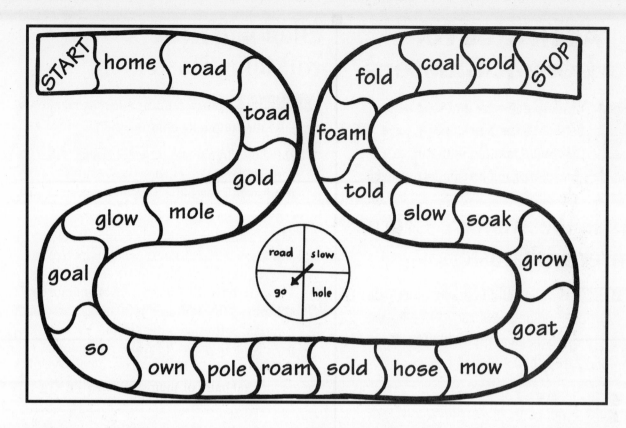

Go Slow on the Road

INDEPENDENT Make a copy of the S-Shape Game Board from pages 115–116. Fill the spaces with words containing the long *o* vowel sound, spelled *oa, o-e, ow,* and *o.* Use the blank spinner pattern from page 120, and draw lines to divide the spinner into four sections. Write one of the following words in each section: *road, slow, go, hole.* **Two or three players** take turns spinning , reading the word on the spinner, moving a game marker along the road to the first word that contains the same spelling for the vowel sound of long *o,* and reading the word.

Guess My Picture Name

INDEPENDENT Provide **each child** with a copy of the Pull-Out Book pattern on page 134. Model how children are to write a list of words with long vowel sounds on the page. Then they are to choose one of those words to illustrate on the pull-out tab. After their books are assembled, they can tell a **partner** clues , and ask him or her to read the list and guess which word is pictured on the hidden tab.

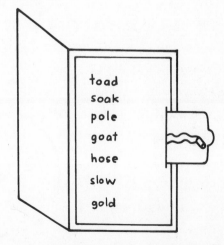

Activities for Consonant Clusters

You can duplicate and send home School-Home Newsletter 4, page 105, to provide families with fun, easy-to-do activities for reinforcing consonant clusters.

This Is the Way We Learn Consonant Clusters

TEACHER DIRECTED Provide children with individual Letter Cards, found on pages 136–137. Sing the following song to the tune "Here We Go 'Round the Mulberry Bush":

Listen to the words I sing:
    black, blue, blow; black, blue, blow;
Now repeat the words with me:
    black, blue, blow.
Show the letters that start these words:
    black, blue, blow; black, blue, blow;
Then name some other words you know
    that start the same.

Children are to form the initial cluster, using the letter cards. Then invite them to name other words that begin with the cluster. These can be written on the board or Word Wall. Repeat the song, focusing on another consonant cluster.

Blending Letters to Make Clusters

TEACHER DIRECTED When reinforcing consonant clusters, use the following chart method.

1. Have children make large letter cards that form a consonant cluster you wish to reinforce. Example: **b** **l**

2. Make a chart with three columns labeled *b, l,* and *bl* on the board or on chart paper. Write two familiar examples under each heading. Use action words for the consonant cluster column so that children will always associate a certain action with the cluster. You will be reviewing /b/*b* and /l/*l* while introducing /bl/*bl*.

b	l	bl
bat	look	blink
box	like	blow

3. After reading the chart words together, say new words that begin with *b, l,* or *bl.* Have children repeat each word and indicate in which column to write the word by holding up one or both of the letter cards. Ask a child with a correct response to tell you where to write the word on the chart. Children can help you spell the word. Use words such as *boy, blue, lap, ball, black, bloom, bit, last, leaf, block, blind, lion, blouse,* and *band* to fill the chart. Once the chart is finished, read the words in each column together. Follow a similar procedure to reinforce other consonant clusters. As children become more proficient, they can have their own charts to fill in.

Moving Right Along

TEACHER DIRECTED When reinforcing the initial clusters, use action words as your examples. Children will remember and associate the consonant cluster with the action. Here are some examples:

blow	*breathe*	*creep*	*clap*	*drive*
fly	*frown*	*grab*	*skip*	*slither*
smile	*sniff*	*spin*	*stomp*	*trot*

Use the words to sing the following action song to the tune of "Row, Row, Row Your Boat." Hold up letter cards, such as *s* and *k,* and have children name the action word. *(skip)* Insert the action word *skip* in each blank to sing and act out the song. Continue the song, using another initial cluster and action word.

_____, _____, _____ with me.
I will show you how.
You can _____ so easily.
Do it with me now!

Action Track

INDEPENDENT Make copies of the Racetrack Game Board found on page 113. Fill in or have children fill in each blank with an action word that begins with a consonant cluster. **Two to four players** can use a numbered spinner, found on page 120, to move game markers along the board while naming and acting out the word landed on. Play until everyone has finished the race.

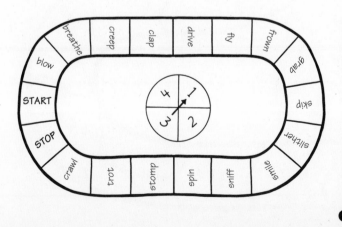

Tongue Twister a Day

TEACHER DIRECTED Tongue twisters are a great way to use a collection of words having a common consonant cluster. You may want to begin each day by saying a tongue twister and having children repeat it, saying it faster each time. Write the words on chart paper as children watch. A volunteer can underline initial clusters that are repeated. As you add to your chart each day, review some of the old tongue twisters. Invite children to say their favorites. Eventually children can create tongue twisters for the chart. Here are some examples:

- Blindfolded Blanche blew a blizzard of blue bubbles.
- Brandy's brother Brian brought brown bread for brunch.
- Grady Grocer groans when grouchy Greta grabs a group of green grapes.
- Flexible Floyd flips flat flapjacks.
- Sleepy Slick slipped on slippery slime in his slippers.

Flexible Floyd flips flat flapjacks.

Children may want to publish tongue twisters they write, using the Pop-Up Book pattern from page 131. They can write the tongue twister on the cover and illustrate a picture to glue on the pop-up inside.

Cluster Word Wheels

INDEPENDENT Provide copies of the Word Wheel pattern on page 129. Show children how to cut out and assemble the wheels. Model how to write a consonant cluster on the right side of the top wheel and add letters around the bottom wheel to form words. Plan with children so that different clusters are represented on the wheels. In this way children can trade wheels to read.

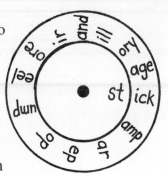

Traveling Along

INDEPENDENT **Partners** can play a game to reinforce words with the final clusters *st, ft, nt, mp, nk, nd, ld, lk.* Use the S-Shape Game Board patterns found on pages 115–116. In each section, write a word that ends with a cluster and is associated with traveling through a town or city. Suggested words: *pavement, restaurant, ramp, hydrant, honk, sidewalk, bump, newsstand, playground, fast, left, lost, walk, dead end, find, went, trunk, bank, past, west, east, signpost, shift, gas pump, crank, bend, behind, wind,* and *child.* Players can use the numbered spinner, found on page 120, to determine the number of moves. They read the word landed on and name the letters that form the final cluster. Play until everyone has reached the *end of the road.* Use toy cars for playing pieces.

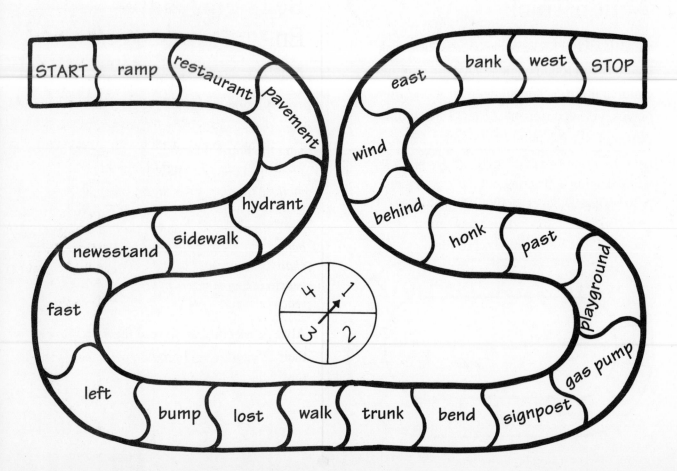

Activities for Consonant Digraphs

 You can duplicate and send home School-Home Newsletter 5, page 106, to provide families with fun, easy-to-do activities for reinforcing consonant digraphs.

Making Words with Digraphs

TEACHER DIRECTED Provide copies of the individual Letter Cards and the Word Builder pattern from pages 136–138. Children can make words with single consonant beginnings and then move on to words beginning with digraphs. Example: First, have children make the word *in*. Then, have them add beginning consonants to form the words *fin, pin, tin,* and *win*. Continue by making four-letter words with beginning digraphs: *chin, shin, thin*. As words are made, have volunteers add them to a Word Wall.

Other word sets to form could be:

> *hip, rip, sip, tip, chip, ship, whip*
> *hop, mop, top, chop, shop*
> *heat, meat, seat, cheat, wheat*
> *lick, sick, tick, chick, thick*

Partners can work on their own to form other word groups and add these new groups to the Word Wall or individual word files.

Sorting Out Words

INDEPENDENT Use index cards or the Word Cards pattern on page 135 to make packs of twenty-four word cards. In each pack, include words that begin with *c, ch, s, sh, t, th, w,* and *wh* (three of each). Choose words that can be sorted in various ways. Sample pack:

> *cot, corn, cow   chow, chip, chop*
> *seat, sick, sink   shin, ship, shop*
> *ten, tin, top   thorn, thick, think*
> *win, wink, worn   whip, when, wheat*

Allow children to figure out how they want to sort the words. After sorting one way, have them try another way. Words can be sorted by initial sounds; ending sounds; vowel sounds; words that rhyme; and three-, four-, and five-letter words. Provide blank cards for children to add more words to each sort.

Beginning and Ending Sorts

INDEPENDENT Use the Word Cards pattern on page 135 to make cards with words that begin or end with the digraphs *sh, th,* and *ch*. Allow children to figure out how they want to sort the words. Words you might include:

shell, shop, shoe, shirt, show, sheep, push, dish, wash, wish, sash, flash, fish, think, thank, thirty, thunder, thorn, thing, thick, thin, both, cloth, teeth, path, bath, with, math, fourth, chair, cheese, cheek, chalk, child, chin, cherry, chew, beach, catch, each, inch, lunch, march, much, reach, watch.

Always ask children to read the words in each of their categories, and provide blank cards in case they want to add more words.

Consonant Digraph Relay

TEACHER DIRECTED Have children form **teams of four** members. Say a word that begins or ends with a digraph. Teammates take turns writing each letter of the word on the board, in order, until the word is complete. If a player makes a mistake, the next teammate can correct it. Play until all teams have finished the word. A point is scored for each correct spelling. Once children become more proficient, make this a timed race to see which team finishes first.

Digraph Word Wheels

INDEPENDENT Have children cut out the blank Word Wheel from the pattern on page 129 . Show them how to assemble the wheels. Then model how to write a digraph on the right side of the top wheel and add letters around the bottom wheel to form words. Plan with children so that different digraphs are represented on the wheels. In this way children can trade wheels to read.

Tongue Twister a Day, Part II

TEACHER DIRECTED If children enjoyed using words with consonant clusters to create tongue twisters, follow a similar procedure for words with initial digraphs. Here are some examples to get you started:

- Charlie Champ cheerfully chomps chicken chili and chocolate cherry cheesecake.
- Shy Sheila sheared seven short shaggy sheep.
- Thankful Thelma threw a thimble on her throbbing thumb.

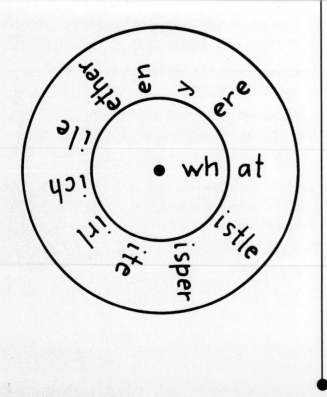

Activities for *R*-Controlled Vowels

 You can duplicate and send home School-Home Newsletter 6, page 107, to provide families with fun, easy-to-do activities for reinforcing *r*-controlled vowels.

Giant Tic-Tac-Toe

TEACHER DIRECTED Select **nine children** to arrange their chairs in tic-tac-toe formation. Provide nine sheets of construction paper with a giant *X* on one side and a giant *O* on the other side. The remaining children form two teams—X's and O's. Alternate saying a word with an *r*-controlled vowel to members of each team. The player must say the word and spell it. Write the word on the board to verify. If correct, the team directs one of the nine children to hold up an *X* or an *O*, as appropriate. Play until one team wins or there is a tie. Follow the same procedure for another round. You can also use this game to focus on words with other phonic elements.

Star Players

INDEPENDENT For each game, reproduce two copies of the 16-Square Grid from page 122. Use one copy as a game board that children can cover by drawing and coloring stars. Write words with the vowel-*r* pattern in the sections on the second copy, and cut apart the cards. To play, **partners** place the word cards face up on the game board to cover the stars. Players take turns choosing a word to read and asking the partner to find and remove the word from the game board. Play until all the words are gone so the stars show.

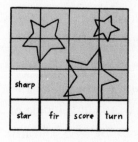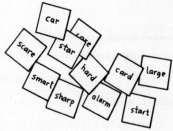

Star Riddle Writers

INDEPENDENT Provide copies of the Pull-Out Book pattern on page 134. Model how to cut out and assemble the books. Then children write riddles about words containing an *r*-controlled vowel. The riddle can be written on the blank page with the answer hidden on the pull-out tab. Encourage children to include as many *r*-controlled words as possible in their writing. Here is a riddle to get them started:

This is a large fish with very sharp teeth.
If you see its fin, hurry and start for the shore.
What is it?
(a shark)

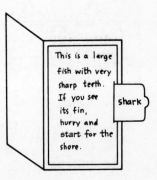

Activities for Vowel Diphthongs and Vowel Variants

 You can duplicate and send home School-Home Newsletter 7, page 108, to provide families with fun, easy-to-do activities for reinforcing vowel diphthongs and vowel variants.

Vowel Cover-Up

INDEPENDENT For each game, you will need the Dot Game Board and the Word Cards from pages 119 and 135. First, fill the dots with the vowel spellings *oo, au, aw, oi, oy, ow, ou,* and *ea.* Write words containing these vowels on the cards. To play, **partners** will turn the word cards face down. They will take turns turning over a card to read and then finding and covering the vowel spelling on the game board. Players can use cotton balls, coins, or plastic markers to cover the dots. Play until all the words have been read and all the dots are covered.

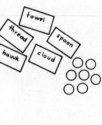

Sort and Split

INDEPENDENT Use the Word Cards pattern on page 135 to make sets of cards with the words *launch, faucet, autumn, sauce, August, sausage, fawn, shawl, straw, hawk, lawn, draw, brown, down, plow, crown, flower, owl, house, mountain, cloud, sound, pouch,* and *blouse.* Children can work **independently or with a partner** to sort the words into two groups according to like vowel sounds (*au* and *aw* words / *ow* and *ou* words). Then have them split the words in each group again to form words with like spellings for those vowel sounds. (*au, aw/ow, ou*)

Loop to Loop

INDEPENDENT Use the Word Cards pattern from page 135 to make a set of cards with words containing the vowels *oi, oy, ow, ou, au, aw,* and *oo.* On each word card, write a numeral from 1 to 4. Use the cards with copies of the Loop Game Board from pages 117–118. Glue the loops together on a file folder to make the game board.

To begin play, stack the cards face down. **Two or three players** take turns picking a card from the stack to read. If read correctly, the card is returned to the bottom of the stack, and the player moves a game marker the number of spaces indicated by the numeral on the word card. If the word is not identified, the player forfeits a move and must give the word card to the next player to read. Play until everyone has moved from loop to loop to the end of the path.

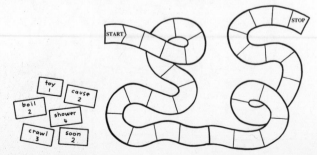

Activities for Contractions

You can duplicate and send home School-Home Newsletter 8, page 109, to provide families with fun, easy-to-do activities for reinforcing contractions. It also includes activities for reinforcing possessives.

We'll Be Coming 'Round the Mountain

INDEPENDENT Use copies of the Mountain Game Board from page 114. Write a contraction on half of the spaces and two words that can form a contraction on the other spaces. **Partners** choose one side of the mountain to begin play, starting at the bottom and taking turns climbing up one side and down the other. To move, they jump over one another, landing on every other word. If a player lands on a contraction, the two words forming the contraction should be identified and spelled. If two words are landed on, the player should say and spell the contraction that can be formed. Once players have reached the other side of the mountain, they can reverse to go back over again so that a new set of words is identified.

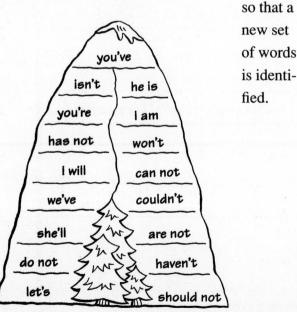

you've

isn't | he is

you're | I am

has not | won't

I will | can not

we've | couldn't

she'll | are not

do not | haven't

let's | should not

Contraction Concentration

TEACHER DIRECTED Write each of the following contractions and word pairs on large cards or sheets of paper: *didn't, did not, wasn't, was not, let's, let us, we'll, we will, they're, they are*. Give the cards to **ten volunteers** who will stand across the front of the room with the blank side of the card facing the group of players. The group will play a game of Concentration, with players taking turns asking two card holders to turn around their word cards. If a match between a contraction and corresponding word pair is made, the card holders stand off to the side. If a match is not made, the cards are turned around again. Play Concentration until all matches have been made. Make new cards for another game. **Individual** games can be made using Word Cards from page 135.

Contraction Builders

TEACHER DIRECTED Provide children with sets of Letter Cards and a Word Builder, found on pages 136–138. Blank cards can be used to make an apostrophe and additional letter cards that are needed. Children build pairs of words you say by placing the letter cards in the pocket of the Word Builder. Then have them replace one or more letters with an apostrophe to make the contraction that means the same. Use these words: *let us, was not, I am, has not, he is, you are, are not, is not, you have.*

Activities for Possessives

 You can duplicate and send home School-Home Newsletter 8, page 109, to provide families with fun, easy-to-do activities for reinforcing possessives. It also includes activities for reinforcing contractions.

Silly Sentences with 's

TEACHER DIRECTED Use silly alliterative sentences to reinforce and provide examples of names with the possessive form 's. Write examples on the board or on chart paper, and read them with children.

- Kevin's kangaroo kicked Karen's cousin Kyle.
- Luisa's load of lemons landed in Larry's lap.
- Papa will pay for Pepe's peck of pickled peppers and Polly's pound of peaches.
- Floyd's flapjacks flew and fell flat on Flora's flowerpot.

The sentences could be written on strips and the words then cut apart so that children can arrange them in a pocket chart. The words can be arranged in more than one way.

Have children write their silly sentences, and suggest that they publish them using the Step-Page Book pattern, page 132. Each child's sentence can be written on the first step, and classmates' sentences can be copied onto the other pages.

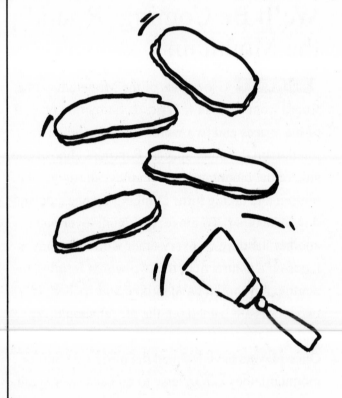

| Floyd's | flowerpot | flew | and | fell | on | Flora's | flat | flapjacks | . |

| Flora's | flapjacks | flew | and | fell | on | flat | Floyd's | flowerpot | . |

Activities for Inflected Endings

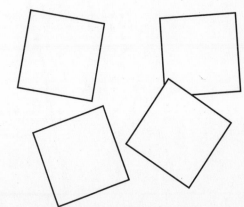

You can duplicate and send home School-Home Newsletter 9, page 110, to provide families with fun, easy-to-do activities for reinforcing inflected endings.

Action Word Wall

TEACHER DIRECTED One way to start or add to a Word Wall featuring words with inflected endings is to involve children in performing actions. Your Word Wall might be divided into four sections like this:

base word	ending s or -es	ending -ing	ending -ed

Add words to the wall while using the word in context and having children demonstrate the action. Use a procedure like this: Ask who can *twirl*. Write the word *twirl* in the first column. Then tell children to watch as a volunteer *twirls*. Write the word *twirls* in the second column. As the child is moving, ask the group to name what he or she is doing. Write their response *twirling* in the third column. Once the child is seated, ask the group what the child did. Write *twirled* in the last column. When several words are on the wall, read them together and talk about the base words and the endings. For older children, you could include words that require spelling changes, such as *carry, carries, carrying, carried*.

Wordo

TEACHER DIRECTED Provide **each child** with a copy of the 16-Square Grid found on page 122 and game markers. Call on children to pick words from the Word Wall that will be included in the game. As each word is chosen, all players write the word in one space on their game sheet as you write it on an index card. All children will have the same words on their sheets but in different spaces. Once the sheets are filled, shuffle the cards and start to play. As each word is called, have children repeat the word, chant its spelling, and cover it on their sheets. Play until someone has covered all the words in a row.

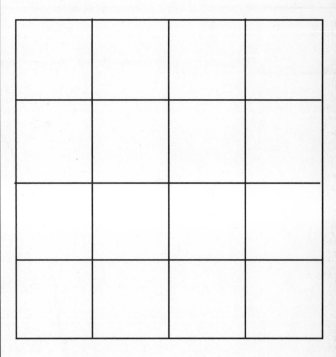

Sort and Spell

INDEPENDENT Use the Word Cards pattern found on page 135 to make a set of base word cards to which inflected endings can be added. Include words such as *jump, carry, smile, run, stop, wash, hurry, copy, paint, sleep, chase, fix, skip, clap, bake, help, reach, splash, dance, erase, hum, plan, sneeze,* and *work*. First, have children sort the words into base words that require spelling changes when an ending is added and those that do not. (Spelling changes are required of words ending with *y* or *e* and most words ending with a single consonant.) Then, children can add *-s,-es, -ing,* or *-ed* to each word and write it on paper to verify.

Hiking Up Word Mountain

INDEPENDENT Use copies of the Mountain Game Board found on page 114. In each space, write a word with the inflected ending *-s, -es, -ed,* or *-ing,* including words that require spelling changes. **Partners** choose one side of the mountain to begin play, starting at the bottom and taking turns climbing up one side and down the other. To move, they jump over one another, landing on every other word. They must read the word and spell the base word. Once players have reached the other side of the mountain, they should reverse to go back over again so that a new set of words is identified.

Activities for Prefixes

You can duplicate and send home School-Home Newsletter 10, page 111, to provide families with fun, easy-to-do activities for reinforcing prefixes. It also includes activities for reinforcing suffixes.

Know and Don't-Know Sorts

INDEPENDENT Use the Word Cards pattern from page 135 to make a pack of cards with words having prefixes: *retell, unsafe, dislike, reload, unpack, disobey, rewrite, unable, distrust, refill, unclear, displease, repaint, unload, disappear, reuse, unroll, disagree, retie, unafraid, recheck, unbutton, dishonest, unhappy.* Children can read and sort the words according to the prefix. Then they can sort again into groups of words they can define and those they do not know. You may want to write the meaning on the back of each word card or provide an answer key.

Run the Bases

TEACHER DIRECTED Create a baseball diamond in the room, labeling home plate and first, second, and third base. Write words with suffixes on the board or have children refer to a Word Wall they have created. Then, children take turns standing at home plate to choose a word to read. They get to first base by reading the word, to second base by identifying the base word, to third base by defining the word, and to home plate by using the word in a sentence. Form **two teams** if children wish.

A Game Board of Sorts

INDEPENDENT Make copies of the Loop Game Board pattern on pages 117–118. Use the blank spinner pattern, page 120, and divide it into three sections. Write the words *return, undo,* and *dislike* on the spinner. Fill the spaces on the game board with words beginning with *re-, un-,* and *dis-.* **Two or three players** take turns spinning the spinner and moving a marker along the game board until they reach the first word that begins with the same prefix as that shown on the spinner. Players must read the words along the way and use the word landed on in a sentence. Play until everyone has traveled the loops.

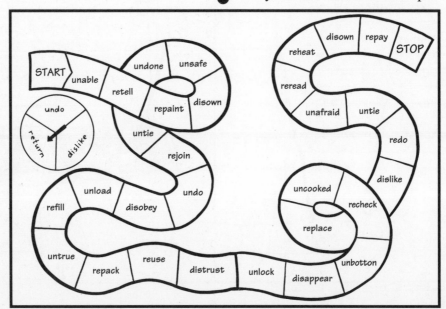

Activities for Suffixes

You can duplicate and send home School-Home Newsletter 10, page 111, to provide families with fun, easy-to-do activities for reinforcing suffixes. It also includes activities for reinforcing prefixes.

Climb the Highest Mountain

INDEPENDENT Make a copy of the Mountain Game Board found on page 114. In each section, write a word with the suffix *-er* or *-est*. **Partners** choose one side of the mountain to begin play, starting at the bottom and taking turns climbing up one side and down the other. To move, they jump over one another, landing on every other word. Players must read the word landed on and use it in a sentence to illustrate meaning. If the word is not identified, the partner can help out. Once players have reached the other side of the mountain, they should reverse to go back over again so that a new set of words is identified.

Seeing Spots

INDEPENDENT Make a copy of the Dot Game Board found on page 119. On each dot, write a word that ends with a suffix, including *-er, -est, -ful, -less, -ness,* and *-ly*. Use the spinner pattern, page 120, and draw lines to make four sections. Write the numerals 1, 2, 1, 2 in the sections. **Partners** take turns spinning the spinner, reading one or two words, and naming and spelling the base words. As words are read, they can be covered with cotton balls or game markers. When all the words are covered, the partners may want to invite two more players to join them to spin, remove one or two markers at a time, and read the words.

Reproducible
Phonics Resources

School ←→ Home Newsletter

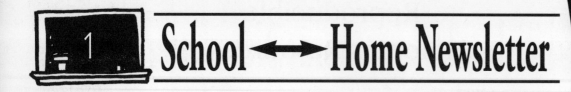

DEAR FAMILY,

Your child has been learning about consonants. As your child continues to learn about consonant letters and the sounds they make in words, you can participate too by trying some activities at home. These activities will help your child become a better reader and writer.

PHONICS FOCUS

The letters *b, c, d, f, g, h, j, k, l, m, n, p, q, r, s, t, v, w, x, y,* and *z* are **consonants**.

AFTER-SCHOOL ACTIVITIES

Everyone's name has consonant letters in it. So do the names of things you use every day.

✓ Have your child write his or her name and circle all the consonant letters. See how many words your child can say that begin or end with each of those letters. Then help your child list the words. You can use books or a dictionary to find words, too.

M o n i c a

mud	nuts	cat
money	nose	car
mail	net	cow
hum	van	corn

✓ Work together to think of the names of foods that begin with each consonant. Look in kitchen cupboards and recipe books for ideas. Make a book of the names. Draw a picture or cut a picture from a magazine to go with each food name. Then create menus in which all the foods must begin with the same consonant.

Cut out this bookmark and take it to the library.

GET INTO BOOKS

Look for these alphabet books. Help your child notice the words that begin with consonants:

Librarians A to Z by Jean Johnson. Walker, 1989.

Alpha Beta Chowder by Jeanne Steig. HarperCollins, 1992.

I Spy: An Alphabet in Art by Lucy Micklethwait. Greenwillow, 1992.

The Calypso Alphabet by John Agard. Henry Holt, 1989.

Potluck by Anne Shelby. Orchard, 1991.

The Monster Book of ABC Sounds by Alan Snow. Dial, 1991.

PROJECT TIME

Fill an empty container with dirt or clay. Put a branch in the container so it stands up. Your child can cut paper leaves and write words on them that begin with consonants and name things that tell about the current season or an upcoming holiday. Read the words together.

2 School ←→ Home Newsletter

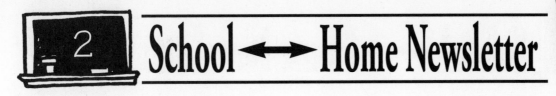

DEAR FAMILY,

Your child has been learning about words with short vowel sounds. As your child continues to learn about vowel sounds and the letters that spell these sounds, you can participate too by trying some activities at home.

AFTER-SCHOOL ACTIVITIES

Use the names of items found in your home to give your child practice with reading and writing words with short vowel sounds.

✓ Invite your child to go on a scavenger hunt. Write a list of things for your child to find, and read it together. If your child needs extra help, draw a picture of each thing. Here are some things to find:

hat	bell	big pan
toy	sock	ten spoons
nut	jam	six rocks

✓ Read the words on your list aloud, and ask your child to say another word that rhymes with the name of each thing found. For example, *cat* rhymes with *hat*.

PROJECT TIME

The word *map* has a short *a* in it. Give your child a large sheet of paper or a paper bag that has been cut and opened. Ask your child to draw a room map showing his or her bedroom and the things in it. Have your child label things that have names with short vowels, such as the *bed, desk, rug,* and *clock.*

PHONICS FOCUS

The letters *a, e, i, o,* and *u* are **vowels**. The words *cat, bed, six, box,* and *cup* have **short vowel** sounds. If a short word or a syllable in a longer word has only one vowel and it is positioned between two consonants, the vowel is likely to have a short vowel sound as in the words above.

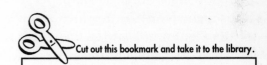

Cut out this bookmark and take it to the library.

GET INTO BOOKS

Look for these books that feature words with short vowel sounds:

Who Is Tapping at My Window? by A. G. Deming. Puffin, 1994.
short *a*

Emma's Pet by David McPhail. Dutton, 1985.
short *e*

It's My Birthday by Helen Oxenbury. Candlewick, 1994.
short *i*

Fox in Socks by Dr. Seuss. Random House, 1965.
short *o*

Caps, Hats, Socks, and Mittens by Louise Bordon. Scholastic, 1992.
short *u*

Thump and Plunk by Janice May Udry. Harper Collins, 1981.
short *u*

101 Ways to Make Your Students Better Decoders and Readers   103

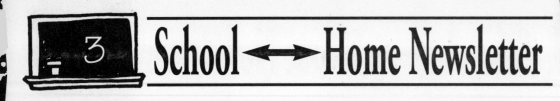 

School ←→ Home Newsletter

3

DEAR FAMILY,

Your child has been learning about words with long vowel sounds. As your child continues to learn about vowel sounds and the letters that spell these sounds, you can participate too by trying some activities at home. These activities will help your child become a better reader and writer.

AFTER-SCHOOL ACTIVITIES

Do you recycle? What kinds of things do you use again—boxes, cans, glass jars, plastic containers, toys, or clothing?

✓ Help your child recycle word parts. Write the following word parts on paper. Help your child make as many words as possible by adding different beginning letters and saying the words aloud.

    _ain _ame _ale _one
    _eet _ite _eam _ide
    _ight _oat _oke _ube

Help your child write them on small separate pieces of paper. Sort the words according to vowel sound and put them in separate bags.

✓ Use the words from one bag to play a guessing game. Give clues about a word and have your child guess the word. Then your child can take a turn. Example: "I'm thinking of a word that has the sound of long *a*, and it names the water that falls from the clouds."

PROJECT TIME

Help your child recycle newspapers, magazines, and junk mail by cutting out interesting words with long vowel sounds. Create a sign, a poster, a greeting card, or a message using the words.

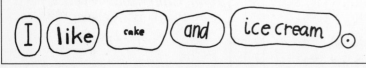

PHONICS FOCUS

The letters *a, e, i, o,* and *u* are **vowels**. The words *cake, leaf, bike, boat,* and *flute* have **long vowel** sounds. There are different ways to spell long vowels, such as with one letter as in *me,* with two letters as in *meet,* or with a vowel and final *e* as in *bake.*

GET INTO BOOKS

Look for these great books that feature words with long vowel sounds:

The Great Kapok Tree: A Tale of the Amazon Rain Forest by Lynne Cherry. Harcourt Brace, 1990.

Look What I Did with a Leaf! by Morteza E. Sohi. Walker, 1993.

Sheep Out to Eat by Nancy Shaw. Houghton Mifflin, 1992.

Small Green Snake by Libba Moore Gray. Orchard, 1994.

Jake Baked the Cake by B. G. Hennessy. Puffin, 1992.

z

Harcourt Brace School Publishers

DEAR FAMILY,

Your child has been learning about the sounds of consonant clusters in words and the letters that form them. As your child continues to learn about consonant clusters, you can participate too by trying some activities at home. These activities will help your child become a better reader and writer.

AFTER-SCHOOL ACTIVITIES

What is the weather forecast for today? Your child can learn about weather while reading and writing words that have consonant clusters.

✓ Give your child three paper plates or sheets of paper to label with these words: *sunny weather, snowy weather, rainy weather*. Write the following words on small self-stick notes: black clouds, freezing rain, sunglasses, damp, sled, clear blue sky, floods, ski slope, warm front, gray skies, snowflakes, swimming, raindrops, sleet, sand, swings, cold front, mild breeze, wool gloves, summer camp, scarf, bright sunshine, plants grow, strong wind, ice skating. Together read the words and underline the consonant clusters. Your child can stick each word on the paper plate that names the weather associated with it.

PROJECT TIME

Your child might want to write a weather forecast for the following day. He or she can tell what the sky will look like, predict the high and low temperatures for the day, and describe any other weather conditions. See how many words with consonant clusters are used.

PHONICS FOCUS

A **consonant cluster** is two or three consonants that are blended together at the beginning or end of a word. The sound of each letter is heard. Consonant clusters found at the beginning of words include *br, cr, dr, fr, gr, pr, tr, bl, cl, fl, gl, pl, sl, sp, sk, st, sc, sl, sm, sn, sw, str, scr, squ,* and *thr*. Some clusters found at the end of words are *st, ft, nt, lk, lt, ld, mp, nd,* and *pt.*

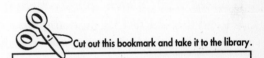
Cut out this bookmark and take it to the library.

GET INTO BOOKS

Look for these books that feature words with consonant clusters:

In the Small, Small Pond by Denise Fleming. Henry Holt, 1993. initial clusters with *s*

There's a Nightmare in My Closet by Mercer Mayer. Puffin, 1992. initial clusters with *l*

Cloudy with a Chance of Meatballs by Judi Barrett. Macmillan, 1978. variety of initial clusters

Starring First Grade by Miriam Cohen. Greenwillow, 1985. final clusters with *t*

The Milk Makers by Gail Gibbons. Macmillan, 1985. final cluster *lk*

The Grumpalump by Sarah Hayes. Clarion, 1991. final clusters *mp, nd*

5 School ←→ Home Newsletter

DEAR FAMILY,

Your child has been learning about words with consonant digraphs. As your child continues to learn about digraphs, you can participate too by trying some activities at home.

AFTER-SCHOOL ACTIVITIES

Ask your child to name the five senses. Then use <u>seeing</u>, <u>smelling</u>, <u>touching</u>, <u>hearing</u>, and <u>tasting</u> to help your child learn more about words that begin and end with consonant digraphs.

✓ On paper or a small chalkboard, write the following words that contain digraphs: *shop, lunch, quilt, chew, photo, sting, watch, whipped, skunk, thorn, thumb.* Read the words together, and have your child find and underline the letters that spell the digraph in each word: *sh, ch, qu, ch, ph, ng, tch, wh, nk, th, th-mb.*

✓ Play a guessing game using the words from above in questions like these:

- What do you smell when you go in a bake *shop*?
- What do you taste when you eat your favorite *lunch*?
- How do you feel when you snuggle under a *quilt*?
- What do you hear when you *chew* celery and carrot sticks?
- Whom would you see in a *photo* of your friends?
- What do you feel if you get a bee *sting*?
- What do you hear when you listen to a *watch*?
- What do you taste when you eat *whipped* potatoes?
- What do you smell if a *skunk* gets scared?
- What do you feel if a *thorn* pricks your *thumb*?

PROJECT TIME

The words *chocolate chips, chewy,* and *crunchy* have the *ch* digraph. Look in a favorite recipe book for a dessert that fits that description, and ask your child to be a dessert chef by helping you make it for an after-dinner treat. Ask family members how it tastes.

PHONICS FOCUS

A **consonant digraph** in a word is two consonants together that stand for one unique sound. A digraph may begin or end a word, as in these examples: *<u>sh</u>ip, fi<u>sh</u>, <u>wh</u>eel, thin<u>k</u>, ba<u>th</u>, <u>ph</u>one, laug<u>h</u>, <u>wr</u>ite, <u>kn</u>ow, <u>gn</u>aw, <u>ch</u>ew, crun<u>ch</u>, sin<u>g</u>, ban<u>k</u>, <u>qu</u>een.* The consonants *tch* form a three-letter digraph, as in the word *watch*.

Cut out this bookmark and take it to the library.

GET INTO BOOKS

Look for these books featuring words with digraphs:

The Quilt by Ann Jonas. Greenwillow, 1984. *qu*

Is This a House for Hermit Crab? by Megan McDonald. Orchard, 1990. *ch, tch*

Sheep on a Ship by Nancy Shaw. Houghton Mifflin, 1989. *sh, wh*

The Fish Who Could Wish by John Bush and Corky Paul. Kane-Miller, 1991. *sh, wh*

Elmer by David McKee. Lothrop, 1989. */f/ gh, ph*

Lionel in the Spring by Stephen Krensky. Dial, 1990. *ng, nk*

Agatha's Feather Bed by Carmen Agra Deedy. Peachtree, 1991. variety of digraphs

Harcourt Brace School Publishers

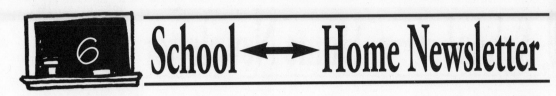

DEAR FAMILY,

Your child has been learning about words in which the letter *r* gives the vowel a new sound. As your child continues to learn about *r*-controlled vowels, you can participate too by trying some activities at home.

AFTER-SCHOOL ACTIVITIES

Do you live in the city or the country? Use words that tell about these two places to help your child read and write words that have vowels with *r*.

✓ Make a category game. Write these words on small pieces of paper: *farm, corn, deer, garden, curbs, barn, herd, park, steer, birds, yard, turkey, fair, cart, bear, squirrel, circus, cable cars, horse, burro, turtle, sports arena, sheep shearing*. Help your child read the words, and categorize them into <u>city things</u> and <u>country things</u>. Do some of the words fit both categories?

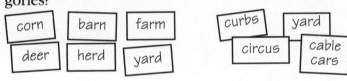

✓ Choose one group of words to tell or write a story together, using as many words as possible.

PROJECT TIME

Have your child color or paint a city scene or a country scene, including pictures of some of the categorized words from the activities. When your child has finished, ask her or him to tell you about the picture and label the details, using words with a vowel + *r*.

PHONICS FOCUS

In some words, the letter r gives the vowel a new sound. The spellings of these **r-controlled vowels** include *ar, er, ir, or, ur, air, ear, eer, ore, our, oor,* and *oar*. Help your child notice words with these vowels and the sounds they make as you read and write together.

Cut out this bookmark and take it to the library.

GET INTO BOOKS

Look for these books that feature words with *r*-controlled vowels:

Watch Out, Ronald Morgan! by Patricia Reilly Giff. Viking, 1985. words with *ear, eer*

Farmer Goff and His Turkey Sam by Brian Schatell. Lippincott, 1982. words with *ar, ur, air, ear*

Farm Noises by Jane Miller. Simon & Schuster, 1992. words with *ar*

Garden in the City by Gerda Muller. Dutton, 1992. words with *ar*

The Wednesday Surprise by Eve Bunting. Clarion, 1989. words with *er, ur*

The Lady and the Spider by Faith McNulty. HarperCollins, 1986. words with *or, ore, our*

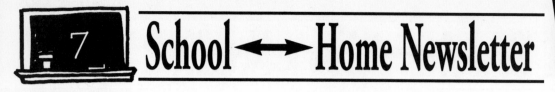 

School ←→ Home Newsletter

7

DEAR FAMILY,

Your child has been learning about words with vowel pairs. These vowel pairs have special spellings and stand for unique sounds. As your child continues to learn about vowel sounds and letters that stand for the sounds, you can try these activities at home.

AFTER-SCHOOL ACTIVITIES

Take a close look at words with special vowel pairs. Discover the fun and games suggested by some of these words.

✓ Write these words on separate cards or pieces of paper to create a sorting game:

> *yawn, lawn, taught, caught, thought, bought*
> *glue, blue, drew, chew*
> *coil, foil, soy, toy*
> *cow, now, out, shout*
> *could, should, would, book, cook, look*

Ask your child to read the words and then sort and stack words that have the same vowel sound.

✓ Mix the word cards and place them face down to play a game of concentration. Your child can turn over two cards at a time to read. If the words rhyme and have the same vowel spelling, the pair can be removed. If they do not, turn the cards face down again.

PROJECT TIME

How about having some outdoor fun? Some words that have vowel pairs suggest things you might do.

- *Draw* chalk pictures or a hopscotch game on the sidewalk or driveway.
- Play a game of tag or other running game on the *lawn*.
- Plan a family *cookout* with your favorite foods.
- Make up water *shower* games using empty dishwashing liquid bottles. They are great for squirting targets and people!
- Lie on the *ground* and find shapes in the *clouds*.

PHONICS FOCUS

In some words, two vowels appear together and stand for a special sound. In the words *saw*, *launch*, and *thought*, the vowel pairs *aw*, *au*, and *ou(gh)* stand for the same sound. In the words *clue* and *new*, the vowel sounds are the same but are spelled *ue* and *ew*. The vowels *ou* in *should* and *oo* in *brook* sound the same. These special vowel pairs are called **vowel variants**.

Vowel pairs *oi* and *oy* sound the same in *coin* and *toy*. The *ow* and *ou* in *cow* and *out* sound the same, too. These vowel pairs are called **diphthongs**.

 Cut out this bookmark and take it to the library.

GET INTO BOOKS

Look for these books featuring words with vowel variants and diphthongs:

The Luckiest Kid on the Planet by Lisa Campbell Ernst. Bradbury, 1994. *ue, ew*

The Monkey and the Crocodile by Paul Galdone. Clarion, 1987. *aw, au, ou*

Green Eggs and Ham by Dr. Seuss. Random House, 1960. *oo, ou*

Too Much Noise by Ann McGovern. Houghton Mifflin, 1992. *oi, oy*

Harcourt Brace School Publishers

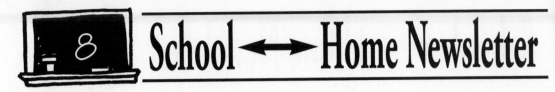

DEAR FAMILY,

Your child has been learning about using an apostrophe in words. As your child continues to discover how to use an apostrophe to write contractions and possessive forms of words, you can participate too by trying some activities at home.

AFTER-SCHOOL ACTIVITIES

Contractions and possessive forms of words are used every day in your conversations. Here are some ideas to help your child read and write these words.

✓ Ask your child what a *shortcut* is. Talk about shortcuts that can be taken to go to school, to a nearby store, or to a friend's house. See if your child recognizes word shortcuts called **contractions**. Make a matching game by writing the following on paper or on a small chalkboard:

don't	I will	**you've**	I have
you're	let us	**we'd**	we would
I'll	do not	**they're**	you have
let's	you are	**I've**	they are

Your child can read the words and draw lines to match each contraction to the words it stands for. Then read a book together and look for contractions that the writer used.

✓ Have your child ask to borrow one favorite thing owned by each family member. Place the items on a table. Help your child make signs to show who owns what, using the possessive form of each person's name.

PROJECT TIME

Provide construction paper and help your child figure out how to make fancy place cards and napkin holders for your family dinner table, using the possessive form of names to mark each person's place.

FOCUS ON WORD STRUCTURE

A **contraction** is a short way of writing two words as one word. An **apostrophe** replaces the one or more letters that are left out. Here are some examples: *did not = didn't I am = I'm, we will = we'll.*

An apostrophe is also used in **possessives** to show ownership. Use *'s* to show that something belongs to one person, animal, or thing: *the girl's bike.*

Cut out this bookmark and take it to the library.

GET INTO BOOKS

Look for these books that feature words with apostrophes:

Where's My Teddy? by Jez Alborough. Candlewick, 1992. contractions

"I Can't" Said the Ant by Polly Cameron. Coward, McCann, 1961. contractions

I'm the Best! by Marjorie Weinman Sharmat. Holiday House, 1991. contractions

Moonbear's Friend by Frank Asch. Simon & Schuster, 1993. possessives

The Day Jimmy's Boa Ate the Wash by Trinka Hakes Noble. Dial, 1980. possessives

School ←→ Home Newsletter

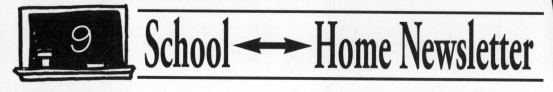

DEAR FAMILY,

Your child has been learning about endings that can be added to words to make new words. As your child continues to learn about words and their endings, you can participate too by trying some activities at home.

AFTER-SCHOOL ACTIVITIES

Numbers and time influence what we do every day. Help your child connect counting and time to learning about words with endings.

✓ Visit your local library and ask the librarian to help you find counting books. Some are listed on the bookmark. As you read the counting books with your child, look for words that mean more than one. Have your child spell some of the words aloud and notice whether the ending *-s or -es* was added.

✓ Model using words that tell about the present and the past (words with the endings *-s, -ing; -ed*). For example, you might pull out the family photo album and talk about what is happening in the photos, occasionally prompting "Remember when you . . ." Listen to the words your child is using.

FOCUS ON WORD STRUCTURE

The **endings** *-s, -es, -ing*, and *-ed* can be added to words to make new words. The endings *-s* and *-es* are added to make a word mean "more than one," such as *dogs* and *foxes*. The endings *-s, -es*, and *-ing* are added to an action word to tell about something that is happening now: *runs, fixes, helping*. The ending *-ed* is added to an action word to tell about a past action: *worked*.

Cut out this bookmark and take it to the library.

GET INTO BOOKS

Look for these books that feature words with endings:

Count-a-Saurus
by Nancy Blumenthal. Macmillan, 1989. *-s*

Counting Sheep
by John Archambault. Henry Holt, 1989. *-s, -es*

Who Wants One? by Mary Serfozo. Margaret McElderry, 1989. *-s, -es*

The Silly Tail Book by Marc Brown. Parents Magazine Press, 1983. *-s, -ing*

Walking Through the Jungle by Julie Lacome. Candlewick, 1993. *-ed, -ing*

PROJECT TIME

Do you have a special relative or family friend who lives far away? Ask your child to make a decorative greeting card or stationery. Work together to write a letter to this person, telling about things you have done. Then, reread the letter and check the spelling of words with endings.

Dear Grandpa,
How are you doing?
I visited Jungle World at the zoo last week.
Monkeys were swinging in the trees.

10 School ←→ Home Newsletter

DEAR FAMILY,

Your child has been learning about words with prefixes and suffixes. As your child continues to learn about word parts and their meanings, you can participate too by trying some activities at home.

AFTER-SCHOOL ACTIVITIES

Do you plant a garden at home? What must you do to make your garden grow? Tell your child that words can grow too—when a prefix or a suffix is added, that is!

✓ After sharing a book with your child, go back and together look for words that have prefixes, such as *re-, dis-, pre-,* and *un-,* and suffixes, such as *-ful, -ness, -ly, -er, -est, -less,* and *-y.* Read the words and ask your child to name the word to which the prefix or suffix was added.

✓ Your child can make each of these words grow by adding the suffix *-ful: spoon, cup, mouth, hand, plate.* Then use the words to make up sentences related to eating and cooking. Here are a few more words with prefixes to use in sentences about cooking or kitchen appliances: *preheat, precooked, reheat, refreeze, disconnect, unload, refill, reuse, remove.*

PROJECT TIME

Make word flowers to show how words grow by adding a prefix or a suffix. Cut circles and petal shapes from construction paper. Write a prefix or a suffix on a circle shape. Your child will write words that contain that prefix or suffix on the petals. Use books or a dictionary to look for words. Glue the petals to the circle to form a flower. Add a pipe cleaner stem and paper leaves.

FOCUS ON WORD STRUCTURE

A **suffix** is a word part added to the end of a base word to make a new word and change the meaning. Some suffixes are *-ful, -ness, -ly, -er, -est, -less,* and *-y.* A **prefix** is a word part added to the beginning of a base word to make a new word and change the meaning. Some prefixes are *re-, un-, dis-,* and *pre-.*

Cut out this bookmark and take it to the library.

GET INTO BOOKS

Look for these books that feature words with prefixes and suffixes:

The Bad Dream by Jim Aylesworth. Whitman, 1985.
suffixes *-ful, -ly*

The Story of Jumping Mouse: A Native American Legend retold by John Steptoe. Lothrop, 1984.
suffixes *-ful, -ly*

Learning to Swim in Swaziland by Nila K. Leigh. Scholastic, 1993.
suffixes *-ly, -y*

Better Homes and Gardens *Step-by-Step Kid's Cookbook.* Meredith Press, 1984.
prefixes and suffixes

Mufaro's Beautiful Daughters by John Steptoe. Lothrop, 1987.
prefixes and suffixes

School ←→ Home Newsletter

DEAR FAMILY,

PHONICS FOCUS

Cut out this bookmark and take it to the library.

GET INTO BOOKS

AFTER-SCHOOL ACTIVITIES

You may want to try these activities at home.

PROJECT TIME

Racetrack Game Board

1. Make two copies.   2. Cut out.   3. Glue onto a file folder.

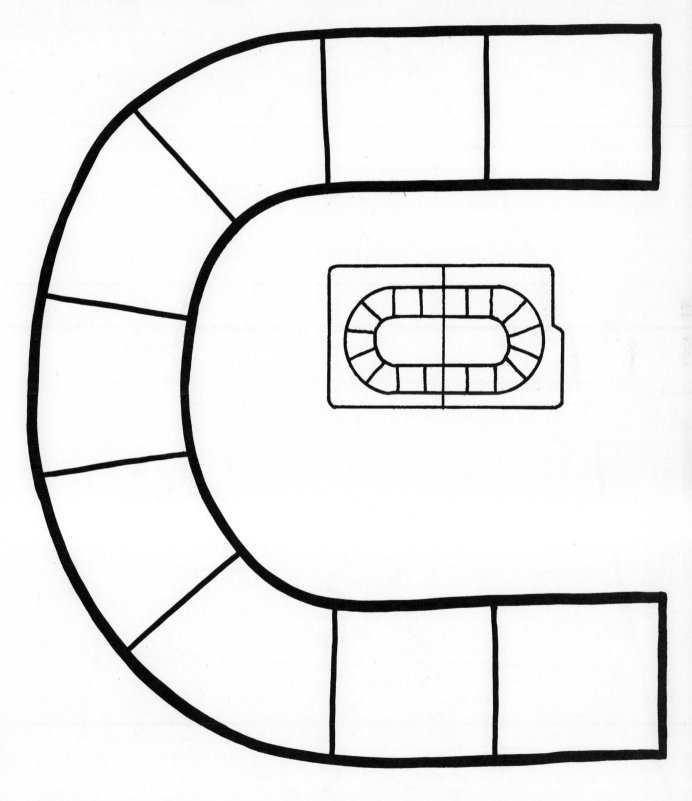

Mountain Game Board

1. Cut out.   2. Glue onto construction paper.

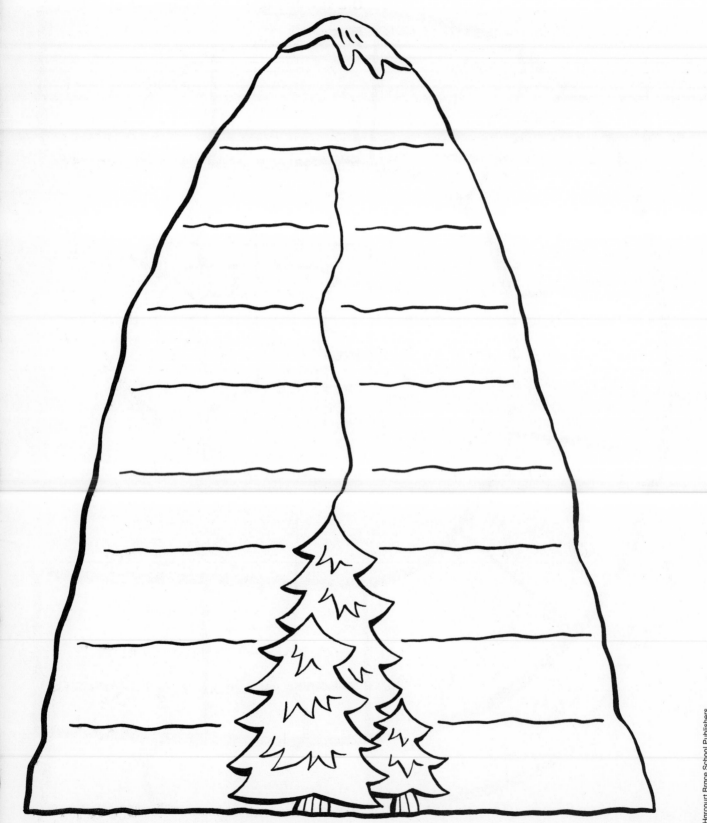

Harcourt Brace School Publishers

S-Shape Game Board (left side)

1. Make a copy of both S-Shape Game Boards. 2. Cut out.

3. Glue onto a file folder.

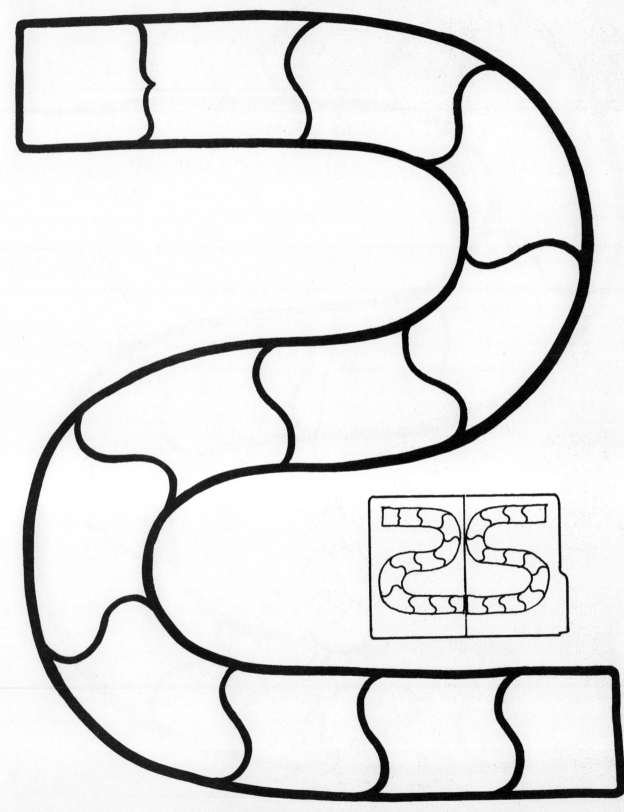

Harcourt Brace School Publishers

S-Shape Game Board (right side)

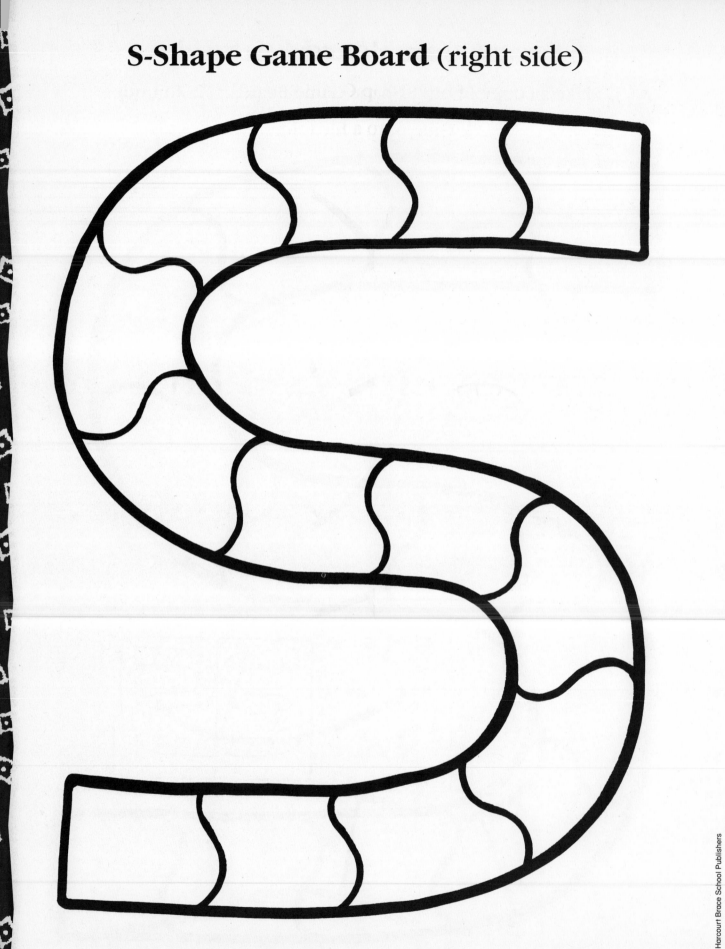

Loop Game Board (left side)

1. Make a copy of both Loop Game Boards.   2. Cut out.

3. Glue onto a file folder.

Loop Game Board (right side)

Harcourt Brace School Publishers

Dot Game Board

1. Cut out.   2. Glue onto construction paper.

Spinners

1. Cut out a wheel and glue it onto thick paper.
2. Put on a paper clip with a brad.

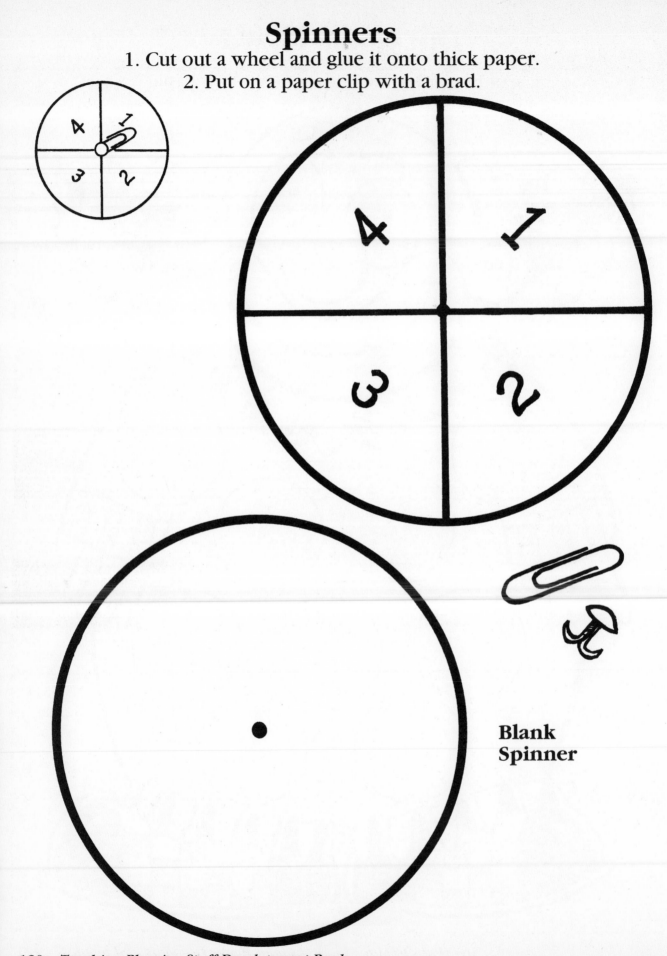

Blank Spinner

Harcourt Brace School Publishers

9-Square Grid

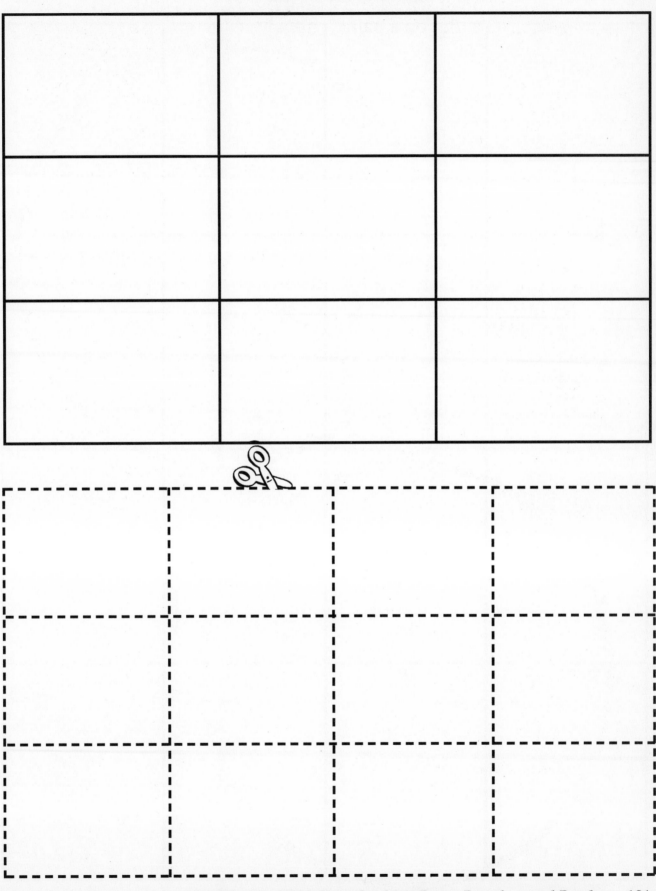

16-Square Grid

Teaching Phonics: Staff Development Book

Harcourt Brace School Publishers

Finger Puppets

1. Cut.

2. Draw or write.

3. Tape.

4. Wear.

Crab Word Slide

Cut out the strip. Write a word with short *a* in each box.
The crab will give you ideas. Cut the slits on the crab.
Pull the strip and read the words.

Harcourt Brace School Publishers

Hen Word Slide

Cut out the strip. Write a word with short *e* in each box. The hen will give you ideas. Cut the slits on the hen. Pull the strip and read the words.

Pig Word Slide

Cut out the strip. Write a word with short *i* in each box.
The pig will give you ideas. Cut the slits on the pig. Pull
the strip and read the words.

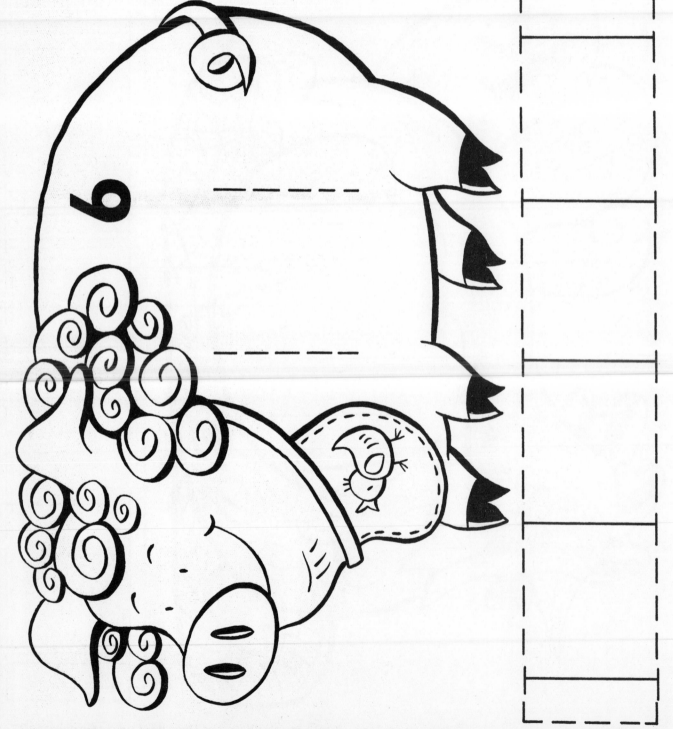

Harcourt Brace School Publishers

Fox Word Slide

Cut out the strip. Write a word with short *o* in each box. The fox will give you ideas. Cut the slits on the fox. Pull the strip and read the words.

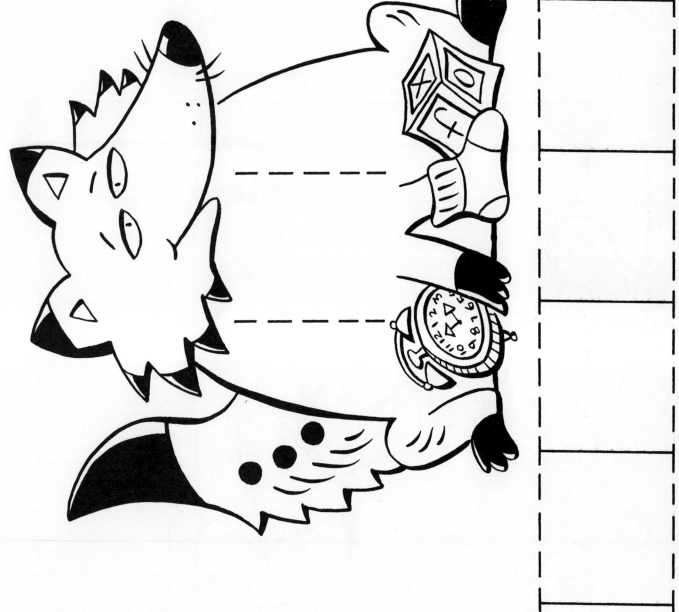

Bug Word Slide

Cut out the strip. Write a word with short *u* in each box. The bug will give you ideas. Cut the slits on the bug. Pull the strip and read the words.

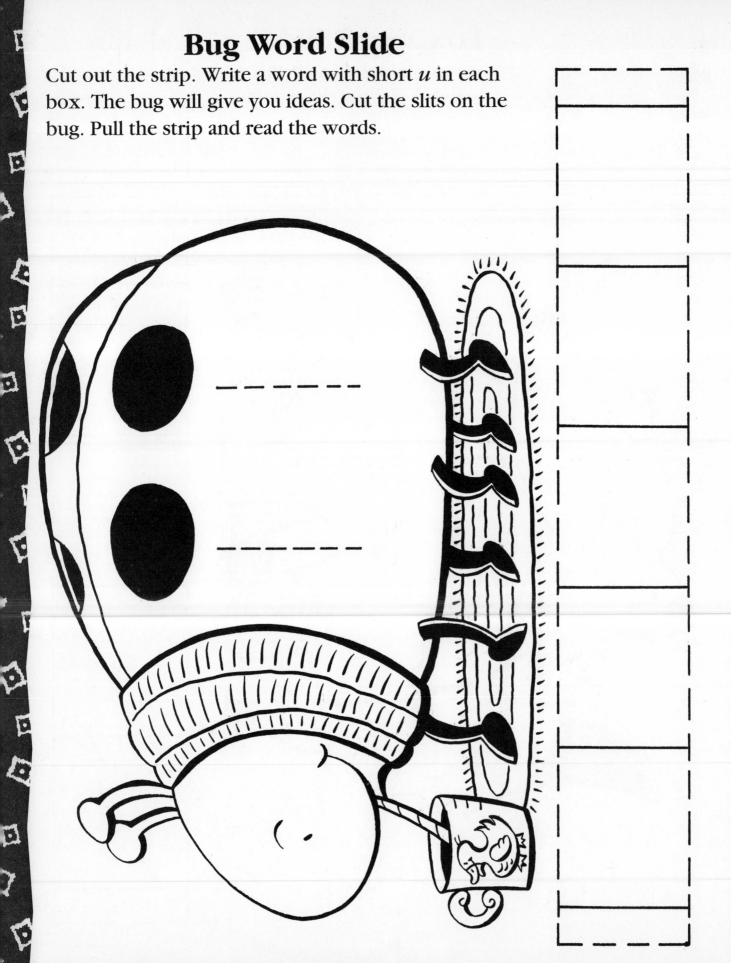

Word Wheel

1. Cut out each wheel.   2. Attach with a brad.

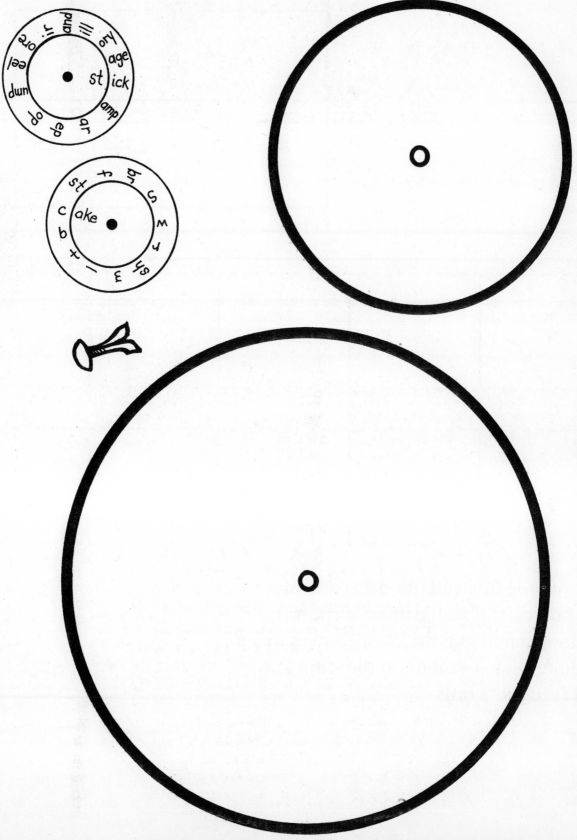

Wordscope

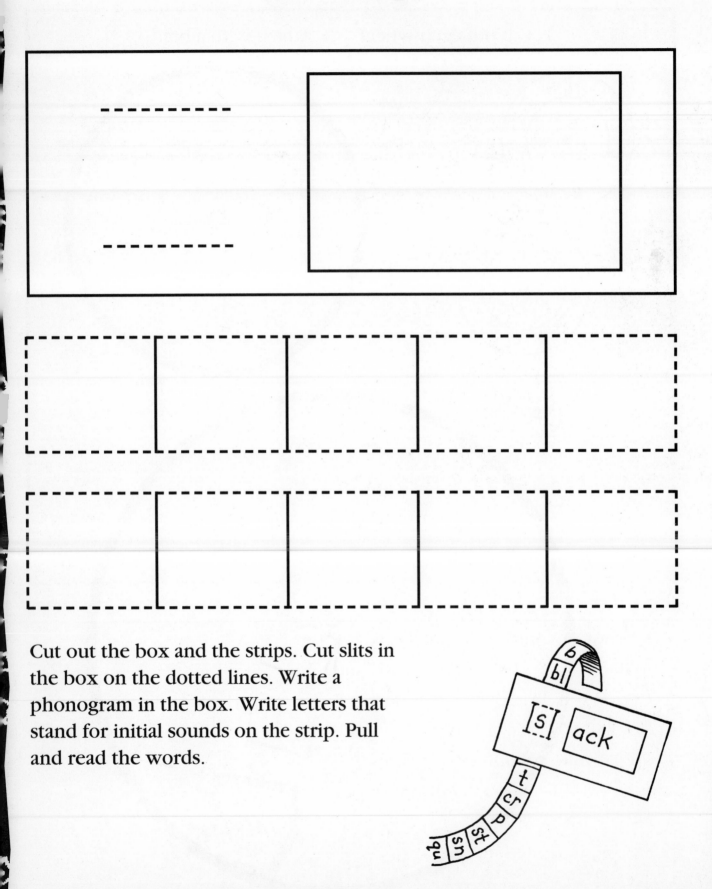

Cut out the box and the strips. Cut slits in the box on the dotted lines. Write a phonogram in the box. Write letters that stand for initial sounds on the strip. Pull and read the words.

Harcourt Brace School Publishers

Pop-Up Book

Fold 1

Fold 2

1. Cut out the book. Fold the book in half.

2. Cut on the dotted lines through both layers.

3. Fold on the solid lines. Open and refold so the box will pop out.

4. Glue it inside a cover.

5. Glue a picture on the pop-up.

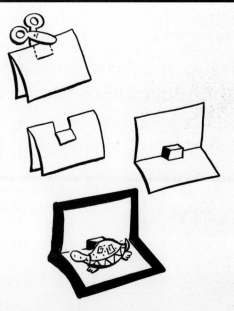

Step-Page Book

1. Cut out the four pages.

2. Lay the pages one on top of the other.

3. Bind the pages at the top.

Harcourt Brace School Publishers

Flip Book

Cut out the book back and the pages. Write a phonogram on the right side of the book back. Write letters that stand for beginning sounds on the pages. Staple the pages to the book back. Flip the pages to read the words.

Pull-Out Book

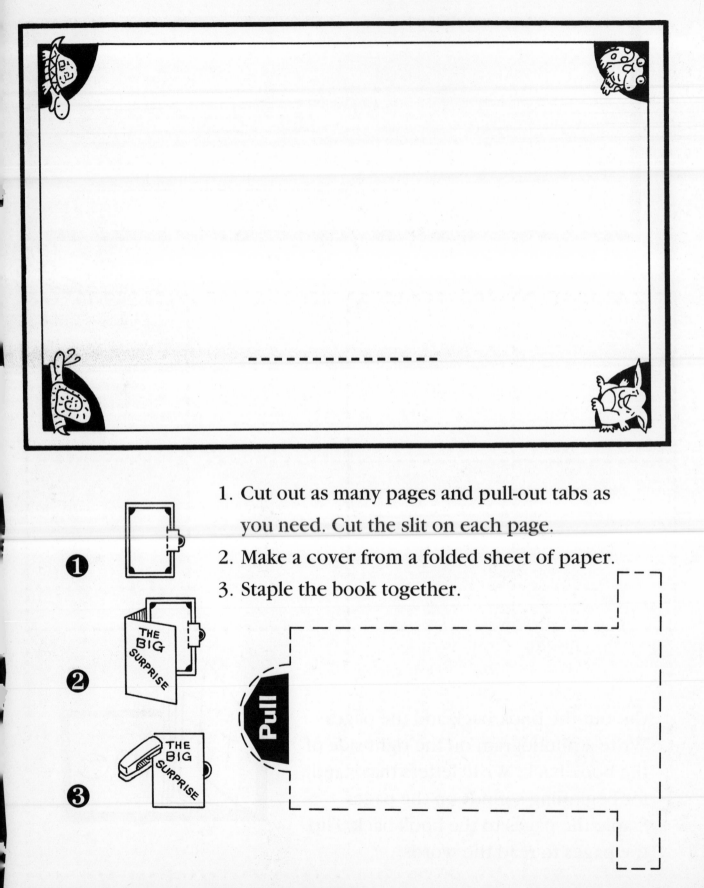

1. Cut out as many pages and pull-out tabs as you need. Cut the slit on each page.
2. Make a cover from a folded sheet of paper.
3. Staple the book together.

Pull

Harcourt Brace School Publishers

Word Cards

Letter Cards (Lowercase)

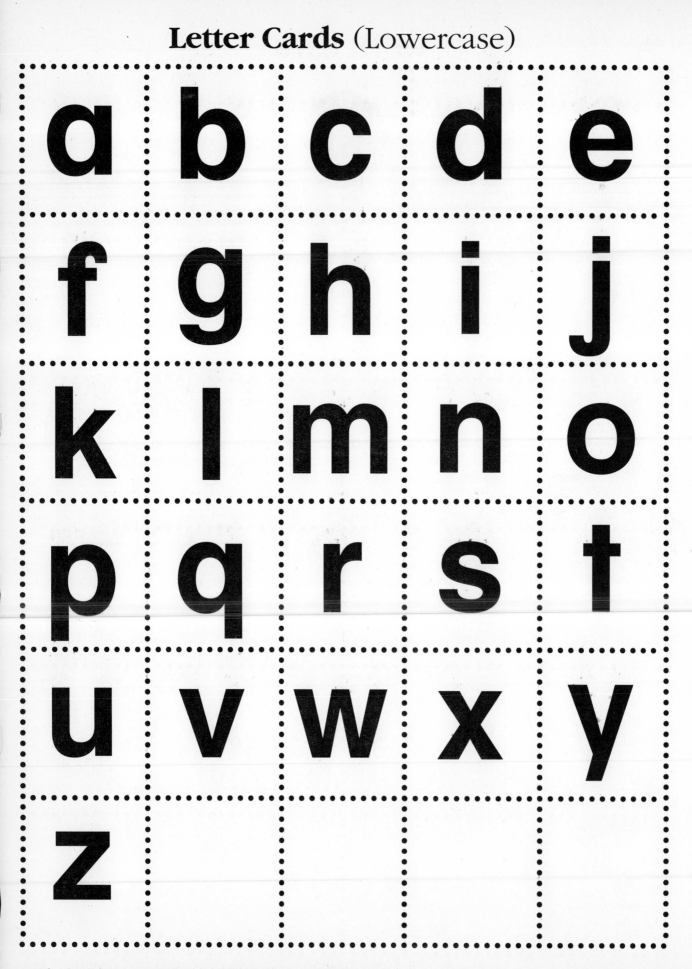

a b c d e

f g h i j

k l m n o

p q r s t

u v w x y

z

Letter Cards (Uppercase)

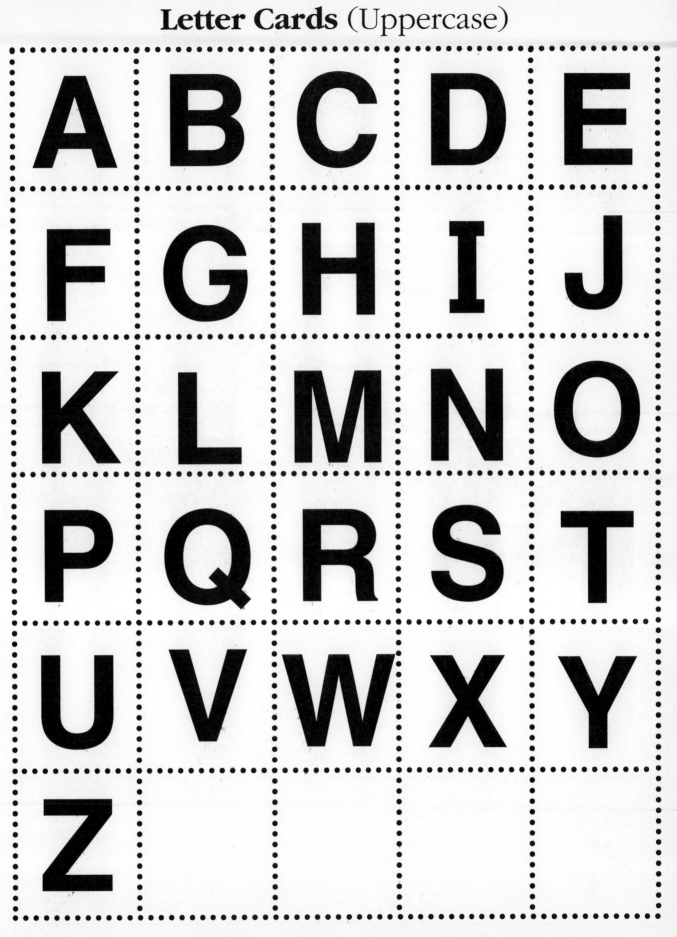

Word Builder

1. Cut out the Word Builder.
2. Fold up the pocket.
3. Staple it on each side.
4. Draw an arrow on
   the pocket.

Word Builder

Word Builder
(name)

Fold. ⬑

Reading Log

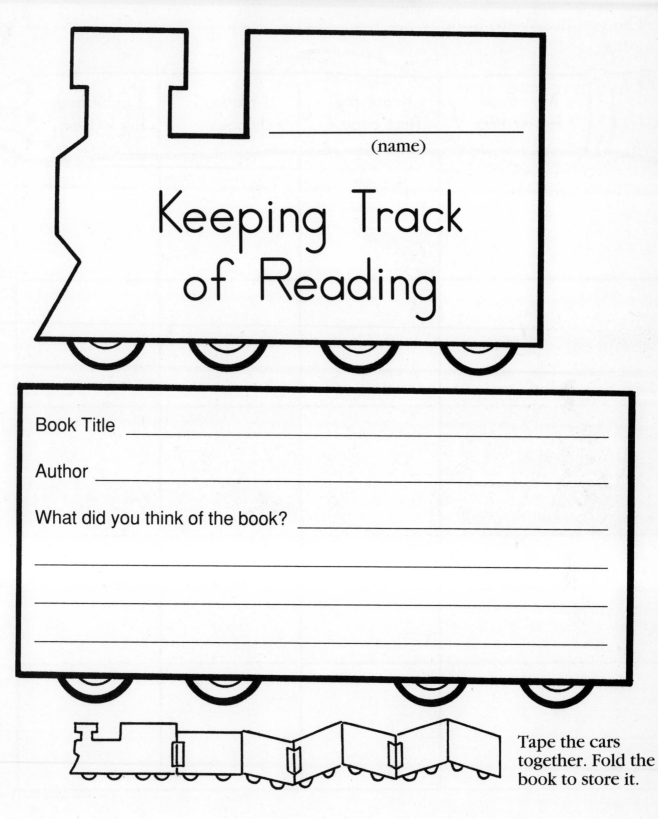

_____
(name)

Keeping Track of Reading

Book Title _____

Author _____

What did you think of the book? _____

_____

_____

_____

Tape the cars together. Fold the book to store it.

Children can make an accordion book to keep a record of books they have read. Make several copies of the train cars to use.

My Writing Log

Name _____

My ideas for writing:	I wrote my first copy.	I made changes.	I published my writing.

Make copies of the Writing Log for children to keep in their portfolios. Keep a log of progress by placing check marks, a rubber stamp, or a date for each writing idea that is developed.

Bookmarks

did a
great job
today!

really got
into
books
today!

did an
amazing job
today!

Start

Finish

Pencil Toppers

You may want to reproduce these on construction paper. Use as rewards, gifts, or reminders. Cut out each topper. Cut on the Xs and insert a pencil.

Wrist Band Messages

1. Reproduce and cut out. Cut the slits.
2. Write a message on the shape.
3. Insert the tail through the slits to close.
4. Place around child's wrist and close.

Send special messages home with children. You can use the wrist bands for "good work" messages, reminders, and more!

Door Knobber

Cut out this circle
and hang on a
door knob.

should feel
proud because

Cut out a door knobber, and write the child's name and accomplishment. Send the door knobber home for the child to display.

Teacher
Resources

"*Get in touch with what you believe about teaching and learning. Your belief system provides the foundation for everything you do. But always keep the door open for new ideas and insights.*"

Dr. Dorothy S. Strickland

PHONICS PLANNING GUIDE

PHONIC ELEMENT	PHONICS PRACTICE BOOK	PHONICS PRACTICE READERS	BIG BOOK OF RHYMES	PHONICS GAME BOARD PATTERN BOOK	MANIPULATIVES AND OTHER RESOURCES
Initial Consonants					
/b/*b*	pp. 25–26, 29				*Word Builder Cards*
/d/*d*	pp. 33–34, 41				Letter Cards
/f/*f*	pp. 11–12, 17				Phonogram Cards
/g/*g*	pp. 15–16, 17				Digraph Cards
/h/*h*	pp. 13–14, 17				
/j/*j*	pp. 47–48, 51				
/k/*c*	pp. 21–22, 29				*Word Builder*
/k/*k*	pp. 45–46, 51				
/l/*l*	pp. 27–28, 29				
/m/*m*	pp. 9–10, 17				*High-Frequency Word Cards*
/n/*n*	pp. 37–38, 41				
/p/*p*	pp. 39–40, 41				
/r/*r*	pp. 23–24, 29				
/s/*s*	pp. 7–8, 17				*Alphabet Cards*
/t/*t*	pp. 19–20, 29				
/v/*v*	pp. 49–50, 51				
/w/*w*	pp. 35–36, 41				*Big Alphabet Cards*
/y/*y*	pp. 31–32, 41				
/z/*z*	pp. 43–44, 51				*Magnetic Letters*
Final Consonants					
/b/*b*, /n/*n*, /t/*t*, /p/*p*	pp. 57–60, 65	Book 2: *My Cat* Phonograms: *-an, -ap, -at* Book 5: *What Can You Find?* Phonograms: *-an, -ap, -at, -op, -ot*	pp. 14–15	p. 13	*Oo-pples and Boo-noo-noos: Songs and Activities for Phonemic Awareness and Audiocassette*
/k/*k, ck*; /l/*l, ll*, /g/*g, gg*	pp. 61–64, 65	Book 6: *Jack and Mack* Phonograms: *-ack, -ock* Book 17: *Jig to the Jazz* Phonograms: *-ag, -ig, -og, -ug*	pp. 20–21		
/ks/*x*, /m/*m*, /d/*d*	pp. 67–70, 75	Book 11: *Yam Jam* Phonograms: *-ad, -am, -ed, -ix*	p. 25	p. 14	
/z/*s, zz*; /f/*f, ff*	pp. 71–72, 75	Book 17: *Jig to the Jazz* Phonogram: *-uff*	p. 31	pp. 14–15	
/d/*dd*, /t/*tt*, /s/*s, ss*	pp. 73–74, 75	Book 29: *What a Mess!* Phonograms: *-add, -ess, -iss, -itt*	p. 42		
Double Consonants					
bb, pp, tt, dd, ll, ff, rr	pp. 79–80, 85	Book 9: *The Lesson*	p. 7		
Medial Consonants					
/b/*b*, /g/*g*, /m/*m*, /p/*p*, /t/*t*	pp. 81–82, 85	Book 16: *Cabot's Bad Habit*	p. 30		
/d/*d*, /l/*l*, /n/*n*, /s/*s*	pp. 83–84, 85	Book 27: *Colin Melon's Seeds*	pp. 38–39		

PHONICS PLANNING GUIDE

PHONIC ELEMENT	PHONICS PRACTICE BOOK	PHONICS PRACTICE READERS	BIG BOOK OF RHYMES	PHONICS GAME BOARD PATTERN BOOK	MANIPULATIVES AND OTHER RESOURCES
Short Vowels					
/a/a	pp. 89–98, 109	Book 1: *Hap* Phonogram: *-ap* Book 4: *Dan and Don* Phonogram: *-at* Book 20: *The Yaks Come Back* Phonograms: *-ack, -ad, -ag, -an, -at*	p. 16	pp. 1, 6-7, 10-12	*Word Builder Cards* Letter Cards Phonogram Cards Digraph Cards
/e/e	pp. 111–120, 131	Book 8: *My Pets* Phonograms: *-et, -en* Book 13: *Pick One* Phonograms: *-ed, -ell, -en, -et* Book 20: *The Yaks Come Back* Phonograms: *-ed, -en, -et*	pp. 20–21	pp. 3, 6-7, 10-12	*Word Builder* *High-Frequency Word Cards*
/e/ea	p. 147	Book 32: *The Health Hop* Phonograms: *-ead, -ealth*	pp. 44–45		*Alphabet Cards*
/i/i	pp. 121–130, 131	Book 10: *This Little Kitten* Phonograms: *-ick, -ip* Book 13: *Pick One* Phonograms: *-ick, -ill, -in, -ip, -it, -ix*	p. 7	pp. 4, 6-7, 10-12	*Big Alphabet Cards*
/o/o	pp. 99–108, 109	Book 3: *Hop a Lot* Phonograms: *-op, -ot* Book 4: *Dan and Don* Phonogram: *-ot*	pp. 11	pp. 2, 6-7, 10-12	*Magnetic Letters*
/u/u	pp. 133–142, 143	Book 15: *Rub-a-Dub Duck* Phonograms: *-ub, -uck, -ud, -un*	pp. 14–15	pp. 5, 6-7, 10-12	*Oo-pples and Boo-noo-noos: Songs and Activities for Phonemic Awareness* and Audiocassette
Long Vowels					
/ō/o, oa, o-e	pp. 149–160, 173	Book 22: *Goat on a Boat* Phonograms: *-o, -oap, -oat, -ope, -oad, -oan, -oke, -oaf, -one, -ose, -ole* Book 40: *The Case of the Green Coat* Phonograms: *-oan, -oke, -ole*	pp. 34–35	pp. 8-9, 34, 35	
/ī/i, igh, i-e	pp. 161–172, 173	Book 24: *Mike's Flight* Phonograms: *-ide, -ike, -ite, -ight, -ine* Book 37: *A Bite of Cheese* Phonograms: *-ight, -ine, -ite*	p. 10	pp. 8-9, 36, 37	
/ē/e, ea, ee	pp. 175–186, 199	Book 25: *Queen Jean's Feast* Phonograms: *-ean, -eed, -een, -eam, -eet* Book 33: *Ice Cream Dream* Phonograms: *-eam, -eat, -eed, -een, -eep* Book 37: *A Bite of Cheese* Phonograms: *-each, -ean, -eat, -ease, -eet* Book 40: *The Case of the Green Coat* Phonograms: *–ead, -ean, -eek, -eeze*	pp. 8–9	pp. 38, 39	
/ā/ai, ay, a-e	pp. 187–198, 199	Book 30: *I Will Take Your Case* Phonograms: *-ail, -ain, -ake, -ane, -ate, -ave*	p. 43	pp. 8-9, 32, 33	
/yōo/u-e	pp. 201–202, 203	Book 39: *Cute Stuff* Phonogram: *-use*	p. 48	pp. 8-9	
/ō/ow	pp. 210–211	Book 34: *Heathrow Forgot* Phonogram: *-ow* Book 40: *The Case of the Green Coat* Phonogram: *-ow*	pp. 4–5	p. 35	
/ā/ea, ei(gh)	pp. 212–213	Book 35: *What's Great?* Phonograms: *-eak, -eigh*	p. 47		

PHONICS PLANNING GUIDE

PHONIC ELEMENT	PHONICS PRACTICE BOOK	PHONICS PRACTICE READERS	BIG BOOK OF RHYMES	PHONICS GAME BOARD PATTERN BOOK	MANIPULATIVES AND OTHER RESOURCES
Consonant Clusters **Initial Clusters** r (*br, cr, gr, fr, dr, tr, pr*)	pp. 214–217, 222	Book 7: *Fran and Tran*	p. 22	pp. 24–26	*Word Builder Cards* Letter Cards Phonogram Cards Digraph Cards
l (*bl, fl, pl, cl*)	pp. 218–221, 222	Book 19: *The Big Blue Blob*	p. 32	pp. 27–28	
s (*sn, sm, sc, st, sk, sl, sp*)	pp. 234–237, 240	Book 28: *Spike and Skip* Book 31: *Sweet Stan*	pp. 40–41	p. 29	
w (*sw, tw*)	pp. 238–239, 240	Book 38: *Twain's Itch*	p. 7		*Word Builder*
Final Clusters t (*st, nt, lt, ft*)	pp. 224–227, 232	Book 21: *The Best Gift* Phonograms: *-aft, -ast, -elt, -ent, -ept, -ift, -unt, -ust*	p. 33	p. 30	*High-Frequency Word Cards*
ld, mp, nd	pp. 228–231, 232	Book 26: *The Grump* Phonograms: *-amp, -and, -ind, -ump*	p. 37	p. 31	*Alphabet Cards*
Digraphs Initial: /kw/*qu*	pp. 244–245, 254	Book 12: *Quack*	p. 27		*Big Alphabet Cards*
Initial and Final: /ch/*ch, tch*	pp. 246–249, 254	Book 14: *Mitch and Chip* Phonogram: *-itch* Book 18: *Froth Broth* Phonograms: *-itch, -uch, -unch*	p. 28	pp. 40–42	*Magnetic Letters*
Initial and Final: /th/*th*	pp. 250–253, 254	Book 14: *Mitch and Chip* Phonogram: *-ath* Book 18: *Froth Broth* Phonogram: *-oth*	p. 28	pp. 40–42	*Oo-pples and Boo-noo-noos: Songs and Activities for Phonemic Awareness and Audiocassette*
Initial and Final: /sh/*sh*	pp. 256–259, 262	Book 23: *Wish Day* Phonograms: *-ash, -ish, -ush*	p. 36	pp. 41–42	
Initial: /hw/*wh*	pp. 260–261, 262	Book 23: *Wish Day*	p. 36	pp. 41–42	
R-Controlled Vowel /är/*ar*	pp. 268–277	Book 36: *A Charming Planet* Phonograms: *-ar, -art, -ark, -arp, -arm*	p. 29	p. 43	
Contractions and Possessives Contractions: *'m, 'll, n't, 's*	pp. 279–280			pp. 21–23	
Possessive: *'s*	p. 281				
Contractions: *'d, 've, 're*	pp. 282–283			pp. 21–23	
Inflected Endings *-s*	pp. 286–287, 302			p. 16	
-ed	pp. 288–289, 302			p. 16	
-ing	pp. 290–291, 302			p. 16	
-ed (double final consonant)	pp. 292–293, 302			pp. 19–20	
-ing (double final consonant)	pp. 294–295, 302			pp. 19–20	
-ed (drop final *e*)	pp. 296–297, 302			pp. 17–18	
-ing (drop final *e*)	pp. 298–299, 302			pp. 17–18	
-es	pp. 300–301, 302				

PHONICS PLANNING GUIDE

PHONIC ELEMENT	PHONICS PRACTICE BOOK	PHONICS PRACTICE READERS	BIG BOOK OF RHYMES	PHONICS GAME BOARD PATTERN BOOK	MANIPULATIVES AND OTHER RESOURCES
Consonants					
Initial	pp. 7–12, 24				*Word Builder Cards*
Final	pp. 13–18, 24				*Letter Cards*
Medial	pp. 19–21, 24				*Phonogram Cards*
					Digraph Cards
Short Vowels					
/o/o	pp. 28–32, 38	Book 1: *How Odd* Phonograms: -on, -op, -ot		pp. 2, 6–7, 10–12	*Word Builder*
/e/e	pp. 33–37, 38	Book 1: *How Odd* Phonograms: -eg, -ell, -en, -ess, -et		pp. 3, 6–7, 10–12	
/a/a	pp. 40–44, 50	Book 2: *The Maps* Phonograms: -ack, -an, -ap, -at		pp. 1, 6–7, 10–12	*High-Frequency Word Cards*
/i/i	pp. 45–49, 50	Book 4: *Jim and Jill* Phonograms: -ill, -in		pp. 4, 6–7, 10–12	
/u/u	pp. 52–56, 57	Book 4: *Jim and Jill* Phonograms: -ug, -ump, -un		pp. 5, 6–7, 10–12	*Alphabet Cards*
/e/ea	pp. 61–62				*Big Alphabet Cards*
/u/ou	p. 63	Book 19: *What Can I Touch?* Phonogram: -ough	pp. 16–17		*Magnetic Letters*
Long Vowels					*Oo-pples and Boo-noo-noos: Songs and Activities for Phonemic Awareness and Audiocassette*
/ā/ai, ay, a-e	pp. 65–76, 90	Book 7: *A Great Place to Play* Phonograms: -ay, -ade, -ake, -ane, -ain, -ale		pp. 8–9, 32, 33	
/ō/oa, o-e, ow, o	pp. 77–89, 90	Book 8: *Jo Frog and Joan Toad* Phonograms: -oan, -oat, -oke, -old, -o, -ope, -ost		pp. 8–9, 34, 35	
/ī/i-e, igh, i, y, ie	pp. 92–106, 121	Book 9: *When I Get a Bike* Phonograms: -ide, -ike, -ile, -ine, -ight, -ime, -in Book 22: *I Spy*	p. 20	pp. 8–9, 36, 37	
/ē/ee, ea, ie, y	pp. 107–120, 121	Book 10: *The Deep, Green Sea* Phonograms: -ean, -eat, -ee, -eet Book 25: *Unlucky Randy* Phonograms: -ief, -unny	p. 24	pp. 38, 39	
/yōō/ u-e	pp. 123–124, 125	Book 5: *What Can You Do with a Tube?* Phonogram: -ube		pp. 8–9	
_R_-Controlled Vowels					
/är/ar	pp. 133–134, 140	Book 11: *Smart Riddles* Phonograms: -ar, -ark, -art, -arm -arn, -arp	p. 4	p. 43	
/ûr/er, ur	pp. 135–136, 140	Book 15: *Desert Fire* Phonograms: -ur, -urn	pp. 10-11		
/ûr/ir	pp. 137–138, 140	Book 15: *Desert Fire* Phonogram: -ird			
/ûr/ear	pp. 139, 140				
/ôr/or, ore, our	pp. 147, 149	Book 18: *Mort's Country Store and More* Phonograms: -ore, -orch , -ort, -orn, -our	p. 15		
/ôr/oor, oar	pp. 148, 149				
/ir/ear, eer	pp. 161, 164	Book 24: *Deer Steers* Phonograms: -eer, -ear	pp. 22–23		
/âr/air, ear, are	pp. 162–163, 164	Book 26: *A Pair of Bears* Phonograms: -ear, -air, -are	p. 25		

PHONICS PLANNING GUIDE

PHONIC ELEMENT	PHONICS PRACTICE BOOK	PHONICS PRACTICE READERS	BIG BOOK OF RHYMES	PHONICS GAME BOARD PATTERN BOOK	MANIPULATIVES AND OTHER RESOURCES
Vowel Diphthongs					Word Builder Cards
/ou/ow, ou	pp. 143–146, 149	Book 16: *Farmer Brown's Hound* Phonograms: -ound, -oud, -out, -own, -ow, -owl	pp. 12–13		Letter Cards Phonogram Cards
/oi/oi, oy	pp. 151–154, 157	Book 20: *Roy Floyd's Shoes* Phonograms: -oy, -oil	p. 18		Digraph Cards
Vowel Variants					Word Builder
/o͝o/oo, ou	pp. 155–156, 157	Book 21: *The Good Crook* Phonograms: -ood, -ook, -ould	p. 19		High-Frequency Word Cards
/o͞o/ue, ew, u-e	pp. 166–169, 173	Book 23: *Sue's Dewdrop Stew* Phonograms: -ew, -ue	p. 21		
/o͞o/oo, ou, ew	pp. 170–171, 173				Alphabet Cards
/o͞o/ou, ui	pp. 172, 173				
/ô/aw, au(gh), ou(gh)	pp. 177–180, 181	Book 30: *The Forest at Dawn* Phonograms: -ause, -aw, -awk, -awl, -awn	p. 32		Big Alphabet Cards
					Magnetic Letters
Schwa					
/ə/a; /əl/le; /ər/er	pp. 175–176, 181	Book 28: *Jennifer Tuttle's Bubble Bath* Phonograms: -able, -ubble, umble	pp. 28–29		Oo-pples and Boo-noo-noos: Songs and Activities for Phonemic Awareness and Audiocassette
Consonant Clusters **Initial Clusters**					
s (sn, sm, sc, st, sk, sp)	pp. 187–188, 195	Book 3: *How to Spot a Swog*		p. 29	
r (br, cr, gr, fr, dr, tr, pr)	pp. 189–190, 195	Book 3: *How to Spot a Swog*		pp. 24–26	
l (bl, fl, pl, cl)	pp. 191–192, 195	Book 3: *How to Spot a Swog*		pp. 27–28	
w (sw, tw)	pp. 193–194, 195	Book 3: *How to Spot a Swog*			
scr, str	pp. 197–198, 203	Book 17: *Screech and Stripes*	p. 14		
spr, shr	pp. 199–200, 203				
squ, thr	pp. 201–202, 203				
Final Clusters					
lk, sk, sp	pp. 216–217, 220	Book 29: *Henry Hasp Had a Task* Phonograms: -ask, -asp, -elk, -ulk	pp. 30–31		
t (st, nt, lt, ft)	pp. 218–219, 220	Book 3: *How to Spot a Swog* Phonogram: -ast		p. 30	
Consonants					
Final: /s/ce	pp. 205–206, 214	Book 27: *The Ridge Village Fair* Phonograms: -ace, -ance, -ice	pp. 26–27		
Initial: /s/ce, ci, cy	pp. 207–208, 214				
Final: /j/ge, dge	pp. 209–210, 214	Book 27: *The Ridge Village Fair* Phonograms: -age, -edge, -idge, -udge	pp. 26–27		
Initial: /j/ge, gi, gy	pp. 211–212, 214				
Final: /m/mb	pp. 213, 214	Book 27: *The Ridge Village Fair*	pp. 26–27		

GRADE 2 PHONICS PLANNING GUIDE

PHONIC ELEMENT	PHONICS PRACTICE BOOK	PHONICS PRACTICE READERS	BIG BOOK OF RHYMES	PHONICS GAME BOARD PATTERN BOOK	MANIPULATIVES AND OTHER RESOURCES
Consonant Digraphs					Word Builder Cards
Initial: /ch/*ch*	pp. 226, 233	Book 6: *Make a Wish*		pp. 40, 41–42	Letter Cards
Final: /ch/*ch, tch*	pp. 227, 233	Book 6: *Make a Wish*		p. 40	Phonogram Cards
Initial: /sh/*sh*	pp. 228, 233	Book 6: *Make a Wish*		pp. 41–42	Digraph Cards
Final: /sh/*sh*	pp. 229, 233	Book 6: *Make a Wish* Phonogram: -*ish*			
Initial: /th/*th*	pp. 230, 233	Book 6: *Make a Wish*		pp. 40, 41–42	
Final: /th/*th*	pp. 231, 233	Book 6: *Make a Wish*		p. 40	Word Builder
Initial: /hw/*wh*	pp. 232, 233	Book 6: *Make a Wish*		pp. 41–42	
Digraph: /f/*gh*	pp. 235, 238	Book 12: *The Phipp Family Photograph*	p. 5		High-Frequency Word Cards
Digraph: /f/*ph*	pp. 235, 238	Book 12: *The Phipp Family Photograph*	p. 5		
Digraph: /ng/*ng*, /ngk/*nk*	pp. 236, 238	Book 13: *Frank's Gift for the King* Phonograms: -*ing*, -*ink*, -*ong*, -*ank*	pp. 6–7		Alphabet Cards
Digraph: /r/*wr*	pp. 237, 238	Book 14: *Knight Knocking-Knees*	pp. 8–9		
Digraph: /n/*kn, gn*	pp. 237, 238	Book 14: *Knight Knocking-Knees*	pp. 8–9		
Initial: /kw/*qu*	pp. 22–23, 24				Big Alphabet Cards
Contractions and Possessives					Magnetic Letters
					Oo-pples and Boo-noo-noos: Songs and Activities for Phonemic Awareness and Audiocassette
Contractions: '*m*, '*re*, '*s*	pp. 244, 246			pp. 21–23	
Contractions: *n't*, '*ve*, '*d*, '*ll*	pp. 245, 246			pp. 21–23	
Possessive: '*s*	pp. 247, 249				
Possessive: *s'*	pp. 248, 249				
Suffixes and Inflected Endings					
Suffix: -*ful*	pp. 252, 257				
Suffix: -*ly*	pp. 252, 257				
-*es*, -*ed* (change *y* to *i*)	pp. 253, 257				
-*es* (change *f* to *v*)	pp. 254, 257				
-*ed*, -*ing* (double final consonant)	pp. 255, 257			pp. 19–20	
-*ed*, -*ing* (drop final *e*)	pp. 256, 257			pp. 17–18	

PHONIC ELEMENT	PHONICS PRACTICE BOOK	PHONICS PRACTICE READERS	PHONICS GAME BOARD PATTERN BOOK	MANIPULATIVES AND OTHER RESOURCES
Consonants				
Initial	pp. 7–12, 22			*Word Builder Cards*
Final	pp. 13–18, 22			Letter Cards
Medial	pp. 19–21, 22			Phonogram Cards
				Digraph Cards
Short Vowels				
/a/*a*	pp. 26–30, 36	Book 1: *Who Has Max?* Phonograms: -ap, -an, -ad, -at, -ack Book 13: *Dave Saves the Planet* Phonograms: -an, -ad, -ash, -and	pp. 1, 6–7, 10–12	*Word Builder*
/e/*e*	pp. 31–35, 36	Book 2: *The Great Rex* Phonograms: -et, -ell, -en, -ed, -eck, -eg Book 14: *The Green Street Team* Phonograms: -et, -est, -ell, -en	pp. 3, 6–7, 10–12	*High-Frequency Word Cards*
/i/*i*	pp. 38–42, 48	Book 3: *The Kid Pit* Phonograms: -ick, -id, -ig, -ip, -it, -ill, -in Book 15: *Prince Quince* Phonograms: -ish, -ip	pp. 4, 6–7, 10–12	*Alphabet Cards*
/o/*o*	pp. 43–47, 48	Book 4: *Bob, Dot, and Tom* Phonograms: -ob, -od, -og, -ox, -ot, -ock, -op Book 16: *The Nose Knows*	pp. 2, 6–7, 10–12	*Big Alphabet Cards* *Magnetic Letters*
/u/*u, ou*	pp. 50–54, 55	Book 5: *Bud's Luck* Phonograms: -ust, -un, -uck, -ub, -usk, -uff, -ug, -ump, -ut	pp. 5, 6–7, 10–12	*Oo-pples and Boo-noo-noos: Songs and*
/e/*ea*	p. 59			*Activities for Phonemic*
Long Vowels				*Awareness and*
/ā/*ai, ay, a-e, ea, ei*	pp. 61–72, 85	Book 13: *Dave Saves the Planet* Phonograms: -ace, -ay	pp. 8–9, 32–33	*Audiocassette*
/ē/*ee, ea, ie, y, ey*	pp. 73–84, 85	Book 14: *The Green Street Team* Phonograms: -eam, -ean, -eet, -each, -eak, -eed, -eat	pp. 8–9, 38–39	
/ī/*i-e, ie, igh, i, y*	pp. 87–98, 111	Book 15: *Prince Quince* Phonograms: -ight, -ind, -ine	pp. 8–9, 36–37	
/ō/*oa, o-e, ow, o*	pp. 99–110, 111	Book 16: *The Nose Knows* Phonograms: -ow, -oan, -old, -oke, -ote, -oat	pp. 8–9, 34–35	
/yo͞o/*u-e*	pp. 113–118, 119		pp. 8–9	
_R_-Controlled Vowels				
/är/*ar*	pp. 128–129, 136	Book 18: *The Clark's Yard Sale* Phonograms: -ar, -ark, -ard, -art, -arn, -arm, -arp Book 22: *The Hairy Bear Suit* Phonograms: -ar, -ard, -ark, -art	p. 43	
/ûr/*er, ur*	pp. 130–131, 136	Book 24: *Derby Circle* Phonogram: -urt		
/ûr/*ir*	pp. 132–133, 136	Book 24: *Derby Circle* Phonogram: -irt		
/ûr/*ear*	pp. 134–135, 136			
/ôr/*or, ore, our*	pp. 142, 144	Book 23: *Morris's Snore* Phonograms: -ort, -orn, -ore		
/ôr/*oor, oar*	pp. 143, 144	Book 23: *Morris's Snore* Phonogram: -oor		
/ir/*ear, eer*	pp. 156, 159			
/âr/*air, ear, are*	pp. 157–158, 159	Book 22: *The Hairy Bear Suit* Phonograms: -are, -air		

PHONIC ELEMENT	PHONICS PRACTICE BOOK	PHONICS PRACTICE READERS	PHONICS GAME BOARD PATTERN BOOK	MANIPULATIVES AND OTHER RESOURCES
Vowel Diphthongs				
/ou/*ow, ou*	pp. 138–141, 144	Book 20: *A Nice Hound* Phonograms: *-ound, -owl, -out, -ouch, -ow, -own*		*Word Builder Cards* Letter Cards Phonogram Cards Digraph Cards
/oi/*oi, oy*	pp. 146–149, 152	Book 19: *The Purloined Coin* Phonograms: *-oy, -oil, -oice*		
Vowel Variants				*Word Builder*
/o͞o/*oo, ou*	pp. 150–151, 152	Book 21: *Shoot for the Moon* Phonograms: *-ood, -ook*		
/o͞o/*ue, ew*	pp. 161–164, 168			*High-Frequency Word Cards*
/o͞o/*oo*	pp. 165–166, 168	Book 21: *Shoot for the Moon* Phonograms: *-ool, -oom, -oon, -oop*		
/o͞o/*ou, ui*	pp. 167, 168			
/ô/*aw, au(gh), ou(gh)*	pp. 172–175, 176			*Alphabet Cards*
Schwa				*Big Alphabet Cards*
/ə/*a*; /əl/*le*; /ər/*er*	pp. 170–171, 176			*Magnetic Letters*
Consonant Clusters				*Oo-pples and Boo-noo-noos: Songs and Activities for Phonemic Awareness and Audiocassette*
Initial Clusters				
s (sn, sm, sc, st, sk, sp)	pp. 182–183, 190		p. 29	
r (br, cr, gr, fr, dr, tr, pr)	pp. 184–185, 190	Book 6: *Grin and Grim*	pp. 24–26	
l (bl, fl, pl, cl)	pp. 186–187, 190	Book 7: *Plots and Plans*	pp. 27–28	
w (sw, tw)	pp. 188–189, 190			
scr, str, spr, squ	pp. 192–195, 200			
shr	pp. 222–223, 228			
thr	pp. 224–225, 228			
Final Clusters				
t (st, nt, lt, ft)	pp. 196–197, 200		p. 30	
lk, sk, sp, ld, mp, nd	pp. 198–199, 200		p. 31	
Hard and Soft *g*	pp. 202–207, 214	Book 11: *Hodgepodge Gems* Phonograms: *-og, -ug, -edge, -idge, -odge*		
Hard and Soft *c*	pp. 208–213, 214	Book 12: *Fifty-Cent Cal* Phonograms: *-ance, -ence, -ince*		
Consonant Digraphs				
Initial: /ch/*ch*	pp. 220, 228		pp. 40, 41–42	
Final: /ch/*ch, tch*	pp. 221, 228	Book 8: *A Way to Be Rich* Phonograms: *-anch, -atch, -itch, -unch*	p. 40	
Initial: /sh/*sh*	pp. 222–223, 228		pp. 41–42	
Final: /sh/*sh*	pp. 222–223, 228	Book 9: *A Real Fish Home* Phonograms: *-ash, -ish, -ush*		
Initial: /th/*th*	pp. 224–225, 228		pp. 40, 41–42	
Final: /th/*th*	pp. 224–225, 228	Book 10: *That Beth!* Phonograms: *-eth, -oth*	pp. 40, 41–42	
Initial: /hw/*wh*	pp. 226–227, 228		pp. 41–42	
Digraph: /f/*gh*	pp. 231, 236			
Digraph: /f/*ph*	pp. 230, 236			
Digraph: /r/*wr*	pp. 232, 236			
Digraph: /n/*kn, gn*	pp. 233, 236			
Digraph: /ng/*ng*, /ngk/*nk*	pp. 234–235, 236			

PHONICS PLANNING GUIDE

PHONIC ELEMENT	PHONICS PRACTICE BOOK	PHONICS PRACTICE READERS	PHONICS GAME BOARD PATTERN BOOK	MANIPULATIVES AND OTHER RESOURCES
### Contractions and Possessives				
Contractions: *'m, n't, 'll, 's*	pp. 240, 242		pp. 21–23	*Word Builder Cards*
Contractions: *'ve, 'd, 're*	pp. 241, 242		pp. 21–23	Letter Cards
Possessive: *'s*	pp. 244, 246			Phonogram Cards
Possessive: *s'*	pp. 245, 246			Digraph Cards
				Word Builder
### Inflected Endings				
				High-Frequency
-s, -es, -ed, -ing	pp. 250–251, 254		p. 16	*Word Cards*
-ed, -ing (double final consonant)	pp. 252–253, 254		pp. 19–20	
-ed, -ing (drop final *e*)	pp. 256–257, 261		pp. 17–18	*Alphabet Cards*
-es (change *f* to *v*)	pp. 258, 261			
-ies (drop final *y*)	pp. 259–260, 261			
				Big Alphabet Cards
### Prefixes, Suffixes, and Word Endings				
				Magnetic Letters
Prefixes: *un-, re-, im-*	pp. 265–267, 271			
Prefixes: *non-, pre-, dis-*	pp. 268–270, 271			*Oo-pples and Boo-noo-noos:*
Suffixes: *-ly, -ful*	pp. 273–274, 277			*Songs and*
Suffixes: *-able, -less*	pp. 275–276, 277			*Activities for*
Comparatives and Superlatives: *-er, -est*	pp. 281–282, 287			*Phonemic Awareness*
Comparatives and Superlatives: *more, most*	pp. 283–284, 287			and
Agents: *-or, -er*	pp. 285–286, 287			Audiocassette

Harcourt Brace School Publishers

Oo-pples and Boo-noo-noos: Songs and Activities for Phonemic Awareness and the Oo-pples and Boo-noo-noos Audiocassette can be used to foster phonemic awareness. This chart lists the songs and the skill(s) that each can be used to develop.

Planning Guide

Oo-pples and Boo-noo-noos: Songs and Activities for Phonemic Awareness

Song	Rhyme	Alliteration	Phoneme Substitution	Phoneme Addition	Nonsense Manipulation
Apples and Bananas			♦		
A Ram Sam Sam					♦
Barnyard Song	♦	♦			
Bibbidi-Bobbidi-Boo		♦	♦		♦
Burgalesa			♦		
Clickety-Clack	♦	♦	♦		
The Corner Grocery Store	♦				
Down By the Bay	♦				
Eletelephony	♦		♦		
Fooba-Wooba John	♦		♦		
The Frog in the Well	♦	♦	♦		♦
Goin' to the Zoo	♦	♦	♦		
Hanstead Boys	♦				
Happy Birthday Little Sally Spingel Spungel Sporn	♦	♦			
His Four Fur Feet		♦		♦	
Hocky Tocky Oombah			♦		♦
Howdido		♦	♦		♦
I Make Myself Welcome	♦	♦			
I've a Pair of Fishes	♦			♦	
Jennie Jenkins	♦	♦	♦		♦
Jig Jog Jig Jog	♦	♦	♦		♦
Jim Along, Josie		♦			
The Kangaroo	♦	♦			♦
Kitty Alone	♦	♦			♦
Lippety-Lip	♦	♦	♦		
Little Arabella Miller	♦				
Little Sacka Sugar			♦		♦
Mary Had a William Goat		♦			♦
Michael Finnegan	♦			♦	
The Name Game	♦		♦		♦
The Old Gray Horse	♦	♦			♦
Old Molly Hare	♦	♦			♦
Once an Austrian Went Yodeling	♦				♦
The Pawpaw Patch		♦			
Plinker Plunker Strummer Zummer Beeper Booper		♦	♦	♦	♦
Sarasponda		♦			♦
Somebody Stole My Hoo-To Foo-To Boo-To BAH!			♦		♦
What Have You Seen?	♦				
Whosery Here?	♦			♦	
Willoughby, Wallaby, Woo	♦	♦	♦		

A Test for Assessing Phonemic Awareness in Young Children

by Dr. Hallie Kay Yopp

THE YOPP-SINGER TEST OF Phoneme Segmentation provides teachers with a new tool for assessing children's phonemic awareness and identifying those children who may experience difficulty in reading and spelling.

WHEN TO USE THE TEST

Kindergarten

There is substantial evidence that phonemic awareness is strongly related to success in reading and spelling acquisition. The Yopp-Singer Test of Phoneme Segmentation was designed for use with English-speaking kindergartners. It may be used as a general assessment tool in order for teachers to learn more about their students and so develop suitable experiences, or it may be used selectively as teachers observe individual children experiencing difficulty with literacy-related tasks. Certainly, it need not be administered to the child who is already reading fluently. Independent reading implies the existence of phonemic awareness. Further, phonemic awareness is not an end in itself—rather, it is one aspect of literacy development.

Revised and adapted from "A test for assessing phonemic awareness in young children" by Hallie Kay Yopp in *The Reading Teacher,* September 1995, Vol. 49, No. 1. Text copyright © 1995 by the International Reading Association. Reprinted by permission of the International Reading Association.

First Grade

First-grade teachers, too, may wish to administer the test to students at the beginning of the school year in order to determine the phonemic awareness needs of the children in the classroom. Reading/language arts specialists or clinicians who work with children experiencing difficulty in literacy acquisition may also wish to assess their students' phonemic awareness as part of a larger diagnostic survey. And, although there are currently no data regarding the use of this particular test with older populations, we know that often older nonreaders lack phonemic awareness.

Beyond First Grade

This instrument may be helpful to teachers of older individuals, including adult emerging readers, as they begin to build a profile of the strengths and needs of the individuals with whom they work. If phonemic awareness is poor, then it is appropriate to include activities that support its development in the larger picture of literacy experiences.

Should students who are limited in English proficiency be given this test? There are no data on using this test with an EL (English learner) population. Further, the issue is problematic since not only is there a potential problem with understanding task directions and familiarity with vocabulary (the items on the test were selected, in part, on the basis of word familiarity), but there is also the possibility that performance on the test could be influenced by the fact that some speech sounds that exist in the English language may not exist in a student's dominant language.

GIVING THE TEST

The Yopp-Singer Test of Phoneme Segmentation measures a child's ability to separately articulate the sounds of a spoken word in order. For example, given the orally presented word *sat*, the child should respond with three separate sounds: /s/-/a/-/t/. Note that sounds, not letter names, are the appropriate response. Thus, given the four-letter word *fish*, the child should respond with three sounds: /f/-/i/-/sh/. Do not let the child see the written words as the items are presented orally. (See the 22-item Test and Answer Key that follow.) Words were selected for inclusion on the basis of feature analysis and word familiarity. (For a complete discussion of the word list rationale, see Yopp, 1988.) The test is administered individually and requires about 5 to 10 minutes per child.

WHAT THE RESULTS MEAN

Students who achieve high scores (segmenting all or nearly all of the items correctly) may be considered phonemically aware. Students who correctly segment some items are displaying emerging phonemic awareness. Students who are able to segment only a few items or none at all lack appropriate levels of phonemic awareness. Without intervention, those students scoring very low on the test are likely to experience difficulty with reading and spelling.

Teachers' notes on the blank lines of the test will be helpful in understanding each child. Some children may partially segment—perhaps dividing words into chunks larger than phonemes. These children are beginning to have an insight into the nature of speech. Others may simply repeat the stimulus item or provide nonsense responses regardless of the amount of feedback and practice given. They have very little insight into the phonemic basis of their speech. Still others may simply offer letter names.

If the letter names are random (e.g., given *red*, the child responds "*n-b-d-o*"), the teacher learns that the child lacks phonemic awareness but knows some letter names. If the letter names are close approximations to the conventional spelling of the words (e.g., given *red*, the child responds "*r-a-d*"), the teacher knows that either the child has memorized the spellings of some words or that he or she is phonemically aware and has mentally segmented the items and then verbally provided the examiner with the letters corresponding to those sounds—an impressive feat! In this case, the examiner should repeat the instructions to make sure the child fully understands the task.

WHAT TO DO FOR STUDENTS WHO LACK PHONEMIC AWARENESS

Can phonemic awareness be taught? Many researchers and teachers have found that children who participate in specific language experiences can learn to become more aware of the sounds of language and have increased success in learning to read and spell.

For more information about phonemic awareness and activities to promote it, see the following articles and sections in this book: "Phonemic Awareness," "Developing Phonemic Awareness with Trade Books," "Intervention Strategies," and 101 Ways to Make Your Students Better Decoders and Readers.

References

Yopp, H. K. (1988). The validity and reliability of phonemic awareness tests. *Reading Research Quarterly*, 23, 159-177.

Yopp, H. K. (1992a). A longitudinal study of the relationships between phonemic awareness and reading and spelling achievement. Paper presented at the annual meeting of the American Educational Research Association, San Francisco, CA.

Yopp, H. K. (1992b). Developing phonemic awareness in young children. *The Reading Teacher*, 45, 696–703.

Yopp, H. K. (1995). Read-aloud books for developing phonemic awareness: An annotated bibliography. *The Reading Teacher*, 48, 538–542.

Harcourt Brace School Publishers

Yopp-Singer Test of Phoneme Segmentation

Student's name _____ Date _____

Score (number correct) _____

Directions: Today we're going to play a word game. I'm going to say a word and I want you to break the word apart. You are going to tell me each sound in the word in order. For example, if I say "old," you should say "/o/-/l/-/d/."

(*Administrator: Be sure to say the sounds, not the letters, in the word.*) Let's try a few together.

Practice items: (*Assist the child in segmenting these items as necessary.*) ride, go, man

Test items: (*Circle those items that the student correctly segments; incorrect responses may be recorded on the blank line following the item.*)

1. dog _____		12. lay _____	
2. keep _____		13. race _____	
3. fine _____		14. zoo _____	
4. no _____		15. three _____	
5. she _____		16. job _____	
6. wave _____		17. in _____	
7. grew _____		18. ice _____	
8. that _____		19. at _____	
9. red _____		20. top _____	
10. me _____		21. by _____	
11. sat _____		22. do _____	

The author, Hallie Kay Yopp, California State University, Fullerton, grants permission for this test to be reproduced for classroom use only. The author acknowledges the contribution of the late Harry Singer to the development of this test.

ANSWER KEY

Yopp-Singer Test of Phoneme Segmentation

Student's name _____ Date _____

Score (number correct) _____

Directions: Today we're going to play a word game. I'm going to say a word and I want you to break the word apart. You are going to tell me each sound in the word in order. For example, if I say "old," you should say "/o/-/l/-/d/."

(*Administrator: Be sure to say the sounds, not the letters, in the word.*) Let's try a few together.

Practice items: (*Assist the child in segmenting these items as necessary.*) ride, go, man

Test items: (*Circle those items that the student correctly segments; incorrect responses may be recorded on the blank line following the item.*)

1. dog	/d/ - /ô/ - /g/	12. lay	/l/ - /ā/
2. keep	/k/ - /ē/ - /p/	13. race	/r/ - /ā/ - /s/
3. fine	/f/ - /ī/ - /n/	14. zoo	/z/ - /o͞o/
4. no	/n/ - /ō/	15. three	/th/ - /r/ - /ē/
5. she	/sh/ - /ē/	16. job	/j/ - /o/ - /b/
6. wave	/w/ - /ā/ - /v/	17. in	/i/ - /n/
7. grew	/g/ - /r/ - /o͞o/	18. ice	/ī/ - /s/
8. that	/th/ - /a/ - /t/	19. at	/a/ - /t/
9. red	/r/ - /e/ - /d/	20. top	/t/ - /o/ - /p/
10. me	/m/ - /ē/	21. by	/b/ - /ī/
11. sat	/s/ - /a/ - /t/	22. do	/d/ - /o͞o/

Phonemic Awareness Interview

Phonemic awareness is an understanding that speech is composed of a series of sounds, or phonemes. Children who have difficulty attending to and manipulating the sounds in their language are likely to have problems learning to read. These children need additional experience with oral language play to heighten their sensitivity to the phonemic basis of their speech.

The Phonemic Awareness Interview is an oral test designed to provide informal assessment of a child's level of phonemic awareness to help the teacher plan for the development of literacy activities. The Phonemic Awareness Interview consists of the following four tasks:

Task 1: Sound Matching
Assesses the child's ability to tell whether the beginning sounds (phonemes) in words are the same or different

Task 2: Sound Isolation
Assesses the child's ability to produce the initial sound (phoneme) in words

Task 3: Sound Blending
Assesses the child's ability to blend isolated sounds (phonemes) together to form words

Task 4: Sound Segmenting
Assesses the child's ability to segment individual sounds (phonemes) in words

GENERAL DIRECTIONS FOR ADMINISTERING

The Phonemic Awareness Interview should be conducted individually in a quiet and comfortable setting. By administering the Interview individually, the teacher can be sure the child is attending to the task and can gain insights into problems the child may be having.

You may use any one, or all, of the tasks. If you wish to obtain a comprehensive understanding of the child's phonemic awareness, administer all four tasks. If you are interested in evaluating a specific aspect of phonemic awareness, administer only those tasks that are relevant to your needs. Whether you administer all four tasks or just selected tasks, the tasks should be given in sequential order.

There is no time limit. However, a period of 15 to 20 minutes is suggested to administer all four tasks. If possible, the tasks should be administered in a single session.

You and the child should be seated at a flat table or desk. The best seating location for you is facing the child, to facilitate clear diction and immediate recording of responses.

Become familiar with the directions and items. Specific directions for administering each task can be found on each "Administering and Recording Form." The text in **bold** type is intended to be read aloud. The other information is for the teacher only and should not be read aloud. You should feel free to rephrase the directions, to repeat the samples, or to give additional examples to make sure the child understands what to do.

Before beginning the Interview, spend a few minutes in light, friendly conversation with the child. Don't refer to the Interview as a "test." Tell the child you would like to play some "word games."

SPECIFIC DIRECTIONS FOR ADMINISTERING

Follow these steps to administer the Phonemic Awareness Interview:

1. Duplicate a copy of the "Administering and Recording Form" for each task you will be administering and one "Summary of Performance Form." You will record a child's responses on the "Administering and Recording Form" and summarize the totals on the "Summary of Performance Form." The child will not need any materials.

2. Explain that the words the child hears and says every day are made up of sounds and that you will be saying some words and sounds and asking questions about them. Be sure to speak clearly.

3. Administer the tasks in sequential order. If the child has difficulty with the first few items or cannot answer them, you may wish to discontinue conducting that particular task until a later time. If the child misses half of the items on any task, move on to the next task.

4. Follow the same basic procedures when administering each task. First, model the task so the child understands what to do. Second, administer the sample item and provide positive feedback to the child. Third, administer the items for that task. Fourth, record the child's responses for each item.

5. After the Interview, record the child's scores on the "Summary of Performance Form." Use the "Level of Performance" scale on the "Summary of Performance Form" to determine the level that best describes the child's understanding of phonemic awareness. Children whose scores reflect minimal or emerging understanding may need additional oral language experiences. You may also wish to record specific observations from the Interview, especially for those areas where the child had obvious difficulty with the task or required additional prompting.

Harcourt Brace School Publishers

PHONEMIC AWARENESS INTERVIEW

Summary of Performance Form

Name _____ Grade _____ Date _____

Task	Score	Comments
Task 1: Sound Matching	_____ / 8	_____
Task 2: Sound Isolation	_____ / 8	_____
Task 3: Sound Blending	_____ / 8	_____
Task 4: Sound Segmenting	_____ / 8	_____
Total Phonemic Awareness	_____ /32	_____

Level of Performance (circle one):		
Minimal	Emerging	Strong
0-12	13-25	26-32

Comments:

PHONEMIC AWARENESS INTERVIEW

Task 1: Sound Matching
Administering and Recording Form

Task: The child will listen to two words and will indicate if the two words do or do not begin with the same sound.

Model: **I am going to say two words. Listen carefully so you can tell me if the two words begin with the same sound: *monkey, mother*. Listen again: *monkey, mother*. The words begin with the same sound. *Monkey* and *mother* begin with the same sound.**

Sample: **Listen to these two words: *rain, snow*. Listen again: *rain, snow*. Do the two words begin with the same sound? (no) You're correct. *Rain* and *snow* do not begin with the same sound.**

   Now listen to some more words. Tell me if the words begin with the same sound.

Name _____ Grade _____ Date _____

Items

Circle child's response.
(Correct response is underlined.)

Items		
1. leg, lunch	<u>Same</u>	Different
2. duck, pan	Same	<u>Different</u>
3. sun, moon	Same	<u>Different</u>
4. fork, fish	<u>Same</u>	Different
5. chocolate, checkers	<u>Same</u>	Different
6. phone, poem	Same	<u>Different</u>
7. ball, banana	<u>Same</u>	Different
8. red, nut	Same	<u>Different</u>

Total Score: _____/8

Comments:

PHONEMIC AWARENESS INTERVIEW

Task 2: Sound Isolation
Administering and Recording Form

Task: The child will listen to a word and then will produce the initial phoneme in the word.

Model: **I am going to say a word. Then I am going to say just the beginning sound. Listen carefully for the beginning sound:** *pig.* **The beginning sound is** */p/.*

Sample: **Listen to another word. This time, you tell me the beginning sound. Listen carefully:** *goat.* **What is the beginning sound in** *goat?* **(/g/) You're correct. /g/ is the beginning sound in** *goat.* If the child tells you a letter name, remind the child to tell you the *sound,* not the letter.

Now listen to some more words. Tell me the beginning sound you hear in each word.

Name _____ Grade _____ Date _____

Items	Correct Response	Child's Response
1. *d*ot	/d/	_____
2. *m*ap	/m/	_____
3. *s*ad	/s/	_____
4. *t*alk	/t/	_____
5. *c*ow	/k/	_____
6. *b*ird	/b/	_____
7. *f*arm	/f/	_____
8. *y*ellow	/y/	_____

Total Score: _____/8

Comments:

Harcourt Brace School Publishers

PHONEMIC AWARENESS INTERVIEW

Task 3: Sound Blending
Administering and Recording Form

Task: The child will listen to individual sounds and will blend the sounds together to say the word.

Model: **I am going to say some sounds. Then I want you to put the sounds together to make a word. I will do the first one. Listen to the sounds: /r/-/u/-/n/. When I put the sounds /r/-/u/-/n/ together, they make the word *run*.**

Sample: **Listen to these sounds: /k/-/a/-/t/. What word do you make when you put /k/-/a/-/t/ together?** (cat) **You're correct. The sounds /k/-/a/-/t/ make the word *cat*.**

Now listen again. I will say some sounds. You put the sounds together to make a word and tell me the word.

Name _____ Grade _____ Date _____

Items	Correct Response	Child's Response
1. /g/-/ō/	go	_____
2. /sh/-/ē/-/p/	sheep	_____
3. /j/-/u/-/m/-/p/	jump	_____
4. /a/-/n/-/t/	ant	_____
5. /h/-/o/-/t/	hot	_____
6. /l/-/i/-/p/	lip	_____
7. /d/-/e/-/s/-/k/	desk	_____
8. /b/-/ī/	by	_____

Total Score: _____/8

Comments:

PHONEMIC AWARENESS INTERVIEW

Task 4: Sound Segmenting
Administering and Recording Form

Task: The child will listen to a word and then will produce each phoneme in the word separately.

Model: **I am going to say a word. Then I am going to say each sound in the word. Listen carefully for each sound. The word is** *go*. **The sounds in** *go* **are** /g/-/ō/. Be sure to articulate each sound separately. Do not simply stretch out the word.

Sample: **Listen to this word. This time, you tell me the sounds in the word. Listen carefully:** *man*. **What sounds do you hear in** *man*? (/m/-/a/-/n/) **You're correct. The sounds in the word** *man* **are** /m/-/a/-/n/.

Now listen to some more words. Tell me the sounds you hear in these words.

Name _____ Grade _____ Date _____

Items	Correct Response	Child's Response
1. dog	/d/-/ô/-/g/	_____
2. keep	/k/-/ē/-/p/	_____
3. no	/n/-/ō/	_____
4. that	/th/-/a/-/t/	_____
5. me	/m/-/ē/	_____
6. do	/d/-/o͞o/	_____
7. race	/r/-/ā/-/s/	_____
8. in	/i/-/n/	_____

Total Score: _____/8

Comments:

Read-Aloud Books for Developing Phonemic Awareness

by Dr. Hallie Kay Yopp

Brown, Margaret Wise. *Four Fur Feet*. Doubleday, 1993.

In this simple book the reader is drawn to the /f/ sound; the phrase "four fur feet" is repeated in every sentence as a furry animal walks around the world. We see four fur feet walk along the river, into the country, and so forth. The book must be turned around as the animal makes its way around the world.

Buller, Jon, and Schade, Susan. *I Love You, Good Night*. Simon & Schuster, 1988.

A mother and child tell each other how much they love one another. When the child says "as much as blueberry pancakes," the mother responds that she loves her child as much as "milkshakes." The child says she loves her mother as much as "frogs love flies," to which the mother responds that she loves her child as much as "pigs love pies." The two go back and forth in this manner until good night is said. The rhyme invites the listener to participate and continue the story.

Cameron, Polly. *"I Can't" Said the Ant*. Coward-McCann, 1961.

Household items discuss the fall of a teapot from a kitchen counter and the means by which to put it back. In a series of brief contributions to the conversation, each item says something that rhymes with its own name. "'Don't break her,' said the shaker" and "'I can't bear it,' said the carrot."

Carle, Eric. *All About Arthur (An Absolutely Absurd Ape)*. Franklin Watts, 1974.

Arthur, an accordion-playing ape who lives in Atlanta, feels lonely, so he travels from Baltimore to Yonkers making friends. In each city he makes a friend whose name matches the initial sound of the city—from a banjo-playing bear in Baltimore to a young yak in Yonkers.

Carter, David. *More Bugs in Boxes*. Simon & Schuster, 1990.

In this pop-up book the reader is presented with a series of questions and answers about make-believe bugs that are found inside a variety of boxes. Both the questions and answers make use of alliteration: "What kind of bug is in the rosy red rectangle box? A bright blue big-mouth bug." Following a similar pattern is the author's *Jingle Bugs* (Simon & Schuster, 1992), which has a Christmas theme and makes use of rhyme: "Who's in the chimney, warm and snug? Ho, ho, ho! It's Santa Bug!"

de Regniers, Beatrice Schenk; Moore, Eve; White, M.; and Carr, J.; editors. *Sing a Song of Popcorn: Every Child's Book of Poems*. Scholastic, 1988.

A number of poems in this book draw attention to rhyme and encourage children to experiment. Also included are poems that play with sounds within words. In "Galoshes" the author describes the slippery slush "as it slooshes and sloshes and splishes and sploshes" around a child's galoshes. In "Eletelephony," sounds are mixed up and substituted for one another—"Once there was an elephant/Who tried to use the telephant—"

Deming, A.G. *Who Is Tapping at My Window?* Puffin, 1994.

A young girl hears a tap-tapping at her window and asks who is there. The farm animals each respond "It's not I," and she discovers that it is the rain. The book is predictable in that the names of each pair of animals rhyme. The loon responds, followed by the raccoon. The dog's response is followed by the frog's.

Ehlert, Lois. *Eating the Alphabet: Fruits and Vegetables from A to Z.* **Harcourt Brace, 1989.**

Fruits and vegetables for each letter of the alphabet are offered in print and pictures. The following are displayed for *B*, for instance: blueberry, brussels sprout, bean, beet, broccoli, banana.

Eichenberg, Fritz. *Ape in a Cape: An Alphabet of Odd Animals.* **Harcourt Brace, 1988.**

In this alphabet book of odd animals, we meet an ape in a cape, a pig in a wig, a rat with a bat, and others. The original publication was named a Caldecott Honor book.

Emberley, B. *One Wide River to Cross.* **Little, Brown, 1992.**

This Caldecott Honor book is a picture-book adaptation of the traditional African American spiritual about Noah's ark. Through the use of rhyme the author describes the animals gathering on board one by one (while "Japhelth played the big bass drum"), two by two ("The alligator lost his shoe"), and so on up to ten, when the rains begin.

Fortunata. *Catch a Little Fox.* **Scholastic, 1968.**

In this repetitive book a group of children talk about going hunting. One by one they identify animals they will catch and decide where they will keep each one. A frog will be put in a log, a cat will be put in a hat, and so forth. The story concludes with the animals in turn capturing the children, putting them in a ring, and listening to them sing. All are then released. The music is included in this book. A different version of this story that includes a brontosaurus (who is put in a chorus) and an armadillo (who is put in a pillow) is John Langstaff's *Oh, A-Hunting We Will Go* (Atheneum, 1974).

Galdone, Paul. *Cat Goes Fiddle-i-fee.* **Clarion, 1985.**

This old English rhyme tells the story of a boy feeding his farm animals. As the animals are fed, they make noises: the pig goes "guffy guffy," the cat goes "fiddle-i-fee," and the hen goes "chimmy-chuck, chimmy-chuck." Sound repetition is a dominant part of this book.

Galdone, Paul. *Henny Penny.* **Clarion, 1984.**

A hen becomes alarmed when an acorn hits her on the head. She believes the sky is falling, and on her way to inform the king she meets several animals who join her until they all get eaten by Foxy Loxy. This classic story is included here because of the amusing rhyming names of the animals. A more recent release of this story is Steven Kellogg's *Chicken Little* (Mulberry Books, 1985).

Geraghty, Paul. *Stop That Noise!* **Crown, 1992.**

A mouse is annoyed with the many sounds of the forest and implores the cicada to stop its "zee-zee-zee-zee" and the frog to stop its "woopoo," until it hears far more disturbing sounds—the "Brrrm" and "Crrrrrr RACKA-DACKA-RACKA-SHOONG" of a bull-dozer felling trees. The presentation of animal and machine sounds makes this book useful in drawing attention to the sounds in our language.

Gilman, Phoebe. *The Wonderful Pigs of Jillian Jiggs.* **Scholastic, 1993.**

"Jillian Jillian Jillian Jiggs, Maker of wonderful, marvelous pigs!" In this rhyming book, a young girl enthusiastically makes pigs to sell. When she realizes that she cannot part with them, she teaches others how to make them. Instructions for making pigs are included.

Gordon, Jeffie R. *Six Sleepy Sheep.* **Puffin, 1993.**

Six sheep try to fall asleep by slurping celery soup, telling spooky stories, singing songs, sipping simmered milk, and so on. The use of the /s/ sound is prevalent throughout and amuses listeners as they anticipate the sheep's antics.

Hague, Kathleen. *Alphabears: An ABC Book.* **Henry Holt, 1991.**

In this beautifully illustrated book, 26 teddy bears introduce the alphabet and make use of alliteration. Teddy bear John loves jam and jelly. Quimbly is a quilted bear, and Pam likes popcorn and pink lemonade.

Hawkins, Colin, and Hawkins, Jacqui. *Tog the Dog.* **G.P. Putnam's Sons, 1986.**

This book tells the story of Tog the Dog, who likes to jog, gets lost in a fog, falls into a bog, and so forth. Emphasis is on words that rhyme with *dog*. With the exception of the final page, the pages in the book are not full width. On the final page the letters *og* appear in large bold type. As the reader turns the narrower pages throughout the text, a new letter appears and lines up with the *og*—thus presenting a new word on each page. When Tog falls into the bog, a large letter *b* lines up with the *og* to make the word *bog*. This is a great book for both developing phonemic awareness and pointing out a spelling pattern. Also by the authors are *Jen the Hen, Mig the Pig,* and *Pat the Cat.*

Harcourt Brace School Publishers

Hymes, L., and Hymes, J. *Oodles of Noodles.* **Young Scott Books, 1964.**

Several of the poems in this collection make use of non-sense words in order to complete a rhyme. In the poem "Oodles of Noodles," the speaker requests oodles of noodles because they are his/her favorite "foodles." In a poem titled "Spinach," the authors list a series of words, each beginning with the /sp/ sound, until they finally end with the word *spinach*. Words include *spin, span, spun,* and *spoony*. Many of the other poems point out spelling patterns; these will be entertaining for an older audience.

Krauss, Ruth. *I Can Fly.* **Golden Press, 1992.**

In this simple book, a child imitates the actions of a variety of animals. "A cow can moo. I can too." "I can squirm like a worm." "Howl howl howl, I'm an old screech owl." The rhyming element combined with the charm of the child's imaginative play is what makes the story so engaging. On the final page, non-sense words that rhyme are used, encouraging listeners to experiment with sounds themselves: "Gubble, gubble, gubble, I'm a mubble in a pubble."

Kuskin, Karla. *Roar and More.* **HarperTrophy, 1990.**

This book includes many poems and pictures that portray the sounds made by a variety of animals. Both the use of rhyme and the presentation of animal sounds ("Ssnnaaaarrll" for the tiger, "Hsssssss. . ." for the snake) draw children's attention to sounds. An earlier edition of this book won the 1979 NCTE Award for Excellence in Poetry for Children.

Lewison, Wendy. *Buzz Said the Bee.* **Scholastic, 1992.**

A series of animals sit on top of one another in this story. Before each animal climbs on top of the next, it does something that rhymes with the name of the animal it approaches. For instance, the hen dances a jig before sitting on the pig. The pig takes a bow before sitting on the cow.

Lindbergh, Reeve. *The Day the Goose Got Loose.* **Dial, 1990.**

Chaos results when a goose gets loose in this rhyming book. The horses were glad; they ran like mad. Mom was upset because the goose was a pet. The sheep were scared; they huddled and stared.

Martin, Bill, Jr. *The Happy Hippopotami.* **Voyager Books, Harcourt Brace, 1992. (Text copyright by Holt, Rinehart and Winston, 1970.)**

This clever book makes use of rhyme and phoneme substitution as happy hippopotamamas wearing pretty beach pajamas and happy hippopotapoppas strolling about the candy shoppas have fun with family and friends at the beach.

Martin, Bill, Jr. *Sounds of a Powwow.* **Holt, Rinehart and Winston, 1974.**

Included in this volume is the song "K-K-K-Katy," in which the first consonant of several words is isolated and repeated, as in the song title. This song presents the opportunity for teachers to work with children on segmenting the sounds of their language.

Martin, Bill, Jr., and Archambault, John. *Chicka Chicka Boom Boom.* **Scholastic, 1989.**

The letters of the alphabet meet at the top of the coconut tree. Rhyme and silly play with sounds ("Skit skat skoodle doot. Flip flop flee.") make this book a must for preschool, kindergarten, and first-grade teachers.

Martin, Bill, Jr., and Archambault, John. *Listen to the Rain.* **Henry Holt, 1988.**

This delightful book plays with language as the authors describe the rain, "Leaving all outdoors a muddle, a mishy, mushy, muddy puddle" and "The tiptoe pitter-patter, the splish and splash and splatter," making use of rhyme and medial sound substitution.

Martin, Bill, Jr., and Egielski, Richard. *"Fire! Fire!" Said Mrs. McGuire.* **Harcourt Brace, 1995.**

In this version of the well-known rhyme in which everyone's name rhymes with an exclamation for help, the fire is caused by the many candles on a birthday cake. The text is accompanied by colorful and often humorous illustrations.

Marzollo, Jean. *The Teddy Bear Book.* **Puffin Pied Piper, 1992.**

Poems about teddy bears that the author adapted from songs, jump-rope rhymes, ball-bouncing chants, cheers, and story poems are presented. Use of rhyme is considerable, from the well-known "Teddy bear, teddy bear, turn around/Teddy bear, teddy bear, touch the ground" to the less familiar "Did you ever, ever, ever see a teddy bear dance with his wife" and the response, "No I never, never, never. . . ." Play with sounds is obvious in the poem "Teddy Boo and Teddy Bear," where the author says, "Icabocker, icabocker, icabocker, boo! Icabocker, soda cracker, phooey on you!"

Marzollo, Jean. *Ten Cats Have Hats.* **Scholastic, 1994.**

A young child proudly shows a different hat on each page of this counting book as she tells of the possessions of others: "Five ducks have trucks, but I have a hat" "Eight crabs have cabs, but I have a hat." The story is predictable, beginning with one bear and ending with ten cats, and makes strong use of rhyme.

McDonald, Amy. *Rachel Fister's Blister.* **Houghton Mifflin, 1990.**

Rachel Fister gets a blister on her little toe. Her family enlists the aid of many people ("Find her brothers and some others . . ." "Call the palace. Ask Queen Alice . . .") and finally discovers that her mother's kiss makes the pain disappear.

Moerbeek, Kees. *Can't Sleep.* **Price Stern Sloan, 1994.**

In this highly repetitive pop-up book, a number of animals have difficulty sleeping because they think they are being watched. The /w/ sound is repeated more and more on each page as the fear mounts until the vulture shrieks, "Somebody is w-w-w-w-watching me!" The iteration of the /w/ and the elongation of the /s/ sound when a snake "ssssighs" serve to focus attention on sounds in this story.

Obligado, Lillian. *Faint Frogs Feeling Feverish and Other Terrifically Tantalizing Tongue Twisters.* **Puffin, 1986.**

For each letter of the alphabet, one or more tongue twisters using alliteration is presented in print and with humorous illustrations. "S" has smiling snakes sipping strawberry sodas, a shy spider spinning, and a swordfish sawing. "T" presents two toucans tying ties, turtles tasting tea, and tigers trying trousers.

Ochs, Carol P. *Moose on the Loose.* **Carolrhoda, 1991.**

A moose escapes from the zoo in the town of Zown and at the same time a chartreuse caboose disappears. The zookeeper runs throughout the town asking citizens if they've seen a "moose on the loose in a chartreuse caboose." No one has seen the moose but each has seen a different animal. Included among the many citizens is Ms. Cook, who saw a pig wearing a wig; Mr. Wu, who saw a weasel paint at an easel; and Mrs. Case, who saw a skunk filling a trunk. Each joins in the search.

Otto, Carolyn. *Dinosaur Chase.* **HarperTrophy, 1991.**

A mother dinosaur reads her young one a story about dinosaurs in which "dinosaur crawl, dinosaur creep, tiptoe dinosaur, dinosaur sneak." Both alliteration and rhyme are present in this simple, colorful book.

Parry, Caroline, compiler. *Zoomerang-a-Boomerang: Poems to Make Your Belly Laugh.* **Puffin, 1993.**

Nearly all of the works included in this collection of poems play with language, particularly through the use of predictable and humorous rhyme patterns. In "Oh my, no more pie," the meat's too red, so the writer has some bread. When the bread is too brown, the writer goes to town, and so forth. In "What they said," each of twelve animals says something that rhymes with the type of animal it is. For instance, a pup says "Let's wake up," and a lark says "It's still dark." This pattern is similar to that presented in *I Can't* Said the Ant by Polly Cameron.

Patz, Nancy. *Moses Supposes His Toeses Are Roses.* **Harcourt Brace, 1983.**

Seven rhymes are presented here, each of which plays on language to engage the listener. Rhyme is predictable in "Sweetie Maguire" when Sweetie shouts "Fire! Fire!" and Mrs. O'Hair says, "Where? Where?" Alliteration makes "Betty Botter" a tongue twister: "But a bit of better butter—that will make my batter better!" Assonance adds humor to "The tooter" when a tooter tries to tutor two tooters to toot!

Pomerantz, Charlotte. *If I Had a Paka: Poems in Eleven Languages.* **Mulberry, 1993.**

A selection of twelve poems is included in this volume, and eleven languages are represented. The author manipulates words as in "You take the blueberry, I'll take the dewberry. You don't want the blueberry. OK, take the bayberry. . . ." Many berries are mentioned, including a novel one—the "chuckleberry." Attention is drawn to phonemes when languages other than English are introduced. The Vietnamese translation of the following draws attention to rhyme and repetition: I like fish, Toy tik ka; I like chicken, Toy tik ga; I like duck, Toy tik veet; I like meat, Toy tik teet."

Prelutsky, Jack. *The Baby Uggs Are Hatching.* **Mulberry, 1989.**

Twelve poems describe unusual creatures, such as the sneepies, the smasheroo, and the numpy-numpy-numpity. Though some of the vocabulary is advanced (the Quossible has an irascible temper), most of the poems will be enjoyed by young children, who will delight in the humorous use of words and sounds. For instance, "The Sneezysnoozer sneezes in a dozen sneezy sizes; it sneezes little breezes and it sneezes big surprises." In the poem that lends its name to the title of the book, children will hear sounds manipulated in nonsense words: "Uggily wuggily zuggily zee, the baby Uggs are fierce and free. Uggily wuggily zuggily zay, the baby Uggs come out today."

Harcourt Brace School Publishers

Prelutsky, Jack. *Poems of A. Nonny Mouse.* **Knopf, 1991.**

A. Nonny Mouse finally gets credit for all her works, which were previously attributed to "Anonymous," in this humorous selection of poems that is appropriate for all ages. Of particular interest for developing phonemic awareness are poems such as "How much wood would a woodchuck chuck," and "Betty Botter bought some butter."

Provensen, Alice, and Provensen, Martin. *Old Mother Hubbard.* **Random House, 1992.**

In this traditional rhyme, Old Mother Hubbard runs errand after errand for her dog. When she comes back from buying him a wig, she finds him dancing a jig. When she returns from buying him shoes, she finds him reading the news. The rhyme element is a critical feature of this story.

Raffi. *Down by the Bay.* **Crown, 1988.**

In this story two young children try to outdo one another in making up rhymes with questions like "Did you ever see a goose kissing a moose?" and "Did you ever see a bear combing his hair?" Music is included.

Raffi. *Tingalayo.* **Crown, 1993.**

Another of Raffi's songs is made into a book. Here the reader meets a man who calls for his donkey, Tingalayo, and describes its antics through the use of rhyme and rhythm. Phrases such as "Me donkey dance, me donkey sing, me donkey wearin' a diamond ring" will make children laugh, and they will easily contribute additional verses to this song/story.

Rosen, Michael, editor. *Poems for the Very Young.* **Kingfisher Books, 1993.**

The editor provides a selection of poems sure to engage young listeners. Many make use of rhyme ("Goodness gracious, fiddle dee dee,/Somebody's grandmother's out to sea"). Some make use of alliteration ("Lily likes lollipops, lemonade and lime-drops"). Some make nonsensical play with sounds ("Whipper-snapper, rooty-tooty, Helter-skelter, tutti-frutti").

Sendak, Maurice. *Alligators All Around: An Alphabet.* **HarperTrophy, 1991.**

Using alliteration for each letter of the alphabet, Sendak introduces the reader to the alphabet with the help of alligators who have headaches (for *H*) and keep kangaroos (for *K*).

Seuss. *Dr. Seuss's ABC.* **Random House, 1963.**

Each letter of the alphabet is presented along with an amusing sentence in which nearly all of the words begin with the targeted letter. "Many mumbling mice are making midnight music in the moonlight . . . mighty nice."

Seuss. *Fox in Socks.* **Random House, 1965.**

Before beginning this book the reader is warned to take it slowly because the fox will try to get the reader's tongue in trouble. The play with language is the very obvious focus. Assonance patterns occur throughout, and the listener is exposed to vowel-sound changes when beetles battle, ducks like lakes, and ticks and clocks get mixed up with the chicks and tocks.

Seuss. *There's a Wocket in My Pocket.* **Random House, 1974.**

A child talks about the creatures he has found around his house. These include a "nooth grush on my toothbrush" and a "zamp in the lamp." The initial sounds of common household objects are replaced by other sounds to make the nonsense creatures. A wonderful example of play with language!

Shaw, Nancy. *Sheep on a Ship.* **Houghton Mifflin, 1992.**

Sheep sailing on a ship run into trouble when facing a sudden storm. This entertaining story makes use of rhyme (waves lap and sails flap), alliteration (sheep on a ship), and assonance ("It rains and hails and shakes the sails"). Also by this author are *Sheep in a Jeep, Sheep Out to Eat,* and *Sheep Take a Hike.*

Shelby, Anne. *Potluck.* **Orchard, 1991.**

Two friends, Alpha and Betty, organize a potluck, and each of their friends contributes something. Christine came with carrot cake and corn on the cob. Monica made mounds and mounds of mashed potatoes. Alliteration draws attention to initial sounds throughout this book.

Showers, Paul. *The Listening Walk.* **HarperTrophy, 1993.**

A little girl and her father go for a walk with their dog, and the listener is treated to the variety of sounds they hear while walking. These include "thhhhh . . .," the steady whisper sound of some sprinklers, and "whithh whithh," the sound of other sprinklers that turn around and around. Some phonemes are elongated, as in "eeeeeeyowwwoooo . . .," the sound of a jet overhead. Some phonemes are substituted, as in "bik bok bik bok," the sounds of high heels on the pavement.

Silverstein, Shel. *Falling Up.* **HarperCollins, 1996.**

Few children will not be entertained by the poetry of Shel Silverstein. His latest collection includes many selections that play with sounds. For example, "My Nose Garden" begins, "I have rowses and rowses of noses and noses, And why they all growses I really can't guess." Sound substitution, sound repetition, and rhyme abound in these humorous and occasionally poignant poems.

Silverstein, Shel. *A Giraffe and a Half.* **HarperCollins, 1964.**

Using cumulative and rhyming patterns, Silverstein builds the story of a giraffe who has a rose on his nose, a bee on his knee, some glue on his shoe, and so on until he undoes the story by reversing the events.

Slepian, Jan, and Seidler, Ann. *The Hungry Thing.* **Scholastic, 1988.**

One day a Hungry Thing shows up in town. Only a little boy can understand what the Hungry Thing would like to eat when the creature tells the townspeople he wants shmancakes. Shmancakes, says the little boy, "sound like Fancakes . . . sound like . . . Pancakes to me." Using sound substitution, the authors develop a clever tale in which the townspeople must play with sounds in common words (for example, "boop with a smacker" is "soup with a cracker") in order to communicate with the Hungry Thing. Although out of print, two other Hungry Thing books may be found at libraries: *The Hungry Thing Returns* and *The Hungry Thing Goes to a Restaurant.*

Staines, Bill. *All God's Critters Got a Place in the Choir.* **Puffin, 1993.**

This lively book makes use of rhyme to tell of the place that numerous animals—an ox and a fox, a grizzly bear, a possum and a porcupine, bullfrogs—have in the world's choir. "Some sing low, some sing higher, some sing out loud on the telephone wire."

Tallon, Robert. *Zoophabets.* **Scholastic, 1979.**

Letter by letter the author names fictional animals and in list form tells where each lives and what it eats. They all, of course, begin with the targeted letter. "Runk" lives in "Rain barrels" and eats "raindrops, rusty rainbows, ripped rubbers, raincoats, rhubarb."

Van Allsburg, Chris. *The Z Was Zapped: A Play in Twenty-Six Acts.* **Houghton Mifflin, 1987.**

A series of mishaps befalls the letters of the alphabet. "A" is crushed by an avalanche, "B" is bitten badly, "C" is cut to ribbons, and so forth. Other alphabet books using alliteration include *Animalia* by Graeme Base (Abrams, 1987); *A Apple Pie* by Kate Greenaway (Derrydale, 1993); and *An Amazing Alphabet* by J. Patience (Random House, 1993).

West, Colin. *"I Don't Care!" Said the Bear.* **Candlewick, 1996.**

A cocky bear (with his nose in the air) is not afraid of a loose moose, a big pig, a snake from a lake, or other such animals, but he runs from the teeny weeny mouse. Rhyme is used throughout.

Winthrop, Elizabeth. *Shoes.* **HarperTrophy, 1988.**

This rhyming book surveys many familiar and some not-so-familiar types of shoes. The book begins "There are shoes to buckle, shoes to tie, shoes too low, and shoes too high." Later we discover "Shoes for fishing, shoes for wishing, rubber shoes for muddy squishing." This rhythm and rhyme invites participation and creative contributions.

Wood, Audrey. *Silly Sally.* **Harcourt Brace, 1994.**

Rhyme and alliteration are obvious in this book about Silly Sally, who goes to town and makes some acquaintances along the way. She does a jig with a pig, plays leapfrog with a dog, and sings a tune with a loon.

Zemach, Margot. *Hush, Little Baby.* **Dutton, 1976.**

In this lullaby, parents attempt to console a crying baby by promising a number of outrageous things including a mockingbird, a diamond ring, a billy goat, and a cart and bull. The verse is set to rhyme, e. g., "If that cart and bull turn over, Poppa's gonna buy you a dog named Rover," and children can easily innovate on the rhyme and contribute to the list of items being promised.

Harcourt Brace School Publishers

Phonics Word Lists

Common Phonograms and Example Words

-ab /ab/

cab
lab
tab
crab
drab
grab
scab

-ace /ās/

face
lace
pace
race
brace
grace
place
space
trace

-ack /ak/

back
lack
pack
quack
rack
sack
tack
black
crack
knack
shack
smack
snack
stack
track

-ad /ad/

bad
dad
fad
had
lad
mad
pad
sad
glad

-ade /ād/

fade
jade
made
wade
blade
grade
shade
spade
trade

-ag /ag/

bag
gag
lag
rag
sag
tag
wag
brag
drag
flag
snag
stag

-age /āj/

age
cage
page
rage
sage
wage
stage

-aid /ād/

aid
laid
maid
paid
raid
braid

-ail /āl/

fail
hail
jail
mail
nail
pail
quail
rail
sail
tail
wail
frail
snail
trail

-ain /ān/

main
pain
rain
vain
brain
chain
drain
grain
plain
Spain
stain
strain
train

-aint /ānt/

faint
paint
quaint
saint

-air /âr/

air
fair
hair
pair
chair
stair

-ake /āk/

bake
cake
fake
lake
make
quake
rake
take
wake
brake
flake
shake
snake
stake

-ale /āl/

bale
gale
male
pale
sale
tale
scale
stale
whale

-alk /ôk/

talk
walk
chalk
stalk

-all /ôl/

all
ball
call
fall
hall
mall
tall
wall
small
squall

-am /am/

am
dam
ham
jam
ram
yam
clam
cram
gram
slam
swam
tram

-ame /ām/

came
fame
game
name
same
tame
blame
flame
frame
shame

-amp /amp/

camp
damp
lamp
ramp
champ
clamp
cramp
stamp

-an /an/

an
can
fan
man
pan
ran
tan
van
bran
plan
scan
span
than

-ance /ans/

dance
lance
chance
France
glance
prance
trance

-and /and/

and
band
hand
land
sand
bland
brand
gland
stand
strand

-ane /ān/

cane
lane
mane
pane
vane
crane
plane

-ang /ang/

bang
fang
gang
hang
rang
sang
clang
sprang

-ank /ank/

bank
rank
sank
tank
yank
blank
clank
crank
drank
plank
prank
spank
thank

-ant /ant/

ant
pant
chant
grant
plant
slant

-ap /ap/

cap
gap
lap
map
nap
rap
sap
tap
chap
clap
flap
scrap
slap
snap
strap
trap
wrap

-ape /āp/

cape
tape
drape
grape
scrape
shape

-ar /är/

bar
car
far
jar
tar
scar
star

-ard /ärd/

card
guard
hard
lard
yard

-are /âr/

bare
care
dare
fare
hare
mare
pare
rare
blare
flare
glare
scare
share
snare
spare
square
stare

-arge /ärj/

barge
large
charge

-ark /ärk/

bark
dark
lark
mark
park
shark
spark
stark

-arm /ärm/

farm
harm
charm

-arp /ärp/

carp
harp
sharp

-art /ärt/

art
cart
dart
part
tart
chart
smart
start

-ase /ās/

base
case
vase
chase

-ash /ash/

ash
cash
dash
gash
lash
mash
rash
sash
clash
flash
smash
trash

-ask /ask/

ask
mask
task

-asp /asp/

gasp
clasp
grasp

-ast /ast/

cast
fast
last
mast
past
blast

-aste /āst/

baste
haste
paste
taste
waste

-at /at/

at
bat
cat
fat
hat
mat
pat
rat
sat
vat
chat
flat
gnat
scat
that

-atch /ach/

batch
catch
hatch
latch
match
patch
scratch
thatch

-ate /āt/

ate
date
fate
gate
hate
late
mate
rate
crate
grate
plate
skate
state

-ath /ath/

bath
math
path

-aught /ôt/

caught
taught

-ave /āv/

cave
gave
pave
rave
save
wave
brave
crave
grave
shave
slave

aw /ô/

jaw
law
paw
raw
saw
claw
draw
flaw
gnaw
slaw
straw

-awn /ôn/

dawn
fawn
lawn
pawn
yawn
drawn

-ay /ā/

bay
day
hay
jay
lay
may
pay
ray
say
way
clay
gray
play
pray
spray
stay
stray
sway
tray

-aze /āz/

daze
gaze
haze
maze
blaze
glaze
graze

-ea /ē/

pea
sea
tea
flea
plea

-each /ēch/

each
beach
peach
reach
teach
bleach
preach

-ead /ed/

dead
head
lead
read
bread
dread
spread
thread

-ead /ēd/

bead
lead
read
knead
plead

-eak /ēk/

beak
leak
peak
teak
weak
creak
sneak
speak
squeak
streak

-eal /ēl/

deal
heal
meal
real
seal
squeal
steal

-eam /ēm/

beam
seam
team
cream
dream
gleam
scream
steam
stream

-ean /ēn/

bean
lean
mean
clean

-eap /ēp/

heap
leap
reap
cheap

-ear /ir/

ear
dear
fear
gear
hear
near
rear
tear
year
clear
shear
smear
spear

-ear /âr/

bear
pear
wear

-east /ēst/

east
beast
feast
least
yeast

-eat /ēt/

eat
beat
feat
heat
meat
neat
seat
cheat
treat
wheat

-eck /ek/

deck
neck
peck
check
speck
wreck

-ed /ed/

bed
fed
led
red
wed
bled
fled
shed
shred
sled
sped

-edge /ej/

edge
hedge
ledge
wedge
dredge
pledge

-ee /ē/

bee
fee
see
tee
wee
flee
free
glee
knee
tree

-eed /ēd/

deed
feed
need
reed
seed
weed
bleed
freed
greed
speed
steed

-eek /ēk/

leek
meek
peek
reek
seek
week
cheek
creek
Greek
sleek

-eel /ēl/

eel
feel
heel
keel
peel
reel
kneel
steel
wheel

-een /ēn/

keen
queen
seen
teen
green
screen

-eep /ēp/

beep
deep
jeep
keep
peep
seep
weep
creep
sheep
sleep
steep
sweep

-eer /ir/

deer
jeer
peer
cheer
sneer
steer

-eet /ēt/

beet
feet
meet
fleet
greet
sheet
sleet
street
sweet

-eeze /ēz/

breeze
freeze
sneeze
squeeze
wheeze

-eg /eg/

beg
leg
peg

-eigh /ā/

weigh
sleigh

-ell /el/

bell
cell
fell
sell
tell
well
yell
dwell
shell
smell
spell
swell

-elt /elt/

belt
felt
melt
knelt

-em /em/

gem
hem
stem
them

-en /en/

den
hen
men
pen
ten
then
when
wren

-ench /ench/

bench
clench
drench
French
quench
trench
wrench

-end /end/

end
bend
lend
mend
send
tend
blend
spend
trend

-ense /ens/

dense
sense
tense

-ent /ent/

bent
cent
dent
lent
rent
sent
tent
vent
went
scent
spent

-ept /ept/

kept
wept
crept
slept
swept

-erve /ûrv/

nerve
serve
swerve

-esh /esh/

mesh
flesh
fresh

-ess /es/

guess
less
mess
bless
chess
dress
press
stress

-est /est/

best
guest
nest
pest
rest
test
vest
west
chest
quest

-et /et/

bet
get
jet
let
met
net
pet
set
wet
yet
fret

-ew /o͞o/

new
blew
brew
chew
crew
drew
flew
grew
knew
stew
threw

-ib /ib/

bib
fib
rib
crib

-ice /īs/

ice
dice
lice
mice
nice
rice
price
slice
twice

-ick /ik/

kick
lick
pick
quick
sick
tick
wick
brick
chick
click
flick
slick
stick
thick
trick

-id /id/

bid
did
hid
kid
lid
rid
grid
skid
slid

-ide /īd/

hide
ride
side
tide
wide
bride
glide
pride
slide
stride

-ie /ī/

die
lie
pie
tie

-ied /īd/

died
lied
dried
fried
tried

-ief /ēf/

brief
chief
grief
thief

-ield /ēld/

field
yield
shield

-ies /$\bar{\text{i}}$z/

dies
lies
pies
ties
cries
dries
flies
fries
skies
tries

-ife /$\bar{\text{i}}$f/

life
wife
knife

-ift /ift/

gift
lift
rift
sift
drift
shift
swift
thrift

-ig /ig/

big
dig
fig
jig
pig
rig
wig
sprig
twig

-igh /$\bar{\text{i}}$/

high
sigh
thigh

-ight /$\bar{\text{i}}$t/

light
might
night
right
sight
tight
bright
flight
fright
knight
slight

-ike /$\bar{\text{i}}$k/

bike
dike
hike
like
spike
strike

-ild /$\bar{\text{i}}$ld/

mild
wild
child

-ile /$\bar{\text{i}}$l/

file
mile
pile
tile
smile
while

-ill /il/

ill
bill
dill
fill
gill
kill
mill
pill
quill
sill
till
will
chill
drill
grill
skill
spill
still
thrill

-im /im/

dim
him
rim
brim
grim
slim
swim
trim
whim

-ime /$\bar{\text{i}}$m/

dime
lime
mime
time
chime
crime
grime
prime
slime

-imp /imp/

limp
blimp
chimp
primp
skimp

-in /in/

in
bin
fin
kin
pin
tin
win
chin
grin
shin
skin
spin
thin
twin

-inch /inch/

cinch
finch
pinch
winch
clinch
flinch

-ind /īnd/

bind
find
kind
mind
rind
wind
blind
grind

-ine /īn/

dine
fine
line
mine
nine
pine
vine
shine
spine
whine

-ing /ing/

king
ring
sing
wing
bring
cling
fling
spring
sting
string
swing
thing
wring

-ink /ink/

ink
link
pink
rink
sink
wink
blink
drink
shrink
slink
think

-int /int/

hint
lint
mint
tint
print
splint
sprint
squint

-ip /ip/

dip
hip
lip
rip
sip
tip
zip
chip
clip
drip
flip
grip
ship
skip
slip
snip
strip
trip

-ipe /īp/

pipe
ripe
wipe
gripe
stripe

-ir /ûr/

fir
sir
stir
whir

-ire /īr/

fire
tire
wire
spire

-irt /ûrt/

dirt
shirt
skirt
squirt

-ish /ish/

dish
fish
wish

-isk /isk/

disk
risk
brisk
whisk

-iss /is/

hiss
kiss
miss
bliss
Swiss

-ist /ist/

fist
list
mist
twist
wrist

-it /it/

it
bit
fit
hit
kit
lit
pit
quit
sit
wit
knit
skit
slit
split

-itch /ich/

itch
ditch
hitch
pitch
switch

-ite /īt/

bite
kite
quite
site
spite
white
write

-ive /īv/

dive
five
hive
live
drive
strive
thrive

-ix /iks/

fix
mix
six

-o /o͞o/

do
to
who

-o /ō/

go
no
so

-oad /ōd/

load
road
toad

-oak /ōk/

oak
soak
cloak
croak

-oal /ōl/

coal
foal
goal

-oar /ôr/

oar
boar
roar
soar

-oast /ōst/

boast
coast
roast
toast

-oat /ōt/

oat
boat
coat
goat
moat
float
gloat
throat

-ob /ob/

cob
job
mob
rob
sob
knob

-ock /ok/

dock
lock
mock
rock
sock
block
clock
flock
knock
shock
smock
stock

-od /od/

cod
nod
pod
rod
sod
clod
plod
prod

-ode /ōd/

code
rode
strode

-oe /ō/

doe
foe
hoe
toe
woe

-og /og/

bog
fog
hog
jog
log
clog
frog
smog

-oil /oil/

boil
coil
foil
soil
broil
spoil

-oke /ōk/

joke
poke
woke
yoke
broke
choke
smoke
spoke
stroke

-old /ōld/

old
bold
cold
fold
gold
hold
mold
sold
told
scold

-ole /ōl/

hole
mole
pole
role
stole
whole

-oll /ōl/

poll
roll
toll
scroll
stroll
troll

-olt /ōlt/

bolt
colt
jolt
molt
volt

-ome /ōm/

dome
home
gnome
chrome

-omp /omp/

romp
chomp
stomp

-on /un/

son
ton
won

-ond /ond/

bond
fond
pond
blond
frond

-one /ōn/

bone
cone
lone
tone
zone
phone
shone
stone

-ong /ong/

long
song
strong
wrong

-oo /o͞o/

moo
too
zoo

-ood /o͝od/

good
hood
wood
stood

-ood /o͞od/

food
mood

-ook /o͝ok/

book
cook
hook
look
nook
took
brook
crook
shook

-ool /o͞ol/

cool
fool
pool
tool
school
spool
stool

-oom /o͞om/

boom
doom
loom
room
zoom
bloom
broom
gloom
groom

-oon /o͞on/

moon
noon
soon
spoon

-oop /o͞op/

coop
hoop
loop
droop
scoop
snoop
stoop
swoop
troop

-oose /o͞os/

goose
loose
moose

-oot /o͞ot/

boot
hoot
root
scoot
shoot

-op /op/

hop
mop
pop
top
chop
crop
drop
flop
prop
shop
stop

Harcourt Brace School Publishers

-ope /ōp/

cope
hope
mope
rope
scope
slope

-orch /ôrch/

porch
torch
scorch

-ord /ôrd/

cord
chord
sword

-ore /ôr/

ore
bore
core
more
pore
sore
tore
wore
chore
score
shore
snore
store
swore

-ork /ôrk/

cork
fork
pork
stork

-orn /ôrn/

born
corn
horn
torn
worn
scorn
thorn

-ort /ôrt/

fort
port
sort
short
snort
sport

-ose /ōz/

hose
nose
pose
rose
chose
close
those

-oss /ôs/

boss
loss
moss
toss
cross
floss

-ost /ôst/

cost
lost
frost

-ost /ōst/

host
most
post

-ot /ot/

cot
dot
got
hot
jot
lot
not
pot
rot
blot
clot
knot
plot
shot
slot
spot
trot

-ote /ōt/

note
quote
vote
wrote

-oth /ôth/

moth
broth
cloth

-ouch /ouch/

couch
pouch
crouch
grouch
slouch

-oud /oud/

loud
cloud
proud

-ough /uf/

rough
tough

-ought /ôt/

ought
bought
fought
sought
brought
thought

-ould / o͝od/

could
would
should

-ounce /ouns/

ounce
bounce
pounce

-ound /ound/

bound
found
hound
mound
pound
round
sound
wound
ground

-our /our/

our
hour
sour
flour
scour

-ouse /ous/

house
mouse
blouse

-out /out/

out
pout
scout
shout
snout
spout
sprout
stout
trout

-outh /outh/

mouth
south

-ove /ōv/

cove
wove
clove
drove
grove
stove

-ove /uv/

dove
love
glove
shove

-ow /ō/

bow
low
mow
row
sow
tow
blow
crow
flow
glow
grow
know
show
slow
snow

-ow /ou/

bow
cow
how
now
sow
brow
plow

-owl /oul/

owl
fowl
howl
growl
prowl
scowl

-own /oun/

down
gown
town
brown
clown
crown
drown
frown

-own /ōn/

own
blown
flown
grown
known
shown
thrown

-ox /oks/

ox
box
fox

-oy /oi/

boy
joy
soy
toy

-ub /ub/

cub
hub
rub
sub
tub
club
scrub
shrub
stub

-uck /uk/

buck
duck
luck
tuck
cluck
pluck
stuck
struck
truck

-udge /uj/

budge
fudge
judge
nudge
smudge
trudge

-ue /ōō/

blue
clue
flue
glue
true

-uff /uf/

cuff
puff
bluff
fluff
gruff
scuff
stuff

-ug   /ug/

bug
dug
hug
jug
mug
rug
tug
plug
shrug
snug

-ull   /ul/

dull
gull
hull
lull
skull

-ull   /o͞ol/

bull
full
pull

-um   /um/

gum
hum
sum
chum
drum
glum
plum
strum
swum

-umb /um/

numb
crumb
thumb

-ump /ump/

bump
dump
hump
jump
lump
pump
clump
grump
plump
slump
stump

-un   /un/

bun
fun
gun
pun
run
sun
spun
stun

-unch /unch/

bunch
hunch
lunch
munch
punch
brunch
crunch

-ung   /ung/

hung
lung
rung
sung
flung
sprung
stung
strung
swung

-unk   /unk/

bunk
dunk
hunk
junk
sunk
chunk
shrunk
skunk
trunk

-unt   /unt/

bunt
hunt
punt
runt
blunt
grunt
stunt

-up   /up/

up
cup
pup

-urn   /ûrn/

burn
turn
churn

-urry /ûr' ē/

curry
furry
hurry
blurry
flurry
scurry

-us   /us/

us
bus
plus

-ush /ush/

hush
rush
blush
brush
crush

-ust   /ust/

bust
dust
gust
just
must
rust
crust
thrust
trust

-ut   /ut/

but
cut
hut
nut
rut
shut
strut

-ute / o͞ot/

lute
chute
flute

-y /ī/

by
my
cry
dry
fly
fry
pry
shy
sky
sly
spy
spry
try
why

Harcourt Brace School Publishers

Phonics Elements Lists

Consonant Sounds

B
Consonant Sound: / b / b

Initial

back
ball
barn
bear
bed
before
below
better
big
boy
bus
button
by

Medial

able
baby
cable
fable
labor
number
table

Final

club
crab
cub
grab
job
rib
rub
tub
verb

Consonant Sound: / b / bb

Medial

babble
bubble
nibble
pebble
rabbit
ribbon
rubber
scribble

C
Consonant Sound: / k / c

Initial

cake
call
camp
can
car
carry
cat
cold
color
come
corn
could
cow
cub
cup
cut

Final

electric
music
rustic

Consonant Sound: / k / ck

Final

back
black
clock
duck
kick
lock
pick
rock
stick
truck

Consonant Sound: / s / c

Initial

ceiling
celebrate
celery
cement
cent
center
cereal
circle
circus
city
cycle
cyclone

Final

face
fence
ice
mice
nice
once
practice
twice

D
Consonant Sound: / d / d

Initial

day
dear
December
deep
deer
desk
dig
dinosaur
dish
doctor
dog
doll
door
down

Medial

body
garden
idea
order
ready
shady
study
under

Final

and
did
end
find
food
good
had
hid
old
red
said
would

Consonant Sound: / d / dd

Medial

buddy
cuddle
daddy
fiddle
ladder
middle
paddle
pudding
puddle
saddle
waddle

Final

add
odd

F

Consonant Sound: / f / *f*

Initial

face
family
farm
father
February
few
fire
first
fish
five
follow
food
foot
fork
four
fox
Friday
funny

Medial

after
beautiful
before
careful
safety
wonderful

Final

beef
chief
grief
if
leaf
myself
roof
wolf

Consonant Sound: / f / *ff*

Medial

baffle
muffin
raffle
sniffle
traffic
truffle
waffle

Final

bluff
cliff
fluff
off
stiff
stuff

G

Consonant Sound: / g / *g*

Initial

game
garden
gas
gate
gave
get
gift
girl
give
go
goat
good
grade
great
gum
gust

Medial

again
ago
agree
begin
dragon
English
figure
magazine
sugar
wagon

Final

bag
big
bug
dig
dog
fig
flag
fog
frog
leg
log
pig

Consonant Sound: / g / *gg*

Medial

baggage
giggle
jogger
juggle
shaggy
struggle
wiggle

Final

egg

Consonant Sound: / j / *ge, dge*

Initial

gel
gem
general
genius
gentle
gerbil
germ

Final

age
badge
bridge
change
cottage
edge
fudge
huge
large
ledge
page
strange
village

Consonant Sound: / j / *gi, gy*

Initial

giant
ginger
giraffe
gym
gymnast
gypsy

Final

biology
clergy
energy

H

Consonant Sound: / h / *h*

Initial

hand
happy
he
help
hen
her
here
hero
hide
hill
hit
home
hook
horse
hose
house

J

Consonant Sound: / j / *j*

Initial

jacket
January
jar
jaw
jeep
jet
job
join
joke
joy
juice
July
jump
June
jungle

K

Consonant Sound: / k / k

Initial

kangaroo
keep
key
kick
kind
king
kiss
kitchen
kite
kitten

Final

bank
beak
break
cook
look
mark
milk
shook
speak
took
work

L

Consonant Sound: / l / l

Initial

ladder
lamp
land
large
last
late
law
leaf
leap
left
letter
light
like
line
lion
little
live
lock
log
long
look

Medial

along
always
belong
children
elbow
family
only
telephone

Final

April
bowl
girl
oil
owl
pool
school
towel
until
vowel

Consonant Sound: / l / ll

Medial

fellow
follow
gallon
hello
jelly
million
pillow
silly
wallet
yellow

Final

all
ball
bill
doll
full
hall
hill
sell
small
spell
spill
stall
still
tall
tell
wall
well
will

M

Consonant Sound: / m / m

Initial

made
mail
make
man
map
March
May
milk
mine
Monday
moon
more
most
mother
mouse

Medial

army
complete
family
lumber
number
tumble

Final

am
arm
bottom
farm
foam
form
from
him
room
seem
team
them
warm

Consonant Sound: / m / mb

Final

climb
comb
crumb
lamb
limb
numb
thumb

N

Consonant Sound: / n / n

Initial

nail
name
near
neck
need
nest
net
never
next
nice
night
nine
nose
November
now
number
nurse
nut

Medial

animal
any
country
inside
many
under
until

Final

an
been
can
even
fin
fun
hen
in
man
on
open
own
than
then
when

Harcourt Brace School Publishers

P

Consonant Sound: / p / p

Initial

pair
part
pass
pear
pen
pencil
person
pet
picture
piece
pin
pine
point
poor
pull
push

Medial

important
open
September
super
upon

Final

deep
dip
drop
group
help
jump
map
ship
sleep
step
stop
top
up

Consonant Sound: / p / pp

Medial

apple
copper
happy
pepper
puppy
upper
zipper

R

Consonant Sound: / r / r

Initial

rabbit
rain
rake
ram
ran
read
red
rest
ride
right
ring
rip
road
rock
room
rope
run

Consonant Sound: / r / rr

Medial

berry
carrot
carry
furry
horrible
mirror
scurry
sorry
terrible
worry

S

Consonant Sound: / s / s

Initial

sail
same
sand
Saturday
saw
sea
see
September
set
seven
side
six
soap
sock
soon
sound
sun
Sunday

Medial

also
beside
inside
person

Final

bus
gas
pants
socks
this
us
yes

Consonant Sound: / z / s

Final

as
days
does
flies
his
is
news
ours
says
was

Consonant Sound: / s / ss

Final

across
boss
class
cross
dress
grass
kiss
less
mess
miss
press

T

Consonant Sound: / t / t

Initial

table
take
talk
tame
tape
tell
ten
tent
tiger
time
toast
today
told
took
tool
top
toy
Tuesday
turtle
two

Medial

after
city
enter
hotel
into
later
meter
until
water

Final

at
foot
get
hit
it
not
out
part
past
put
set
want
what

Consonant Sound: / t / *tt*

Medial

attic
battle
better
bitter
cattle
cottage
kettle
kitten
lettuce
little
mitten
whittle

V
Consonant Sound: / v / *v*

Initial

van
vase
very
vest
vine
violin
visit
voice
vote

W
Consonant Sound: / w / *w*

Initial

wait
was
water
wave
way
web
Wednesday
week
well
win
window
wise
with
word
work
worm
would

X
Consonant Sound: / ks / *x*

Final

ax
box
fix
fox
mix
ox
relax
six
tax
wax

Y
Consonant Sound: / y / *y*

Initial

yam
yard
yarn
yawn
year
yell
yellow
yes
you
young
your

Z
Consonant Sound: / z / *z*

Initial

zebra
zero
zing
zip
zipper
zone
zoo
zoom

Final

quiz

Consonant Sound: / z / *zz*

Medial

buzzard
drizzle
fizzle
fuzzy
muzzle
nuzzle
puzzle

Final

buzz
fizz
fuzz
jazz

CONSONANT CLUSTERS

B

Consonant Cluster: / bl / bl

Initial

black
blew
blimp
blink
block
blood
blow
blue

Consonant Cluster: / br / br

Initial

brag
brain
brave
bread
break
brick
bridge
bring
broom
brown

C

Consonant Cluster: / cl / cl

Initial

clam
clap
class
clay
clean
clear
climb
clip
clock
cloth
cloud
clown
club
clue

Consonant Cluster: / cr / cr

Initial

crab
crack
crash
crayon
cream
creek
crops
cross
crow
crowd
crown
cry

D

Consonant Cluster: / dr / dr

Initial

draw
dream
dress
drew
drink
drip
drive
drop
drove
drum
dry

F

Consonant Cluster: / fl / fl

Initial

flag
flame
flap
flat
flea
flew
flight
flip
float
flock
floor
flower
fly

Consonant Cluster: / fr / fr

Initial

France
free
freedom
fresh
Friday
friend
frog
from
front
frost
frown
fruit
fry

Consonant Cluster: / ft / ft

Final

craft
gift
left
lift
loft
raft
rift
sift
soft
swift

G

Consonant Cluster: / gl / gl

Initial

glad
glare
glass
gleam
glitter
globe
glove
glue

Consonant Cluster: / gr / gr

Initial

grab
grade
grand
grape
grass
gray
great
green
grew
grin
ground
grow

L

Consonant Cluster: / ld / ld

Final

build
cold
fold
gold
mold
scold
sold
told

Consonant Cluster: / lk / lk

Final

chalk
milk
silk
talk
walk
yolk

Consonant Cluster: / lt / lt

Final

belt
built
felt
kilt
knelt
melt
quilt
salt
wilt

M

Consonant Cluster: / mp / mp

Final

blimp
bump
camp
champ
clamp
damp
dump
jump
lamp
limp
pump

ramp
shrimp
stamp
stump

N

Consonant Cluster: / nd / *nd*

Final

and
band
bend
find
found
friend
ground
hand
kind
land
lend
mend
mind
pond
round
sand
send
sound
tend

Consonant Cluster: / nt / *nt*

Final

ant
aunt
bent
hint
hunt
lint
mint
plant
sent
slant
tent
tint
went

P

Consonant Cluster: / pl / *pl*

Initial

place
plan
plane

planet
plant
plate
play
please
plow
plug
plum
plus

Consonant Cluster: / pr / *pr*

Initial

practice
present
president
press
pretty
price
print
prize

S

Consonant Cluster: / sk / *sc*

Initial

scale
scare
scarf
scoop
score
scout

Consonant Cluster: / s / *sc*

Initial

scene
science
scissors

Consonant Cluster: / skr / *scr*

Initial

scramble
scrap
scrape
scratch
scream
screech
screen
scribble
scrub

Consonant Cluster: / shr / *shr*

Initial

shred
shriek
shrimp
shrink
shrub

Consonant Cluster: / sk / *sk*

Initial

skate
sketch
ski
skid
skill
skin
skip
skirt
skunk
sky

Final

ask
desk
disk
dusk
mask
risk
task

Consonant Cluster: / sl / *sl*

Initial

slam
sled
sleep
sleet
sleeve
slid
slide
slight
slim
slow

Consonant Cluster: / sm / *sm*

Initial

small
smart

smash
smell
smile
smock
smoke
smooth

Consonant Cluster: / sn / *sn*

Initial

snack
snail
snake
snap
sneakers
sneeze
sniff
snip
snore
snow
snug

Consonant Cluster: / sp / *sp*

Initial

spark
speak
special
speed
spend
spider
spill
spin
spoke
spoon
sport
spot

Final

clasp
crisp
gasp
grasp
wasp

Consonant Cluster: / spr / *spr*

Initial

spray
spring
sprinkle
sprout
spry

Consonant Cluster: / skw / *squ*

Initial

squall
square
squash
squeak
squeeze
squid
squint
squirm
squirrel

Consonant Cluster: / st / *st*

Initial

stamp
stand
star
state
stay
steam
steep
steer
stem
step
stick
still
stood
stop
store
story
study

Final

best
cast
crust
dust
east
fast
just
least
list
lost
mast
mist
most
must
nest
past
rest
rust

toast
vest
west

Consonant Cluster: / str / *str*

Initial

strap
straw
stream
street
stretch
stride
strike
string
struggle

Consonant Cluster: / sw / *sw*

Initial

swan
sway
sweater
sweep
sweet
swell
swept
swift
swim
swing
swirl
switch
swoop

T

Consonant Cluster: / tw / *tw*

Initial

twelve
twenty
twice
twig
twine
twinkle
twins
twirl
twist

DIGRAPHS

C

Digraph: / ch / *ch*

Initial

chain
chalk
chance
change
chart
chase
check
cheer
cheese
chest
chief
children
chin

Final

beach
branch
each
inch
lunch
much
peach
ranch
reach
rich
such
teach
touch
which

Digraph: / ch / *tch*

Final

catch
ditch
hatch
itch
match
patch
pitch
scratch
stitch
stretch
switch
watch

G

Digraph: / f / *gh*

Final

cough
enough
laugh
rough
tough

Digraph: / n / *gn*

Initial

gnat
gnaw
gnu

K

Digraph: / n / *kn*

Initial

knead
knee
knew
knife
knight
knit
knob
knock
knot
know
knuckle

N

Digraph: / ng / *ng*

Final

among
bring
hang
king
long
ring
sing
song
spring
string
strong
thing
wing
wrong
young

Digraph: / ngk / *nk*

Final

bank
blink
chunk
drink
honk
ink
link
pink
rink
sank
sink
thank
think
trunk
wink

P

Digraph: / f / *ph*

Initial

pheasant
phone
photo

Medial

alphabet
biography
elephant
gopher
nephew
telephone

Final

autograph
graph
paragraph
photograph

Q

Digraph: / kw / *qu*

Initial

quack
quart
quarter
queen
question
quick
quiet
quill
quilt
quit
quite
quiz

S

Digraph: / sh / *sh*

Initial

shade
shadow
shape
share
she
sheep
shell
shine
ship
shirt
shock
shoe
shop
short
shout
shovel
show
shy

Final

ash
brush
bush
crash
dish
finish
fish
flash
fresh
leash
push
rush
splash
wash
wish

T

Digraph: / th / *th* (unvoiced)

Initial

thank
thick
thimble
thin
thing
think
third
thirteen
thirty
thorn
thought
thumb
thunder

Final

bath
both
cloth
earth
fifth
health
moth
mouth
ninth
north
path
south
teeth
tooth
truth
with
worth
wreath

Digraph: / th / *th* (voiced)

Initial

than
that
the
their
them
then
there
these
they
this
though

Final

smooth

W

Digraph: / hw / *wh*

Initial

whale
what
wheat
wheel
when
where
whether
which
while
whisker
whisper
whistle
white
why

Digraph: / r / *wr*

Initial

wrap
wreath
wreck
wren
wrench
wring
wrinkle
wrist
write
wrong
wrote

Harcourt Brace School Publishers

SHORT VOWELS

Short Vowel: / a / *a*

Initial

act
add
after
am
and
apple
ask
at
ax

Medial

back
bag
bat
black
can
cat
fan
fast
flag
had
hand
has
last
man
map
pan
plant
stand
that

Short Vowel: / e / *e*

Initial

echo
egg
elephant
empty
end
enter
ever
exit

Medial

bed
desk
dress
get
help
hen
jet
left
men
nest
next
pen
red
shell
sled
spell
then
web
went
wet
when

Short Vowel: / e / *ea*

Medial

ahead
bread
breath
dead
feather
head
heavy
instead
ready
spread
steady
sweat
thread
weather

Short Vowel: / i / *i*

Initial

if
in
inch
India
insect
inside
into
is
it

Medial

big
chin
city
crib
dig
fin
him
his
kick
little
miss
pig
pin
ship
sit
six
thin
this
wig
win

Short Vowel: / o / *o*

Initial

oblong
October
octopus
odd
olive
otter
ox

Medial

body
box
clock
copy
drop
fox
frog
got
hob
hot
lock
mop
not
pot
rock
sock
stop
top

Short Vowel: / u / *u*

Initial

ugly
umbrella
uncle
under
up
upon
upset
us

Medial

bus
but
cut
drum
duck
dug
fun
gum
hug
hundred
hunt
jump
just
much
must
number
run
study
summer
sun
truck
tub

Short Vowel: / u / *ou*

Medial

country
couple
cousin
double
enough
rough
touch
tough
trouble
young

LONG VOWELS

Long Vowel: / ā / a-e

age
ape
ate
cage
came
cane
face
frame
game
gate
gave
grape
lake
late
made
make
name
place
plate
rake
same
shape
skate
space
state
tale
tape
wave

Long Vowel: / ā / ai

braid
brain
chain
jail
nail
pail
pain
paint
plain
rain
sail
snail
tail
train
wait

Long Vowel: / ā / ay

away
bay
clay
day
gray
hay
may
pay
play
say
stay
tray
way

Long Vowel: / ā / ea

break
great
steak

Long Vowel: / ā / ei (gh)

eight
freight
neighbor
sleigh
weigh
weight

Long Vowel: / ē / e

be
Egypt
equal
even
he
maybe
me
secret
she
we
zebra

Long Vowel: / ē / ea

beach
bead
beat
clean
dream
each
eagle
east
easy
eat
flea
heat
jeans
leaf
least
meal
meat
neat
pea
peach
peanut
read
sea
seal
tea
team
weak

Long Vowel: / ē / ee

agree
bee
eel
eerie
feel
feet
flee
free
green
heel
keep
knee
peel
queen
screen
see
sleep
street
teeth
three
tree
week
wheel

Long Vowel: / ē / ie

believe
chief
field
grief
shield
thief

Long Vowel: / ē / ey

donkey
honey
journey
key
money
monkey
turkey

Long Vowel: / ē / y

any
baby
body
city
country
early
easy
every
family
funny
happy
lady
many
only
pretty
ready
really
story
study
very

Long Vowel: / ī / i

child
find
kind
mild
mind
rind
spider
tiny
wild

Long Vowel: / ī / ie

lie
pie
tie

Long Vowel: / ī / i-e

bike
bite
bride
dive
drive
fire

five
glide
hive
ice
kite
life
like
line
mice
mile
mine
nice
nine
pine
ride
shine
side
size
slide
tide
vine
white
wide
wife
wire
write

Long Vowel: / ī / igh

fight
high
light
might
night
right
sight
tight
bright
flight
fright
slight

Long Vowel: / ī / y

by
cry
cycle
dry
fly
fry
July
my
shy
sky
why

Long Vowel: / ō / o

ago
also
cold
fold
go
gold
hello
hero
hold
no
obey
ocean
odor
Ohio
open
over
piano
potato
radio
so
soda
sofa
sold
told
total
zero

Long Vowel: / ō / oa

boat
coach
coal
coast
coat
float
goal
goat
load
loaf
loan
oak
oat
oatmeal
road
roast
soak
soap
throat
toad

Long Vowel: / ō / o-e

bone
broke
cone

drove
hole
home
hope
joke
nose
note
phone
pole
robe
rope
rose
smoke
stone
stove
those
vote
zone

Long Vowel: / ō / ow

arrow
blow
borrow
bow
crow
flow
follow
glow
grow
know
low
mow
owe
own
owner
row
show
slow
snow
throw
window
yellow

Long Vowel: / yōō / u-e

cube
cute
excuse
fume
fuse
huge
mule
perfume
use

R-CONTROLLED VOWELS

R-Controlled Vowel: / âr / air

Final

air
chair
fair
flair
hair
lair
pair
stair

R-Controlled Vowel: / âr / are

Final

care
dare
flare
glare
hare
rare
scare
share
snare
spare
square
stare

R-Controlled Vowel: / âr / ear

Final

bear
pear
tear
wear

R-Controlled Vowel: / är / ar

Initial

arm
army
art
artist

Medial

bark
barn
card
cart
chart

dark
dart
farm
garden
hard
large
marble
March
mark
Mars
park
part
party
scarf
shark
sharp
smart
spark
start
yard
yarn

Final

bar
car
far
jar
scar
tar

R-Controlled Vowel: / ir / *ear*

Final

clear
dear
ear
fear
gear
hear
near
rear
tear
year

R-Controlled Vowel: / ir / *eer*

Final

cheer
deer
jeer
peer
sheer
steer

R-Controlled Vowel: / ôr / *oar*

Final

boar
roar
soar

R-Controlled Vowel: / ôr / *oor*

Final

door
floor
poor

R-Controlled Vowel: / ôr / *or*

Initial

or
orbit
orchard
orchestra
order
organ

Medial

born
corn
corner
forest
fork
form
forty
horn
horse
morning
porch
port
short
sort
sport
storm
story
thorn
torn
worn

R-Controlled Vowel: / ôr / *ore*

Final

before
bore
chore

core
explore
more
score
shore
store
tore
wore

R-Controlled Vowel: / ôr / *our*

Final

four
pour
your

R-Controlled Vowel: / ûr / *ear*

Initial

early
earn
earth

Medial

heard
learn
search

R-Controlled Vowel: / ûr / *er*

Medial

clerk
fern
gerbil
herd
hermit
perch
perfect
person
serve
stern
verse

R-Controlled Vowel: / ûr / *ir*

Medial

bird
birthday
circle
circus
dirt
dirty
first

girl
shirt
skirt
third
thirsty
thirty

Final

fir
sir
stir
whir

R-Controlled Vowel: / ûr / *ur*

Medial

burn
burst
church
curb
curl
curve
hurry
hurt
nurse
purple
purse
Thursday
turkey
turn
turtle

Final

fur
occur

VOWEL DIPHTHONGS

Vowel Diphthong: / ou / *ou*

Initial

ounce
our
out
outline
outside

Medial

about
aloud
amount
around
cloud
count
county
found
ground
hour
house
mountain
mouse
round
scout
shout
sound

Vowel Diphthong: / ou / *ow*

Medial

brown
clown
crowd
crown
down
flower
power
town
vowel

Final

allow
brow
cow
how
now
plow

Vowel Diphthong: / oi / *oi*

Initial

oil
oink

Medial

boil
broil
choice
coin
join
moist
noise
point
soil
spoil
voice

Vowel Diphthong: / oi / *oy*

Medial

loyal
royal
voyage

Final

annoy
boy
employ
enjoy
joy
soy
toy

VOWEL VARIANTS

Vowel Variant: / ô / *au(gh)*

Medial

because
caught
cause
daughter
fault
haul
launch
taught

Vowel Variant: / ô / *aw*

Medial

crawl
dawn
drawn
fawn
hawk
lawn
yawn

Final

claw
draw
jaw
law
paw
raw
saw
straw

Vowel Variant: / ô / *ou(gh)*

Initial

ought

Medial

bought
brought
cough
fought
sought
thought

Vowel Variant: / ŏŏ / *oo*

Medial

book
brook
cook
cookie
foot
good
hook
look
shook
stood
took
wood

Vowel Variant: / ŏŏ / *ou*

Medial

could
should
would

Vowel Variant: / ōō / *ew*

Final

blew
crew
drew
grew
new
stew

Vowel Variant: / ōō / *oo*

Medial

balloon
boot
cool
food
fool
goose
loose
mood
moon
noon
pool
roof
room
school
shoot
smooth

smooth
soon
tool
tooth

Final

igloo
kangaroo
moo
shampoo
too
zoo

Vowel Variant: / $\overline{oo}$ / *ou*

Medial

group
soup
through
toucan

Vowel Variant: / $\overline{oo}$ / *ue*

Final

blue
clue
flue
glue
true

Vowel Variant: / $\overline{oo}$ / *ui*

Medial

fruit
juice
suit

SCHWA
Schwa: / ə / *a*

Initial

again
ago
agree
ahead
alike
alive
alone
away

Schwa: / əl / *le*

Final

angle
apple
bubble
castle
fable
gable
little
marble
middle
purple
table

Schwa: / ər / *er*

Final

baker
center
gopher
maker
never
number
teacher
water

High-Frequency Word Lists

The words on the following lists appear with high frequency in children's reading. They are mainly words from Edward Dolch's list of 220 high-frequency words, supplemented with words from a list compiled by Harris-Jacobson and another by Dale Johnson.

GRADE 1 HIGH-FREQUENCY WORDS

a	he	please
all	her	put
and	here	said
are	his	say
asked	hop	see
be	I	she
because	I'm	so
but	if	that
can	in	the
come	is	then
dad	isn't	there
did	it	they
do	it's	this
does	like	to
doesn't	little	too
don't	me	was
find	mom	we
for	my	were
get	no	what
go	not	will
got	now	with
great	of	would
had	once	you
has	one	your
have	or	

all	I'll	see
another	I'm	some
because	it's	sure
been	like	the
both	many	their
by	·more	there
come	my	these
could	now	they
do	of	to
does	off	was
doesn't	once	were
done	one	what
don't	only	where
for	or	which
found	out	who
give	people	why
have	put	won't
her	said	would
here	says	you
how	school	you're

all	it's	the
are	like	their
because	me	there
come	my	they
do	now	thought
does	of	to
don't	once	too
find	one	use
for	or	was
have	our	were
her	out	what
I'll	people	which
if	said	whose
into	says	you
is	some	your

Professional Bookshelf

Adams, Marilyn J. (1990). *Beginning to Read: Thinking and Learning About Print.* Cambridge, MA: MIT Press.

Allington, R., & Walmsley, S. (eds.) (1995). *No Quick Fix: Rethinking Literacy Programs in America's Elementary Schools.* New York: Teachers College Press.

Anderson, Richard; Hiebert, E.; Scott, J.; & Wilkerson, I. (1985). *Becoming a Nation of Readers.* Washington, D.C.: National Institute of Education.

Ball, E., & Blachman, B. (1988). Phoneme segmentation training: Effect on reading readiness. *Annals of Dyslexia,* 38, 208-225.

Ball, E., & Blachman, B. (1991). Does phoneme awareness training in kindergarten make a difference in early word recognition and developmental spelling? *Reading Research Quarterly,* 26(1) 49-66.

Baskwill, J., & Whitman, P. (1988). *Evaluation: Whole language, whole child.* Toronto: Scholastic.

Bean, Wendy, & Bouffler, Chrystine. (1988). *Spell by Writing.* Portsmouth, NH: Heinemann.

Bear, D. (1991). Learning to fasten the seat of my union suit without looking around: The synchrony of literacy development. *Theory Into Practice,* 30(3), 149-157.

Bear, D.; Invernizzi, M.; Johnston, F.; & Templeton, S. (1996). *Words Their Way: Word Study for Phonics, Vocabulary, and Spelling Instruction.* Englewood Cliffs, NJ: Merrill.

Bear, D.B.; Invernizzi, M.; & Templeton, S. (1995). *Words Their Way: A Developmental Approach to Phonics, Spelling, and Vocabulary, K-8.* New York: Macmillan/Merrill.

Beck, Isabel, & Juel, Connie. (1992). The role of decoding in learning to read. *What Research Has To Say about Reading Instruction.* Newark, Delaware: International Reading Association.

Beers, J.W.; Beers, C.S.; & Grant, K. (1977). The logic behind children's spelling. *The Elementary School Journal,* 77(3), 238-242.

Behm, M., & Behm, R. (1989). *Ideas for Parents to Encourage Reading and Writing: 101 Ideas to Help Your Child Learn to Read and Write.* ERIC (booklet).

Binkley, M. (1988). *Becoming a Nation of Readers: What Parents Can Do.* ERIC.

Bissex, G. (1980). *GNYS at Work: A Child Learns to Write and Read.* Cambridge, MA: Harvard University Press.

Blachman, B. (1991). *Getting Ready to Read: Learning How Print Maps to Speech.* Washington, D.C.: U.S. Department of Health and Human Services.

Bradley, L., & Bryant, P. (1985). *Rhyme and Reason in Reading and Spelling.* Ann Arbor, MI: University of Michigan Press.

Bradley, L., & Bryant, P. (1983). Categorizing sounds and learning to read—A causal connection. *Nature,* 301, 419-421.

Buchoff, R. (1996). Riddles: Fun with language across the curriculum. *The Reading Teacher,* 49(8), 666-668.

Burriss, W. *Storytelling: An Art for All.* ERIC (Special Collection #4), 59-61.

Butler, A., & Turbill, J. (1987). *Towards a Reading-Writing Classroom.* Portsmouth, NH: Heinemann.

Button, K.; Johnson, M.; & Furgerson, P. (1996). Interactive writing in a primary classroom. *The Reading Teacher,* 49(6), 446-454.

Calfee, R. (1991). *Schoolwide Programs to Improve Literacy Instruction for Students At Risk.* Washington, DC: U.S. Department of Education: Office of Planning, Budget, and Evaluation.

California Department of Education (1992). *A Plan for More Parental Involvement in Education: California Strategic Plan.* Sacramento, CA: California Department of Education.

Cambourne, B. (1988). *The Whole Story: Natural Learning and the Acquisition of Literacy in the Classroom.* New York: Ashton Scholastic.

Carbo, M. (1996). Whole language or phonics? Use both! *Education Digest,* Feb., 60-63.

Center, Y.; Wheldall, K.; Freeman, L.; Outhred, L.; & McNaught, M. (1995). An evaluation of reading recovery. *Reading Research Quarterly,* 30(2), 240-263.

Chall, J. (1989). Learning to read: The great debate 20 years later/A response to 'Debunking the great phonics myth.' *Phi Delta Kappan,* 70(7), 521-538.

Chall, J. (1987). *Stages of Reading Development.* New York: McGraw-Hill.

Clark, Reginald (1988). *Critical Factors in Why Disadvantaged Students Succeed or Fail in School.* Washington, DC: Academy for Educational Development.

Clark, H.H., & Clark, E.V. (1977). *Psychology and Language.* New York: Harcourt Brace Jovanovich.

Clarke, L.K. (1988). Invented versus traditional spelling in first graders' writings: Effects on learning to spell and read. *Research in the Teaching of English,* 22(3), 281-309.

Clay, Marie (1994). *Becoming Literate: The Construction of Inner Control.* Portsmouth, NH: Heinemann.

Clay, M. (1985). *The Early Detection of Reading Difficulties* (3rd ed.). Portsmouth, NH: Heinemann.

Clay, M. (1983). *An Observation Survey of Early Literacy Achievement.* Portsmouth, NH: Heinemann.

Clay, M. (1993). *Reading Recovery: A Guidebook for Teachers in Training.* Portsmouth, NH: Heinemann.

Clements, N., & Warncke, E. (1994). Helping literacy emerge at school for less-advantaged children. *Young Children,* 49(3), 22-26.

Clymer, T. (1963). The utility of phonic generalizations in the primary grades. *The Reading Teacher,* 16, 252-258.

Cunningham, A.E. (1990). Explicit versus implicit instruction in phonemic awareness. *Journal of Experimental Child Psychology,* 50, 429-444.

Cunningham, P., & Cunningham, J. (1992). Making words: Enhancing the invented spelling–decoding connection. *The Reading Teacher,* 46(2), 106-115.

Cunningham, P. (1991). *Phonics They Use: Words for Reading and Writing.* New York: HarperCollins.

Cunningham, P. (1991). Research directions: Multi-method, multilevel literacy instruction in first grade. *Language Arts,* 68 (7), 578-584.

Cunningham, P., & Hall, D.P. (1994). *Making Big Words.* Good Apple.

DeFord, D.; Lyons, C.; & Pinnell, G.S. (eds.) (1991). *Bridges to Literacy: Learning from Reading Recovery.* Portsmouth, NH: Heinemann.

Dyson, A.H. (1982). Reading, writing, and language: Young children solving the written language puzzle. *Language Arts,* 59(8), 829-839.

Ehri, L. (1984). The development of spelling knowledge and its role in reading acquisition and reading disability. *Journal of Learning Disabilities,* 22, 356-365.

Ehri, L.C., et al. (1987). Children's categorization of short vowels in words and the influence of spellings. *Merrill-Palmer Quarterly,* 33(3), 393-421.

Ehri, L.C., & Wilce, L.S. (1987). Does learning to spell help beginners learn to read words? *Reading Research Quarterly,* 22(1), 47-65.

Flood, J., et al. (eds.) (1991). Handbook of research on teaching English. *Language Arts,* 721-731. New York: Macmillan.

Freppon, P., & Dahl, K. (1991). Learning about phonics in a whole language classroom. *Language Arts,* 68(3), 190-197.

Fry, E.; Fountoukidis, D.L.; & Polk, J.L. (1995). *The New Reading Teacher's Book of Lists.* Englewood Cliffs, NJ: Prentice-Hall.

Galda, Lee; Strickland, Dorothy; & Cullinan, Bernice (1997). *Language, Literacy, and the Child.* 2nd Edition. Harcourt Brace College Publishers.

Gaskins, I.W.; Downer, M.A.; Anderson, R.C.; Cunningham, P. M.; Gaskins, R.W.; Schommer, M.; & The Teachers of Benchmark School (1988). A metacognitive approach to phonics: Using what you know to decode what you don't know. *Remedial and Special Education,* 9, 36-41.

Geller, L. G. (1982a). Grasp of meaning: Theory into practice. *Language Arts,* 59, 571-579.

Geller, L. G. (1982b). Linguistic consciousness-raising: Child's play. *Language Arts,* 59, 120-125.

Geller, L. G. (1983). Children's rhymes and literacy learning: Making connections. *Language Arts,* 60, 184-193.

Gentry, J.R., & Gillet, J. (1983). *Teaching Kids to Spell.* Portsmouth, NH: Heinemann.

Gentry, Richard (1982). An analysis of developmental spelling in GNYS AT WRK. *The Reading Teacher,* 36(2), 192-200.

Giacobbe, Mary Ellen (1991). Kids can write the first week of school. *Learning,* 10, 130-132.

Goodman, K. (1993). *Phonics Phacts.* Portsmouth, NH: Heinemann.

Goodman, Y. (ed.) (1990). *How Children Construct Literacy: Piagetian Perspectives.* Newark, DE: International Reading Association.

Goodman, Y., & Haussler, M. (1984). *Resources for Involving Parents in Literacy Development.* ERIC.

Griffith, P.L.; Klesius, J.P.; & Kromrey, J.D. (1992). The effect of phonemic awareness on the literacy development of first grade children in a traditional or a whole language classroom. *Journal of Research in Childhood Education,* 6, 86-92.

Griffith, P., & Olson, M. (1992). Phonemic awareness helps beginning readers break the code. *The Reading Teacher,* 45(7), 516-523.

Grinnell, P. (1984). *How Can I Prepare My Young Child for Reading?* International Reading Association (booklet).

Grossen, B., & Carnine, D. (1990). Translating research on initial reading instruction into classroom practice. *Interchange,* 21(4), 15-23.

Gunning, T. (1995). Word building: A strategic approach to the teaching of phonics. *The Reading Teacher,* 48(6), 484-488.

Guszak, F. J. (1992). *Reading for Students with Special Needs.* Dubuque, IA: Kendall/Hunt.

Hall, Nigel (1987). *The Emergence of Literacy.* Portsmouth, NH: Heinemann.

Harp, Bill. (1993). Bringing children to literacy through integrated basic skills instruction. *Bringing Children to Literacy: Classrooms at Work.* Norwood, MA: Christopher-Gordon Publishers.

Harris, Sharon (1986). Evaluation of a curriculum to support literacy growth in young children. *Early Childhood Research Quarterly,* 1(4), 333-348.

Harste, J.C.; Short, K.G.; & Burke, C.L. (1988). *Creating Classrooms for Authors: The Reading-Writing Connection.* Portsmouth, NH: Heinemann.

Harste, J.C.; Woodward, V.A.; & Burke, C.L. (1988). *Language Stories and Literacy Lessons.* Portsmouth, NH: Heinemann.

Heald-Taylor, B. Gail (1984). Scribble in first grade writing. *The Reading Teacher,* 38(1) 4-8.

Heibert, Elfrieda H. (1991). Research directions: The development of word-level strategies in authentic literacy tasks. *Language Arts,* 68(3), 234-240.

Henderson, E. (1981). *Learning to Read and Spell: The Child's Knowledge of Words.* DeKalb, IL: Northern Illinois Press.

Heymsfeld, C.R. (1989). Filling the hole in whole language. *Educational Leadership,* 46(6), 65-68.

Hills, J.R. (1981). *Measurement and Evaluation in the Classroom (2nd ed.).* Columbus, OH: Charles E. Merrill.

Hindley, Joanne (1996). *In the Company of Children.* Stenhouse Publishers.

Holdaway, D. (1979). *The Foundations of Literacy.* Portsmouth, NH: Heinemann.

Holdaway, D. (1982). Shared book experience: Teaching reading using favorite books. *Theory Into Practice,* 21(4), 293-300.

Holdaway, D. (1982). *Independence in Reading,* 3rd ed. Portsmouth, NH: Heinemann.

Jensen, A.R. (1980). *Bias in Mental Testing.* New York: Free Press.

Johns, J.L. (1991). Helping readers at risk: Beyond whole language, whole word, and phonics. *Journal of Reading, Writing, and Learning Disabilities International,* 7(1), 59–67.

Johns, J.L., & Schlesinger, J. *Reading Aloud to Students.* ERIC (Special Collection #4), 39–41.

Joslin, H.K. (1994). *A Comparison of the Effects of Pure and Modified Whole Language Instruction on the Decoding Skills of Kindergartners.* ERIC, 372–367.

Juel, C. (1988). Learning to read and write: A longitudinal study of 54 children from first through fourth grades. *Journal of Educational Psychology,* 80, 437–447.

Juel, C., & Leavell, J. A. (1988). Retention and nonretention of at-risk readers in first grade and their subsequent reading achievement. *Journal of Learning Disabilities,* 21, 571–580.

Kress, J. (1993). *The ESL Teacher's Book of Lists.* Englewood Cliffs, NJ: Prentice-Hall.

Liberman, I.Y.; Shankweiler, D.; Fischer, F. W.; & Carter, B. (1974). Explicit syllable and phoneme segmentation in the young child. *Journal of Experimental Child Psychology,* 18, 201–212.

Lie, A. (1991). Effects of training program for stimulating skills in word analysis in first-grade children. *Reading Research Quarterly,* 23, 263–284.

Londergan, G. *Helping Parents Understand the Stages of Their Child's Reading Development.* ERIC (Special Collection #4), 35–37.

Ludberg, I.; Frost, J.; & Petersen, O. (1988). Effects of an extensive program for stimulating phonological awareness in preschool children. *Reading Research Quarterly,* 23, 263–284.

Martinez, M., & Roser, N. (1985). Read it again: The value of repeated readings during storytime. *The Reading Teacher,* 38(8), 782–786.

Matson, B. (1996). Whole language or phonics? Teachers and researchers find the middle ground most fertile. *The Harvard Education Letter,* 12(2), 1–5.

Mattingly, I. (1984). Reading, linguistic awareness, and language acquisition. In J. Downing & R. Caltin (Eds.), *Language Awareness and Learning to Read,* 9–25. New York: Springer-Verlag.

McCracken, R., & McCracken, M. (1988). *Songs, Stories, and Poetry to Teach Reading and Writing.* Manitoba, Canada: Peguis.

McCracken, M., & McCracken, R. (1996). *Spelling Through Phonics* (2nd ed.). Winnipeg, Canada: Peguis.

Mills, H.; O'Keefe, T.; & Stephens, D. (1992). *Looking Closely: Exploring the Role of Phonics in One Whole Language Classroom.* Urbana, IL: National Council of Teachers of English.

Mooney, M.E. (1990). *Reading to, with, and by Children.* Katonah, NY: Richard C. Owen Publishers.

Morris, D. (1992). *Case Studies in Teaching Beginning Readers: The Howard Street Tutoring Manual.* Boone, NC: Stream Publications.

Morris, D. (1993). Concept of word and phoneme awareness in the beginning reader. *Research in the Teaching of English,* 17(3), 359–373.

Perfetti, C.; Beck, I.; Bell, L.; & Hughes, C. (1987). Phonemic knowledge and learning to read are reciprocal: A longitudinal study of first-grade children. *Merrill-Palmer Quarterly,* 33, 283–319.

Peterson, B. (1988). *Characteristics of Texts That Support Beginning Readers.* Ann Arbor, MI: University Microfilms.

Phenix, Jo (1994). *Teaching the Skills.* Markham, Ontario: Pembroke.

Pinnell, G.S. (1990). Success for low achievers through reading recovery. *Educational Leadership,* 48(1), 17–21.

Powell, D., & Hornsby, D. (1993). *Learning Phonics and Spelling in a Whole Language Classroom.* New York: Scholastic.

Radencich, M.C., & McKay, L.J. (Eds.) (1995). *Flexible Grouping for Literacy in the Elementary Grades.* Boston: Allyn & Bacon.

Richgels, D.; Poremba, K.; & McGee, L. (1996). Kindergartners talk about print: Phonemic awareness in meaningful contexts. *The Reading Teacher,* 49(8), 632–642.

Roser, N. (1989). *Helping Your Child Become a Reader.* International Reading Association (booklet).

Roser, N. (1992). Language charts: A record of story time talk. *Language Arts,* 69(1), 44–52.

Roser, N.; Hoffman, J.; & Farest, C. (1990). Language, literature, and at-risk children. *The Reading Teacher,* 43(8), 554–559.

Roser, Nancy L., & Martinez, Miriam G. (1995). *Book Talk and Beyond.* International Reading Association.

Routman, R. (1994). *Invitations: Changing as Teachers and Learners K/12* (rev. ed.). Portsmouth, NH: Heinemann.

Routman, R. (1996). *Literacy at the Crossroads: Crucial Talk About Reading, Writing, and Other Teaching Dilemmas.* Portsmouth, NH: Heinemann.

Routman, R. (1992). Teach skills with a strategy. *Instructor,* 101(9), 34–37.

Routman, R., & Butler, A. (ed.) (1995). Why talk about phonics? *School Talk,* 1(2), 1–6.

Samuels, S. Jay. (1988) Decoding and automaticity: Helping poor readers become automatic at word recognition. *The Reading Teacher,* 41(8), 756–760.

Schickedanz, J. (1990). *More Than the ABCs: The Early Stages of Reading and Writing.* Washington, DC: NAEYC.

Schmidt, Barbara, et al. (1993). *What Good Teachers Do to Help Literacy Happen: From A to Z: A Practical Handbook of Strategies for Success.* Costa Mesa, CA: The California Reading Association, Inc.

Share, D.; Jorm, A.; Maclean, R.; & Matthews, R. (1984). Sources of individual differences in reading acquisition. *Journal of Educational Psychology,* 76, 1309–1324.

Silberman, A. (1991). *Growing Up Writing: Teaching Our Children to Write, Think and Learn.* Portsmouth, NH: Heinemann.

Slaughter, J.P. (1993). *Beyond Storybooks: Young Children and the Shared Book Experience.* Newark, DE: International Reading Association.

Smith, F. (1992). Learning to read: The never-ending debate. *Phi Delta Kappan,* 73(6), 432-435, 438-441.

Snider, V. (1990). Direct instruction reading with average first graders. *Reading Improvement,* 27(2), 143-148.

Sowers, Susan (1988). Six questions teachers ask about invented spelling. *Understanding Writing: Ways of Observing, Learning, and Teaching* 2nd ed. Portsmouth, NH: Heinemann, 62-79.

Spector, J. E. (1992). Predicting progress in beginning reading: Dynamic assessment of phonemic awareness. *Journal of Educational Psychology,* 84, 353-363.

Spiegel, D. (1992). Blending whole language and systematic direct instruction. *The Reading Teacher,* 46(1), 38-44.

Stahl, S. A. (1992). Saying the "p" word: Nine guidelines for exemplary phonics instruction. *The Reading Teacher,* 45(8), 618-625.

Stahl, S.; Mckenna, M.; & Pagnucco, J. (1993). The effects of whole language instruction: An update and a reappraisal. Presented at the Annual Meeting of the National Reading Conference (43, Charleston, SC, December 1-4, 1993).

Stahl, S.; Osborn, J.; & Lehr, F. (1990). *Beginning to Read: Thinking and Learning About Print: A Summary.* Champaign, IL: Center for the Study of Reading, University of Illinois at Urbana-Champaign.

Stanovich, K. E. (1986). Matthew effects in reading: Some consequences of individual differences in the acquisition of literacy. *Reading Research Quarterly,* 21, 360-407.

Stanovich, K. E. (1994). Romance and reality. *The Reading Teacher,* 47(4), 280-291.

Strickland, D. (1990). Emergent literacy: How young children learn to read and write. *Educational Leadership,* 47(6), 18-23.

Strickland, D. (1994/95). Reinventing our literacy programs: Books, basics, balance. *The Reading Teacher,* 48(4), 294-302.

Strickland, D., & Morrow, L. (eds.) (1989). *Emerging Literacy: Young Children Learn to Read and Write.* Newark, DE: International Reading Association.

Sulzby, E. (1991). Assessment of emergent literacy: Storybook reading. *The Reading Teacher,* 44 (7), 498-500.

Taylor, D., & Strickland, D. (1986). *Family Storybook Reading.* Portsmouth, NH: Heinemann.

Teale, W.H. (1988). Developmentally appropriate assessment of reading and writing in the early childhood classroom. *The Elementary School Journal,* 89(2), 173-183.

Teale, W., & Sulzby, E. (eds.) (1986). *Emergent Literacy: Writing and Reading.* Norwood, NJ: Ablex Publishing Corp.

Temple, C., et al. (1993). *The Beginnings of Writing* (3rd ed.). Boston, MA: Allyn and Bacon.

Templeton, S. (1976). The spelling of young children in relation to the logic of alphabetic orthography. Paper presented at the 26th annual convention of the National Reading Conference at Atlanta, GA.

Trachtenburg, P. (1990). Using children's literature to enhance phonics instruction. *The Reading Teacher,* 43(9), 648-654. *A Treasury of Literature* (1995). Orlando, FL: Harcourt Brace.

Treiman, R., & Baron, J. (1983). Phonemic-analysis training helps children benefit from spelling-sound rules. *Memory and Cognition,* 11, 382-389.

Turnmer, W.; Herriman, M.; & Nesdale, A. (1988). Metalinguistic abilities and beginning reading. *Reading Research Quarterly,* 23, 134-158.

Valencia, S., & Sulzby, E. (1991). Assessment of emergent literacy: Storybook reading. *The Reading Teacher,* 44 (7), 498-500.

Vaughn, S.C., & Milligan, J.L. (1986). If they learn to read by reading, how do we get them started? Paper presented at the 7th Annual Transmountain Regional Conference of the International Reading Association, May 29-31, 1986, at Vancouver, British Columbia.

Wagstaff, Janiel (1994). *Phonics That Work: New Strategies for the Reading-Writing Classroom.* New York: Scholastic.

Weaver, Connie (1994). *Reading Process and Practice: From Sociopsycholinguistics to Whole Language,* 2nd ed. Portsmouth, NH: Heinemann.

Weaver, Connie (1996). *Teaching Grammar in Context.* Portsmouth, NH: Boynton/Cook.

Wells, Jan, & Hart-Hewins, Linda (1994). *Phonics, Too! How to Teach Skills in a Balanced Language Program.* Markham, Ontario: Pembroke.

Wilde, S. (1992). *You Kan Red This!: Spelling and Punctuation for Whole Language Classrooms, K-6.* Portsmouth, NH: Heinemann.

Winthrop, E. (1985). *The Castle in the Attic.* New York: Holiday House.

Wolter, D. (1992). Whole group story reading? *Young Children,* 48(1), 72-75.

Wylie, R.E., & Durrell, D.D. (1970). Teaching vowels through phonograms. *Elementary English,* 47, 787-791.

Yopp, H.K. (1988a). The validity and reliability of phonemic awareness tests. *The Reading Teacher,* 45, 696-703.

Yopp, H.K. (1988b). The validity and reliability of phonemic awareness tests. *Reading Research Quarterly,* 23, 159-177.

Yopp, H.K. (1992a). A longitudinal study of the relationships between phonemic awareness and reading and spelling achievement. Paper presented at the annual meeting of the American Educational Research Association, San Francisco, CA.

Yopp, H.K. (1992b). Developing phonemic awareness in young children. *The Reading Teacher,* 45(9), 696-703.

Yopp, H.K. (1995a). Read-aloud books for developing phonemic awareness: An annotated bibliography. *The Reading Teacher,* 48, 538-542.

Yopp, H.K. (1995b). A test for assessing phonemic awareness in young children. *The Reading Teacher,* 49(1), 20-29.

Phonics Technology Resources

Bailey's Book House by Edmark. Through *Bailey's Book House,* children build language awareness and phonics, vocabulary, and thinking skills through five colorful learning activities. MAC/WIN CD-ROM

Beginning Reading by Sierra. Children engage in activities that build vocabulary and skills related to alphabetizing, two-letter consonant and vowel sounds, and rhyming words by using this program from the *Talking Tutors* series. MAC/WIN CD-ROM

Chugalong's Adventures in Phonics by Maxis. Children learn basic skills that prepare them for reading as they adventure with Chugalong and learn about phonics. WIN CD-ROM

Fisher-Price ABC's by Davidson & Associates. While playing ABC games, children build skills related to letter recognition, beginning sounds, reading readiness and spelling. WIN CD-ROM

Instant Readers CD-ROMs by Harcourt Brace & Company. This program provides 64 stories with accessible, predictable, patterned text that develops children's reading fluency. Games and activities build phonemic awareness and reinforce spelling and phonics skills. MAC/WIN CD-ROM

Kid Phonics by Davidson & Associates. This multimedia software program teaches reading through phonics and features over 50 nursery rhymes, classic and original, and sing-along songs. WIN

Learn to Read With Stickybear by Jones/Optimum Media. This product is a phonics-based learning course for beginning and remedial readers. VIDEODISC (LEVEL 1)

Learning English: Primary, Vol. 1 by Contér Software. Beginning readers and second-language learners use graphics, sound, and animation to develop vocabulary, reading comprehension, and math concepts in this story-based program. MAC/WIN CD-ROM

Learning English: Primary Rhymes, Vol. 1 by Contér Software. Beginning readers use graphics, sound, and animation to build language skills and vocabulary as they read and listen to familiar rhymes like *One, Two, Buckle My Shoe.* MAC/WIN CD-ROM

Reader Rabbit 1 by The Learning Company. Children use four animated games to build phonics, spelling, and language skills. IBM/MAC

Reader Rabbit 2 by The Learning Company. Children build word recognition, spelling-pattern awareness, and alphabetization skills through four interactive language activities. MAC/WIN

Reading Adventures in Oz by Davidson & Associates. Children build comprehension, thinking, and language skills as they complete activities based on *The Wizard of Oz.* MS-DOS

Schaffer Simple Software by Frank Schaffer Publications. With these programs children can learn about the alphabet, beginning consonants, short vowels, long vowels, blends, and digraphs. MAC/WIN

Spell It Plus! by Davidson & Associates. Children review commonly misspelled words and learn spelling rules as they practice spelling words in context, recognize words in syllables, unscramble words, complete words with missing letters, and identify words spelled incorrectly. MAC/IBM

Stickybear's Reading Room by Optimum Resource, Inc. Children use color animation and sound to build vocabulary and to practice word recognition, sentence construction (nouns and verb phrases), comprehension, and phonetics. MAC/MS-DOS

Sugar & Snails & Kitty Cat Tails by Entrex Software, Inc. Young children use graphics and animation to develop familiarity with letters, words, and rhymes to build phonemic and print awareness. MAC

Harcourt Brace School Publishers

Glossary of Professional Terms

ASSESSMENT The process of observing, recording, and otherwise documenting work that children do and how they do it and using these findings as a basis for a variety of educational decisions that affect children. (from NAEYC)

AUDITORY ACTIVITY An activity in which children identify and differentiate sounds, rhyming words, and/or other word patterns.

AUTHOR'S CHAIR A special chair in which a student-author sits to read his/her writing for response from a group or from the class.

AUTOMATICITY A state of mental functioning that produces a seemingly instantaneous understanding of the task. When readers achieve increasing automaticity, they recognize more and more words with a single glance.

BIG BOOK An enlarged book that children can see from a distance and can read in a group; re-creates the lap method of teaching reading in a school setting, since children can see the words as they hear them read aloud.

BRAINSTORMING Expressing ideas without stopping to evaluate them; searching for ideas or solutions through group discussion; a prewriting strategy.

CHORAL READING Reading verse or other patterned language in groups, sometimes by alternating lines or passages.

COMMUNITY OF READERS A classroom in which children have an integral part in defining reading roles, routines, and rules and have a sense that reading is a worthwhile, meaningful experience that should be shared.

CONSTRUCTIVISM The theory that meaningful learning is not passive, but is inquiry-based and student-centered.

CONTEXTUAL CLUES Meaning clues provided by the words surrounding the word to be decoded.

CONVENTIONAL WRITING Writing that exhibits the conventions of English, including sentence structure, spelling, punctuation, capitalization, and grammar.

COOPERATIVE LEARNING Working in pairs or small groups to accomplish goals and generate products interdependently; children may be assigned specific roles, such as Reader, Recorder, and Reporter.

CREATIVE DRAMATICS Informally acting out a story or a poem.

CREATIVE THINKING Generating and expressing thoughts imaginatively, uniquely, and poetically, through relational patterns of language and thought.

CRITICAL THINKING Making judgments about the validity, quality, and accuracy of ideas or text; judging the actions and traits of a character; logical analysis and judgment of worth, based on sound criteria.

CROSS-CHECKING Procedure in which readers take advantage of multiple cueing systems (phonics, syntax, context, and illustrations) to determine and confirm a word's pronunciation.

DECODING Turning print into language; determining letter-sound correspondences; constructing meaning from the graphic symbols of language.

DEVELOPMENTALLY APPROPRIATE PRACTICE A curriculum and an environment that are matched to a particular age group's developmental level.

ECHO READING A form of reading in which students repeat phrases after the teacher.

EMERGENT LITERACY The reading and writing behaviors of young children that precede and develop into conventional literacy.

ENCODING Transcribing spoken language into written symbols.

FLEXIBLE GROUPING Temporary grouping that varies according to instructional goals and students' needs and interests; includes whole groups, teacher-facilitated small groups, cooperative groups, pairs, and individuals.

GRAPHIC ORGANIZER A visual representation that aids meaning; a vehicle for organizing ideas to show relationships among them; webs, charts, and diagrams.

GRAPHOPHONIC A term that relates to print-sound relationships; one part of a cueing system readers use to make sense of text. (from Ken Goodman)

INFORMAL ASSESSMENT Observation of children's progress to diagnose children's needs; a sampling of ability or performance, including portfolios in which representative samples of children's work are gathered over time.

INTEGRATED CURRICULUM Teaching of social studies, science, math, language arts, and other content areas as related parts of a whole.

INTELLIGENCE The ability to solve problems, or to fashion products that are valued in one or more cultural or community settings. (from Howard Gardner)

INVENTED OR TEMPORARY SPELLING The spelling of emergent readers and writers that follows a developmental progression of associating sounds with symbols, moving gradually from drawing and scribbling to closer approximations of words.

KID WATCHING The process of monitoring children's ongoing development as they participate in daily activities that are integral to instruction.

KINESTHETIC ACTIVITY An activity involving physical movement or touch, such as tracing sandpaper letters, jumping, or walking; an activity in which learning is promoted through movement.

LEARNING STYLES Ways in which we learn; visual, auditory, and kinesthetic are the three most frequently used in school.

LITERATURE-BASED Characterized by the use of high-quality stories, poems, plays, and nonfiction to teach reading, writing, listening, and speaking.

METACOGNITION A level of thinking that involves the examination of one's own state of knowledge; awareness of thinking and learning processes; "thinking about thinking."

MINILESSON A brief instructional session, provided when a teacher diagnoses a specific need, in which concepts, skills, or strategies are introduced in a meaningful context through student-teacher interaction.

MODELING Demonstrating behaviors for novices to imitate; "thinking aloud" to make explicit or public what one does or thinks about while reading, writing, listening, or speaking.

MULTI-AGE CLASSROOM A classroom (sometimes called "nongraded") in which children of several ages are taught together.

MULTIPLE INTELLIGENCES A term coined by Howard Gardner, referring initially to seven intelligences, or ways of knowing things—verbal/linguistic, visual/spatial, logical/mathematical, bodily/kinesthetic, musical/rhythmic, interpersonal, and intrapersonal—and is expanding to include additional intelligences.

ONSET A consonant or consonant cluster preceding the vowel in a word; for example, the *w* in *we* or the *dr* in *drop*.

PHONEMIC AWARENESS The understanding that spoken language is composed of a series of separate sounds; the ability to segment language into phonemes.

PHONICS The science of matching speech sounds to printed letters in reading and spelling.

PORTFOLIO ASSESSMENT Evaluation based on the regular collection of samples of children's work over a period of time.

PREDICTABLE TEXT Highly patterned, rhythmic, structured text in which a sentence pattern, a sound, or a rhyme is repeated.

READERS THEATRE A literature response activity in which children translate a narrative or poem into a script and read it aloud; a simply staged performance that requires little preparation.

RIME The final vowel or vowel + consonant element in a word; for example, the *e* in *we* or the *op* in *drop*.

SCAFFOLDING Supporting a novice learner by modeling dialogue and responses and then gradually withdrawing support as a learner becomes increasingly independent.

SECOND-LANGUAGE LEARNER A student who is learning a second language; one whose home language is not English.

SHARED READING The group reading of a book—generally a Big Book—while a teacher or child points to the words.

SHARED WRITING An interactive group-writing process in which teachers and children work together to compose or record meaningful messages and stories.

STORY THEATER Groups of students each reading parts of a selection while other students pantomime the action.

STRATEGY A systematic plan for achieving a specific goal or result; a learning tool that gives children methods for mastering tasks and gaining skills.

SYNTACTIC CLUES Grammatical clues (for decoding a word) provided by the position the word holds within the sentence.

THEME A central or dominating idea around which reading materials, concepts, and instruction can be organized; a message or idea that dominates a work of literature or art.

TRANSITIONAL SPELLING Young writers' attempts to move beyond basic phonetic spelling patterns to handle the irregularities of our language, but are not yet conventional spellings.

VISUAL ACTIVITY An activity that involves discrimination between colors, shapes, and other visual stimuli.

WHOLE LANGUAGE An instructional approach based on the beliefs that learning is a social experience and that children learn from complete texts, high-quality literature, integrated instruction, and ongoing experimentation with language.

WRITER'S WORKSHOP A block of time devoted to writing; can include minilessons and the writing process; a session that provides time to write, ownership of written products, and time to share them.

WRITING PROCESS A framework for writing in which children use some or all of the following steps: prewriting, drafting, responding and revising, proofreading, and publishing; an approach to writing that allows children to shape and reshape their language over a period of time.

Index

See also Assessment; Phonemic awareness; Phonics; Shared reading; Strategic reading.

Reading Recovery strategies, 13–15, 32, 55–57

See also Intervention strategies.

Real-life reading, 48, 106

Real-life writing, 47–48

Reference materials for teachers.
  See Resources.

Reluctant learners, 55–57

Resources
  books for developing phonemic awareness, 41–43, 167-172
  glossary of professional terms, 211–213
  phonemic awareness tests, 156–159, 160–166
  phonics planning guides, 146-154
  phonics technology resources, 210
  professional bibliography, 206-209
  songbook planning guide, 155
  teacher's idea bank, 6
  word lists
    high-frequency words, 203–205
    phonic elements, 188–202
    phonograms, 173–187

Retelling a story, 51

Rhyming texts and activities, 10–12, 31, 42, 53–54, 55–57, 72–73

Rhythm, 57

School-home connection.
  See Family involvement.

Second-language learners.
  See Students Acquiring English.

Self-assessment, 16–18, 51, 54

Shared reading, 13, 19–21, 36–38, 43, 57, 66–68

See also Reading.

Shared writing, 57, 60–62

See also Writing.

Songs, 12, 56, 155

Sorting words, 33–35, 65, 71

Sound-letter relationships.
  See Phonemic awareness; Phonics.

Speaking, 8–9, 10–12, 19–21, 41–43, 56

Spelling, 44–45, 57, 61–62, 63–65, 68, 70–71

See also Phonics; Word building; Writing.

Strategic reading, 13–15, 16–18, 19–21, 33–34, 39–40

Students Acquiring English, 22–24, 36–38, 53–54, 66–68

See also Language acquisition.

Teachable moments, 13–14, 58–59, 60–62

Teacher's idea bank, 6

Teacher resources.
  See Resources.

Technology.
  See Resources.

Testing.
  See Assessment.

Theme teaching, 28

Thinking
  learning styles, 22–24
  theories of intelligence, 22

Total Physical Response (TPR), 23–24

Tracking print, 16–18, 19–21, 53, 67

Trade books
  alliterative, 42
  cumulative, 43
  in literacy programs, 26, 41–43
  patterned language, 43
  for phonemic awareness, 41–43, 167-172
  for phonics, 102–111
  rhyming, 42

Transitional spelling, 63–65, 68

See also Conventional writing; Spelling.

V

Vocabulary strategies, 36–38, 39–40, 66–68

W

Whole-class instruction, 13–15, 60–62

See also Classroom management; Grouping.

Word building
  activities, 33–35, 57, 67, 70
  copying masters for, 136, 137, 138
  with diverse learners, 22, 55–57

Word files, 36–38, 67

Word games and activities, 70–138

Word lists
  high-frequency words, 203–205
  phonic elements, words with, 188–202
  phonograms, words with, 173–187

Word sorts.
  See Sorting words.

Word study, 8–9, 16–18, 36–38, 39–40, 63–65, 66–68

Word wall, 36–38, 71

Writing
  activities, 46–48, 57, 60–62, 105, 110
  assessing, 50–52, 60–62, 63–65
  collaborative, 61
  connection to phonics, 8–9, 36–38, 44–45, 60–62, 63–65, 68
  conventions of, 44–45, 60–62, 63–65, 68
  emergent, 60–62, 63–65
  with families, 47–48, 105, 109, 110
  interactive, 61
  invented spelling, 13–15, 30, 36–38, 44–45, 63–65, 68
  materials, 47
  modeling, by teacher, 60–62
  real-life, 47–48, 103, 105, 109
  shared writing, 57, 60–62
  spelling and, 13–15, 36–38, 44–45, 60–62, 63–65, 68
  writing process, 60–62

See also Assessment; Conventional writing; Shared writing.